America's Maritime Legacy

Also of Interest

Securing the Seas: The Soviet Naval Challenge and Western Alliance Options, Paul H. Nitze, Leonard Sullivan, Jr., and the Atlantic Council Working Group on Securing the Seas

Lend-Lease, Loans, and the Coming of the Cold War: A Study of the Implementation of Foreign Policy, Leon C. Martel

International Politics and the Sea: The Case of Brazil, Michael A. Morris

The Whaling Issue in U.S.-Japan Relations, edited by J. R. Schmidhauser and G. O. Totten III

Superships and Nation-States: The Transnational Politics of the Intergovernmental Maritime Consultative Organization, Harvey B. Silverstein

About the Book and Editor

*America's Maritime Legacy:
A History of the U.S. Merchant Marine and
Shipbuilding Industry since Colonial Times*
edited by Robert A. Kilmarx

This study presents a comprehensive historical analysis of merchant shipping on the high seas and associated shipbuilding under sovereign U.S. jurisdiction from precolonial times to the present.

The volume traces the history of the merchant marine and shipbuilding industries; identifies U.S. policy developments that have affected those industries; and assesses the impact of these policies (or lack thereof) on the abilities of the U.S. shipbuilding industry and merchant fleets to meet U.S. economic and defense requirements, particularly in times of national emergency and conflict. It breaks new ground in its analysis of the contributions of the major segments of these industries to the general development of the United States, its military strength, and its expanding role in world affairs.

Robert A. Kilmarx is director of business and defense research and director of resource studies at the Center for Strategic and International Studies, Georgetown University. He is author of *Special Report, Soviet Sea Power* and *Soviet-United States Naval Balance.*

America's Maritime Legacy:
A History of the U.S. Merchant Marine and Shipbuilding Industry Since Colonial Times
edited by Robert A. Kilmarx

Contributors

Lawrence C. Allin
K. Jack Bauer
John H. Kemble
Lane C. Kendall
Robert A. Kilmarx
Daniel Levine
John J. McCusker
James M. Morris
Sara Ann Platt
Clark G. Reynolds
Jeffrey J. Safford

LONDON AND NEW YORK

First published 1979 by Westview Press, Inc.

Published 2018 by Routledge
52 Vanderbilt Avenue, New York, NY 10017
2 Park Square, Milton Park, Abingdon, Oxon OX14 4RN

Routledge is an imprint of the Taylor & Francis Group, an informa business

Copyright © 1979 by the Center for Strategic and International Studies

All rights reserved. No part of this book may be reprinted or reproduced or utilised in any form or by any electronic, mechanical, or other means, now known or hereafter invented, including photocopying and recording, or in any information storage or retrieval system, without permission in writing from the publishers.

Notice:
Product or corporate names may be trademarks or registered trademarks, and are used only for identification and explanation without intent to infringe.

Library of Congress Cataloging in Publication Data
Main entry under title:
America's maritime legacy.
 1. Merchant marine—United States—History. 2. Shipping—United States—History. 3. Ship-building—United States—History. I. Kilmarx, Robert A.
HE745.A59   387.5'0973   79-11208
ISBN 13: 978-0-367-02091-0 (hbk)
ISBN 13: 978-0-367-17078-3 (pbk)

Contents

List of Figures.................................... ix

Preface xi

About the Contributors and Editors xv

1. *The Rise of the Shipping Industry in Colonial America,*
   John J. McCusker 1

   Origins of Mercantilism and the U.S. Maritime Industry ... 1
   The Colonial Maritime Industry 4
   Colonial Regionalism and Commerce 8
   Policy Consequences 18
   Appendixes A-C 19

2. *The Golden Age,* K. Jack Bauer..................... 27

   The Federalist Period 27
   The Neutral Carrier 31
   The Merchant Marine Revives 36
   Maritime Routes to Western Settlement 48
   Fishing 53
   The California Connection 55

3. *The Civil War and the Period of
   Decline: 1861-1913,* Lawrence C. Allin.............. 65

   Early Attempts to Revise the Merchant Marine......... 70

Agents of Maritime Change 72
The Maritime Revolution 75
Patterns of World Trade 78
The Navy and the Merchant Marine. 80
Factors in the Revival of the Merchant Marine 85
The Changing Maritime Order 94
Theodore Roosevelt and the Great White Fleet. 96
Taft, Wilson, Conspiracy, and the Lobbies 98
Storm Warnings. 101

4. *World War I Maritime Policy and the National Security: 1914-1919*, Jeffrey J. Safford 111

The Wilsonian Approach 114
The Effects of War in Europe 116
The Sinking of the *Lusitania* 120
The United States Enters the War 123
U.S. Shipping in the Postwar World. 130
The Merchant Marine Act of 1920 136
The Aftermath of the Wilson Administration 141

5. *The Years between the Wars: 1919-1939*, John H. Kemble and Lane C. Kendall 149

The Legacy of World War I 149
Postwar Policy. 150
The Postwar Depression in Shipping 151
Achievement and Equilibrium. 155
International Maritime Agreements. 158
Revival of the Subsidy Question 159
The Impact of the Great Depression 163
The Roosevelt Administration. 168
The New Deal 170

6. *The Contribution of U.S. Shipbuilding and the Merchant Marine to the Second World War*, Daniel Levine and Sara Ann Platt 175

The Merchant Marine on the Eve of War 175
The United States Prepares for War. 180

Productivity 187
Incentives 188
Appraisal of Shipbuilding 191
Manning the Merchant Fleet 195
Protection of Merchant Ships 198
Convoying..................................... 200
Shipping the Supplies: Neutral Shipping........ 200
Lend-Lease 201
War Shipping.................................. 203
Appraisal of Ship Operations................... 209
Summary and Overview.......................... 209

7. *American Maritime Power since World War II*,
   Clark G. Reynolds............................ 215

   The Cold War 218
   Return to Traditional Supports.............. 222
   The Age of Détente.......................... 229
   U.S. Initiative on the International Scene .. 232
   Response at the National Level.............. 240
   The Innovations of Business and Labor....... 246

8. *The Shipbuilding Industry:
   A Summary of Developments and Commentary*,
   James M. Morris and Robert A. Kilmarx 255

   The Lessons of Maritime History............. 257
   The Crucial Questions 261

Figures

Figure 1: Relative Shares of U.S. and Allies in Merchant
   Ship Construction............................ 193
Figure 2: Relative Shares of U.S. and Allies in Merchant
   Ship Inventory 194

Preface

Some three years ago the Center for Strategic and International Studies initiated a series of naval studies looking at the maritime policies and problems of the United States. Our longtime interest in regard to the Persian Gulf, beginning in the 1960s, and the possible instabilities there after the British withdrawal, led to our concern with energy and other scarce resources. Our twin concerns for national security and trade led to a reassessment of the adequacy of our maritime structure to meet the challenges of the 1970s and 1980s. As a natural part of this effort, we had long wanted to take a searching look at our merchant marine and shipbuilding industries. We soon found no adequate historical record existed alongside current analysis.

The Center undertook this project in recognition of the fact that the U.S. shipping and shipbuilding industries face a period of major challenges to their viability at a time of increasing global instability. Policies of the United States have proved to be inadequate to meet these challenges. A contributing factor is believed to be a lack of historical understanding on the part of the American public of the relevance of these industries to U.S. national security and foreign policy throughout the nation's history. It is our view that a unique contribution to this understanding could be made by an objective, historical study that is grounded in an appreciation of contemporary issues.

The United States merchant marine and shipbuilding industries have entered a period of unprecedented challenge brought about by the constant evolution in the world environment since U.S. maritime laws were first enacted. Significant changes have taken place in the nature and extent of foreign competition, especially as regards the expanding role of governments. Cost escalation, slow economic growth, developments in technology, regulatory complexities and rigidities, burdensome court decisions, and/or varying fluctuations in international trade patterns have also had significant impact. If present trends continue, a significant decline of these U.S. industries, as presently constituted, is predictable.

This phenomenon raises questions that need to be tested by historical analysis. Is there a need for new maritime laws, for more precise objectives for shipping and shipbuilding, for different institutional arrangements and regulatory approaches, and for fundamentally new attitudes toward these two industries if today's adverse trends are to be checked or reversed? Appropriate solutions are bound to be elusive. Obstacles include competing national objectives and perceptions, differing assumptions on the part of interested parties, a lack of public understanding, and the preoccupation of overly taxed public leadership with other issues and fiscal considerations.

The critical problems of these industries can be effectively overcome only if agreement is reached on an underlying fundamental question: are the privately owned U.S. merchant marine and shipbuilding industries important to the national interests of the United States and relevant to its national security? A derivative of this question is the determination of whether or not these industries should be viewed only in narrow economic terms or be given a broader perspective based on the correlation between economic growth and the goals of U.S. domestic and foreign policy, including national defense.

This study focuses on these topics by illuminating the history of the United States merchant marine and shipbuilding industries from colonial times to the present. It is intended to throw light on why and how these industries evolved in earlier periods; the problems that sequentially arose; how the federal government addressed or failed to address the needs of the industries; and how public attitudes about ships and shipbuilding have varied as our nation grew. The rationale behind earlier and present maritime laws, and other regulatory and legislative approaches, are set forth. The relevance of these industries to U.S.

national security and the contributions they made to the nation in periods of military conflict and economic transition have been explored. The scope of this report includes a discussion of the role of competing special interests, including the part played by leaders of industry and government. The evolution of technology and of industrial relations, including union and management organization, and the impact of international organizations are also examined.

The intent of this analysis is to produce a comprehensive, objective, and readable narrative. Its purpose is to present a meaningful contribution to scholarship and to improve public understanding of the issues at this crucial historical juncture in maritime affairs. In the months and years ahead, changing political administrations and the Congress will have continuing opportunities to assess maritime policies and programs with the realization that some may be wanting, some in disarray, and some in need of revision or replacement. The outcome of this process will greatly influence the future role of the United States in world trade and global economic security.

The Center greatly appreciates the distinguished scholarship of the contributors (listed in the next section) who made possible the production of this work. They are to be commended for their dedication and responsiveness in completing their tasks in a comparatively short period of time. The Center must, of course, accept the responsibility for any revisions, editorial or otherwise, that were made in their draft material to achieve balance and continuity.

Other contributors, advisers, and readers who greatly assisted in this project include: Robert Athay, Albert Blackburn, Robert S. Hope, Admiral George H. Miller, USN (Ret.), David Sasson, and Jim Smalhout.

Invaluable typing assistance was provided by Ms. Shirl G. Clay and Mrs. Deanthia Mebane. The proficient copy editor was Ms. Sylvia Lowe.

Robert A. Kilmarx

About the Contributors and Editors

Lawrence C. Allin took his master's degree in Russian Studies at Syracuse University and his doctoral degree at the University of Maine, where he currently teaches. He is also a Diplomat of the Munson Memorial Institute of American Maritime History and a research affiliate of the Research Institute of the Gulf of Maine.

K. Jack Bauer is professor of history at Rensselaer Polytechnic Institute. A graduate of Harvard University with a Ph.D. from Indiana University, he has served on the staff of the National Archives and with the Marine Corps and U.S. Navy historical sections. In the latter post, he assisted Samuel Eliot Morison.

John H. Kemble received his Ph.D. from the University of California at Berkeley. He is professor emeritus of history at Pomona College, and has been a visiting lecturer or professor of history at many universities, including the University of California at Los Angeles, the U.S. Naval War College, and the University of Texas. He has been a Rockefeller Fellow, a Guggenheim Fellow, and Fellow of the California Historical Society.

Lane C. Kendall has had extensive experience in maritime affairs as professor, executive, and government official. He has held positions with a major shipping company, the faculty of the U.S. Merchant Marine Academy, and the Military Sealift Command. He has lectured at the Munson Institute of American Maritime History, has served as a senior officer in the U.S. Marine Corps, and has published a book, *The Business of Shipping*.

Robert A. Kilmarx is director of Business and Defense Studies, the Center for Strategic and International Studies, Georgetown University. A former intelligence official in the Department of Defense, he has a Ph.D. in international relations and economics, has written on maritime and naval topics, and has been a contributor to conference programs in those fields.

Daniel Levine has a master's degree in economics from George Washington University and a Ph.D. in physics from Catholic University. He has directed studies of the potential use of commercial ships for tasks to support the navy, including mission analysis, and is currently working at the Center for Naval Analyses, a nonprofit research center affiliated with the University of Rochester.

John J. McCusker, an economic historian, is currently associate professor of history at the University of Maryland. A Fellow of the Royal Historical Society, he has received many honors, primarily for his historical research on economic and maritime affairs during the American colonial period.

James M. Morris, senior research editor of the volume, earned his Ph.D. from the University of Cincinnati, concentrating on American economic and labor union history. He is a professor in the Department of History at Christopher Newport College and is the author of *Our Maritime Heritage: Maritime Developments and Their Impact on American Life.*

Sara Ann Platt graduated from Rutgers University in 1977, where she studied American and Russian history. She is currently working at the Center for Naval Analyses, where she is a coauthor of the new quarterly journal, *Naval Abstracts.*

Clark G. Reynolds is a free-lance maritime and naval consultant and writer, currently working on a book on famous U.S. admirals. He received his Ph.D. from Duke University and subsequently taught at several universities and colleges, including the U.S. Naval Academy.

Jeffrey J. Safford is a professor of history at Montana State University. He has lectured at the Munson Institute of Maritime History and is the author of a recent book, *Wilsonian Diplomacy, 1913-1921.*

1
The Rise of the Shipping Industry in Colonial America
John J. McCusker

Our forefathers, mindful of the linkages between the private sector and the public sector, felt the colonists' interests were best served when the government took an active role in promoting private enterprise to the advantage of all.[1] Colonial businessmen and legislators, for instance, quickly discovered that their prosperity was linked to the carrying of trade: the more colonial shipping involved in the import and export of goods at colonial ports, the higher the level of economic benefit for everyone. American leaders throughout the colonies realized the need not only to produce goods for export but also to carry those goods to market themselves in their own ships. Acting upon this premise, colonial governments did all they could to support and promote the shipping industry.

Origins of Mercantilism and the U.S. Maritime Industry

English maritime policies during the colonial period of American history had their origins in the very policies that gave birth to the colonies themselves. Later writers gave the name *mercantilism* to a series of programs and legislation that had a unity of purpose, if not a uniformity in their planning and execution. The overall intent of English mercantilism was to build and strengthen the nation, to allow it to enter the ranks of the rising European nation-states along the Atlantic seaboard, and to maintain itself among them as an independent power. The immediate goals were political and military, but the means to attain them were financial and commercial.

A strong, self-sufficient England required money for the national government to answer to all the requirements of the monarch, including an army and a navy. Wartime emergencies could best be served by loans—forced or voluntary—from a wealthy commercial class. Regular revenues could best be raised from duties on imports and exports. To cultivate both trade and traders and to generate both customs revenues and a class of well-to-do capitalists required that the rulers of England protect and promote English commerce and shipping. Since in policy and in law English colonists were Englishmen, and English colonial ships were English ships, the merchants, ships, and sailors of the American colonies were also protected and promoted.

Colonies played an important part in the world-view of English mercantilism. The colonists established overseas markets to which the mother country could export goods. This stimulated English trade and, it was expected, English manufacturing. The colonists went abroad to improve their standard of living. They presumed that this would be reflected in a higher level of consumption of the goods of the mother country. They then would require the services of merchants, ships, and sailors to carry the goods they needed.

Colonies also provided imports for the mother country. The colonies became for the mother country a source of supply for commodities that the English had previously had to import from outside the empire, transferring a trade that had previously enriched foreign merchants and shippers to English hands. To the degree that the demand at home for those commodities was less than the entire supply imported, there remained a surplus for reexport abroad. Colonial commodities required English hands to process or otherwise prepare them for market, and Englishmen began to work in manufacturing as well as in trade. Colonies fit well into the purposes of mercantilism.

Recognition of the beneficial nature of protectionist policies for England preceded both the founding of colonies and the passing of statutes embodying the principles of mercantilism. Our understanding of the benefits that could be attained during the colonial period can be more clearly articulated if we employ some twentieth-century terminology. It is useful to define a few terms. Mercantilism sought, in effect, to create a permanent, indeed lopsided, surplus in a nation's balance of payments. Economists, looking back on this period, can delineate three separate accounts within that balance. Credits are earned in one or all of the accounts through exports; debits are earned through imports. One account balances debits and credits in the shipment of bullion: the bullion account. Another account deals with capital: the capital account. The third, the current account, concerns the exchange of commodities and the mercantile services—freight charges, insurance, handling costs—involved in moving those commodities.

In the period of the seventeenth and eighteenth centuries, writers often omitted calculating the credits and debits from mercantile services, now called for that reason the "invisibles" in the current account. Nor did they pay much attention to either the bullion or the capital accounts. Instead, most concentrated on the import and export of commodities and spoke only of the balance of trade. It is obvious to us now, even as it was to some people then, that the balance of trade excluded important transactions involved in international trade. Regardless of the manner in which they accounted for it, some writers, merchants, and government officials began to appreciate that the invisibles were an important factor in the balance of payments. A country's trade was even more advantageous if it were carried in its own shipping. Mercantilism was as much a set of policies to promote shipping as it was to stimulate trade.[2]

The perceived need to control and thereby to profit from the shipment of goods—as contrasted with the goods themselves—was an early and continuing feature of mercantilism. While we might indeed be more interested in the expressions of this policy during the seventeenth and eighteenth centuries as the pattern which had a major impact upon the colonies, it is appropriate to note that the earliest of such governmental efforts to promote English shipping can indeed be traced back to the subsidies offered by the legendary King Alfred. He is reported to have given rewards to those of his subjects who carried on at least three overseas ventures in their own vessels. Alfred is remembered, not coincidentally, as the founder of the English navy.

A series of similar measures, all with the purpose of inducing Englishmen to own and to use English shipping, litter the statute books down to the time of Elizabeth I at the end of the sixteenth century. The repetition was necessary simply because the measures enacted were never sufficient, either as threats or as inducements, to overcome the competitive advantage enjoyed by a succession of European rivals. The rights and privileges of aliens trading with England had an ancient origin in the financial needs of successive English monarchs who frequently permitted the foreign merchant even lower duties than those applicable to English merchants. Those measures were not abolished until 1598 when Elizabeth I withdrew the last of the privileges of the Hanseatic merchants. Only then could subsequent monarchs and parliaments frame efficient legislation promotive of English shipping.[3]

The major English mercantilistic legislation dates from the middle of the seventeenth century. That it took another fifty years after the reign of Elizabeth I for these laws to be promulgated is as much a testament to the increasing inability of monarch and parliament to work together as to anything else. Fifty years of quarreling finally ended with the Civil War, the beheading of Charles I, and the rise of Cromwell and the Protectorate in the middle decades of the century. The key acts were those passed in 1651 (which were modified and passed again by the Parliament of Charles II in 1660), in 1663, and in 1673. A later act of 1696 clarified and sharpened some procedures in the system set up in the earlier acts, just as other acts added to or subtracted from their provisions. These English acts of 1651-60, 1663, and 1673 were the core of a mercantilistic system that incorporated maritime and commercial policies under which English colonists grew and prospered. They established a pattern for the mercantile and commercial policies that Englishmen abroad repeated in miniature in colonial, and, later, in state and national laws. In working as well as they did, those policies also contributed to strains within the empire that were resolved only with the destruction of the transatlantic extension of English national interests.

The Colonial Maritime Industry

During the mercantilist period, the key factor for the colonists was that the navigation laws considered them Englishmen and their ships, English ships. In promoting English trade, Parliament promoted colonial trade. In promoting English shipping, Parliament promoted colonial shipping. In promoting English seamen, Parliament promoted colonial seamen. The acts of 1651-60 and 1663 had the effect of closing colonial ports to all but English ships, which were defined as ships owned by, under the captaincy of, and manned by Englishmen.

History emphasizes the restrictive aspects of this closed system for the colonists. The major colonial exports could be sent only to England in English ships. The act of 1663 established bonding procedures and heavy penalties to insure compliance; the act of 1673 set up customs authorities in the colonies to enforce its provisions. The act of 1696, among other things, instituted formal ship-registration procedures, akin to modern measures, that required a formal license to trade within the empire. Yet by "England" and "English" in all of these acts, the law explicitly included not only the residents of England, Wales, and—after 1707—Scotland, but also the residents of the English colonies in America. As shipowners, shipmasters, and sailors, they shared in that same exclusive license to trade within an empire which by 1775 was the richest and the strongest in the world. In the very restrictions and exclusivity of these Navigation Acts, the colonists found considerable opportunities for economic gain.

The growth of English trade and commerce over the century and a quarter after 1650 has been seen by Ralph Davis as a commercial revolution based on the rise of the English shipping industry. Englishmen moved rapidly to take over control not only of the trade to their own country and between England and its colonies, but also a goodly portion of the whole of European waterborne commerce. English builders soon learned to pattern their vessels on the Dutch *flute,* or flyboat, the most efficient carrier of cargo known, to increase their capacity. English captains and seamen contributed an increasing ship-handling ability and a knowledge of winds, currents, and tides to the expanding commercial scene. English merchants evolved networks of correspondents and agents to buy and sell goods in advance of a ship's arrival, to minimize time in port. English brokers and financiers organized credit and insurance techniques that made London the financial capital of the world by the late eighteenth century.

All of these developments served to lower costs and to increase profits for English shipowners and merchants—and to increase the numbers of merchants, ships, and sailors engaged in trade. The English commercial revolution of the seventeenth century set much of the stage for the nation's industrial revolution of the eighteenth century. And the English colonists learned from, patterned themselves upon, and took full advantage of the incentives and opportunities offered them by the commercial revolution in their mother country. As England prospered, so did the colonies.[4]

English maritime policy in the seventeenth and eighteenth centuries varied in its impact upon the colonies depending upon local circumstances. Nevertheless, they may be grouped for purposes of discussion, and we can organize the English colonies in North America roughly into four regions in order to analyze the impact of imperial policies and the colonists' responses to them: the New England colonies of Massachusetts (which after the 1690s included the modern state of Maine), New Hampshire, Rhode Island, and Connecticut; the Middle Atlantic colonies of New York, New Jersey, Pennsylvania, and Delaware; the Chesapeake Bay colonies of Maryland and Virginia; and the Southern colonies of North Carolina, South Carolina, and Georgia.

They can be grouped even more for ease of analysis, with New England standing as surrogate for all of the northern colonies and Virginia and Maryland for the southern colonies. As good colonies they imported increasing quantities of commodities from the mother country, and as good customers they made payment for their purchases. They did so adequately and regularly, and, to put it technically, they established sufficient credits in their balance of payments to match the debits created by their imports from England and elsewhere. This is testimony to how well the colonies integrated themselves within the English commercial revolution. One important measure of this integration, and one important means by which the English colonies established credits in their own balance of payments, was their response to the promotive elements for shipping in English maritime policy. Many of the colonists took advantage of the trading opportunities offered within the empire to earn income for themselves while they earned credits in the colonial balance of payments.

The colonists' responses to these incentives had some common elements that are worth mentioning before detailing the maritime history of each of the major groups of colonies. Ideally, each colony would have been able to do as Virginia did after 1620. Virginia tobacco exported directly from the Chesapeake to English ports and sold there paid directly and immediately for the goods the Virginians wanted from England. The next season, the English goods that the Virginians had ordered were exported to them in the very vessels that would, in turn, load a return cargo of tobacco in America. The cycle repeated itself annually. The colonists earned credits from the exported tobacco; the mother country earned credits both from the goods exported to the colonies and from the invisibles earned in the shipments in both directions because the vessels were owned and manned by Englishmen. Initially at least, while the profits from tobacco were high, everyone was happy with this trade. Similar satisfaction prevailed in other colonies where a staple export like tobacco could be assured; for example, South Carolina's rice or the sugar of the British West Indies.

Where the colonists did not produce a staple commodity for which there was a ready market in England, their continued demand for imported English goods created strains in their balance of payments. One possible answer to this persistent problem was to reduce dependency on imported English goods by producing some of these commodities in the colonies. This solution pleased no one, however. Colonial-produced substitutes were rarely of sufficient quality or low enough in price to satisfy colonial consumers. (This was especially true in the seventeenth century.) Moreover, the production and sale of such goods in the colonies ran counter to the entire rationale of mercantilism. Appropriately, the English government responded both by attempting to stop the colonists' production of such goods and by encouraging instead the production of new staples for export to England.

Another solution was to develop the export of colonial produce for which there was a ready market in some other country or foreign colony and then to transfer to England the credits earned in those places. Both of these solutions addressed themselves directly to the balance of trade in that they were concerned with goods alone. Still other solutions could be found in the bullion account (by colonial export of gold and silver); in the capital account (by investing in English enterprises); and, more importantly, in the current account (by the generation of invisible earnings) through involvement in the carrying trade. Insofar as the colonists began to freight their imports and exports in ships that were owned and manned in the colonies, they earned additional credits in their balance of payments (see Appendixes A and C).[5]

Colonial Regionalism and Commerce

The Chesapeake Bay colonies of Virginia and Maryland were staple-exporting colonies par excellence. They fitted beautifully into the mercantilist's model of how colonies should operate within the English imperial system. Yet, as is discussed below, changing conditions brought some alterations even in the Chesapeake. The earliest years in Virginia and Maryland, from about 1620 until 1660, were a boom time based on the great profits the planters made in the tobacco trade. All during that period the English sale price of tobacco was falling, however, until it reached a level in the 1660s that was effectively unchanged for the next century. Regardless of how stable the price per pound remained, the costs of production and distribution continued to rise in real terms. The resulting squeeze on the profits of tobacco planters was the chief factor in the changes in the economy of the Chesapeake region that altered it from a near monocultural base in the seventeenth century to a diverse agricultural and commercial economy on the eve of the American Revolution.[6]

All the developments that took place during this period are too numerous to detail here. It is sufficient to say that Virginians and Marylanders were very resourceful in their attempts to minimize the impact of declining profits in both the domestic and the foreign sectors of their economy. Many of these stratagems had an impact upon their balance of payments and, therefore, involved matters of maritime policy. As was usual and expected in this era, almost all involved the direct interjection of the colonial governments into the picture which—in the pattern of the English government before them—sought to organize matters and to induce economic behavior that contributed to the common good. That same model, the English government, also provided the colonists with suggestions for the substance of their promotive measures. Themselves a product of mercantilism, the colonists became little mercantilists.

Virginians and Marylanders, in the face of a decline in profits that hurt their ability to import goods they needed, began to produce some of these goods themselves. Particularly after the introduction of slavery, itself a response to the same squeeze on profits, there was an increasing incidence in the Chesapeake of specialized labor on and off the plantations. Occupations such as carpenters, shoemakers, coopers, blacksmiths, wheelwrights, weavers, boat builders, brickmakers, and the like can be discovered with greater frequency over time in the persons either of trained slaves or free whites. A slave with such training on a plantation could be profitably kept at work at his specialty, especially if a market could be found in the neighborhood for the product of his labor beyond the needs of his own plantation.

A small local trade in such goods expanded still further in order to service wider markets. It came to be centered in the towns which grew up during the post-1660 era. These towns, too, were promoted by the colonial legislatures. The agent for such trade, a resident of the town, was the merchant, a new addition to the Chesapeake. The direct trade to England had not required the services of a local merchant to oversee affairs, but this newer trade did. Local merchants had a way of expanding horizons and seeking markets farther away for the surplus produce of the plantations. The rise of Norfolk, Virginia; Baltimore, Maryland; and the numerous smaller Chesapeake towns can be traced directly to this activity.

Virginians and Marylanders could also bolster their balance of payments—besides cutting down on imports—by increasing their exports. They did so indirectly by selling outside the colony their surplus bricks, barrel staves, shingles, and whatever else. They did so directly, and more profitably, if they could find other staple exports. They found two: iron and grain. Large deposits of easily accessible iron ore existed throughout the western shore of the Chesapeake Bay in both Virginia and Maryland. Tobacco planters invested considerable capital setting up furnaces to process the ore for export to England. This was a proper staple, one that the mother country encouraged, because in England the semiprocessed iron could be turned into a variety of products. In 1753, Parliament, in fact, worked to promote the colonial production of the raw ore by instituting a bounty for its delivery to English ports. This nicely complemented the tobacco trade in a second way because it was usually transported as ballast in the tobacco ships at little or no real freight cost to the owner of the vessel, whatever he might charge the colonist.

The colonial tobacco planters had always grown some grains and provisions for their own use and the use of their slaves. As settlements spread away from the shores of the Chesapeake into lands more marginal for growing tobacco, especially after the 1660s, the colonists looked for other crops to plant and harvest. The production of wheat, corn, rye, and oats increased easily as the markets for them were developed first by the merchants of Boston, New York, and Philadelphia and, later, of the new commercial towns of the Chesapeake. Baltimore was, in fact, largely established as an outport of Philadelphia by individuals connected with Philadelphia mercantile houses sent there to take advantage of a closer proximity to the source of grain. Wheat and other grains also had to be milled, so that with the growth of grain production came a concomitant expansion of flour milling.

There were two periods of considerable growth in grain production. One came in the late 1730s and into the 1740s as the traditional West Indian markets for North American grain were increased considerably as a result of the rapid development of the French Islands, especially St. Domingue (Haiti). The second expansion came in the 1760s as the growth of European population coincided with several poor harvests to create a considerable demand for grain, especially in southern Europe. By the 1770s, the Chesapeake was the second largest exporter of grain in North America.

The colonists of Virginia and Maryland benefited from the

decreased imports and increased exports by a better balance of payments than they would have had otherwise. They benefited still further in another way: most of this new trade and some of the old tobacco trade had by the 1770s fallen under American control. It was the merchants of the Chesapeake, not of London, who oversaw and profited from the trade of these commodities inside the colony and overseas. Exports to the West Indies were the exclusive province of colonial merchants; exports to southern Europe usually involved colonial merchants in some kind of joint arrangement, usually with an English merchant resident in a Portuguese or Spanish port. These colonial merchants recognized that their profits would be maximized if exports were shipped in their own vessels so that they could profit not only from the freight but also from the sale of the goods. Again, the carrying trade to the West Indies was exclusively in colonial-owned vessels while exports to southern Europe were sometimes in colonial-owned vessels, sometimes in English-owned vessels, and sometimes in vessels of shared ownership. The trade with the West Indies, be they British, French, Danish, or Dutch, and the trade with Europe, no matter where, could only be in "English" ships because of the provision of the Navigation Acts. That the West Indian carrying trade was exclusively colonial was a function of geography: the merchants of London and Liverpool could not compete at that great distance with the merchants of Baltimore and Norfolk.

The value of the carrying trade as a source of additional credits in the balance of payments was explicitly recognized not only by the merchants of Norfolk and Baltimore who engaged in it, but also by the legislatures of the two colonies which strove to promote it. The subject of government promotion of private enterprise has yet to be fully explored for the colonial period, but that it was a common practice can be clearly seen. In the cases of Virginia and Maryland, the two colonies each sought to promote local ownership of shipping by legislating the remission of a variety of duties and fees for vessels owned in whole or in part by residents of the colony. The ship registry certificate required by the act of 1696 of each vessel that traded in the colonies recorded the name of every owner of the vessel. A shipmaster's certificate that showed Virginia ownership saved him, and the owners, a good bit of money each time he entered and cleared port in that colony; the same was true for Maryland-owned vessels in Maryland. The savings in fees and duties, prorated on the size of the vessel, obviously constituted an indirect subsidy for locally owned vessels. This was in addition to the several incentives that pushed Maryland and Virginia merchants to increase the number and size of their colonial-owned vessels, and to employ them to maximum efficiency.

Any shipping activity by the colonists could be viewed by the merchants of the mother country as competitive with them and as a breach of the spirit, if not the letter, of mercantilism. There were, therefore, some efforts to circumscribe colonial mercantile activity, but these were minor and not effectual; the colonials, after all, had the navigation laws on their side. Actually, the merchants of London and Bristol had no real interest in the intercolonial coasting trades of North America and only little concern over those between North America and the British West Indies. The colonial merchants cut their teeth on these trades, but, having prospered by the promotional efforts of the colonial governments, they began to look elsewhere within the empire to employ their ships by the middle of the eighteenth century. The transatlantic trades beckoned. In the several decades before 1775, colonial-owned ships carried increasing quantities of Chesapeake tobacco to Great Britain, Chesapeake flour to Spain and Portugal, and even some West Indian sugar from the Caribbean to the ports of Europe. Nurtured in and encouraged by the protective arms of mercantilism, the colonists had begun to broaden their carrying trade into areas that put them clearly in direct competition with the merchants of the mother country.

Such competition by Maryland- and Virginia-owned ships was minimal on the eve of the American Revolution. Yet if this happened in the Chesapeake, if the "best" of the colonies, in the view of the mercantilists, could stray in this way, what about the rest of them? None of the others had the advantages that tobacco brought to the Chesapeake. In their attempts to establish themselves on an adequate economic basis, the other North American continental colonies developed even further along some of the lines of Virginia and Maryland. They, in fact, set some of the patterns which the colonists of the Chesapeake followed. But all of them benefited from the maritime policies that were an integral part of the English navigation laws. Some of them developed policies of their own to protect and promote their trade and their shipping. The result was considerable economic growth and development in the colonies—and an emerging sense of a need for political independence, the better to protect that growth and development.[7]

The fields of New England produced grain and rocks, and more of the latter than the former. Neither had a market value in England. If the colonists of Massachusetts were to continue to import from England, they had to find some way to help their balance of payments, in addition to the export of their local produce. The issue came to a head around 1640. With the prospect of a return to parliamentary government at home, the tide of Puritan immigrants to the Bay Colony was stemmed and, with it, the influx of credits in the colony's balance of payments from the mother country dried up. The result was an immediate, sharp depression, the first in American history. Government leaders worked to develop ways to increase exports and to cut down on imports. The General Court, the colony's legislature, offered a range of incentives to induce the colonists to produce at home many of the things that they had previously imported, in order to reduce the flow of imports.[8]

Increasing exports was harder, however. Fur-bearing animals, which had provided some exports in the 1630s, had already begun to run thin as settlement pushed westward. Any material increase in the quantity of fish exported involved several problems, not the least of which was identifying appropriate customers. The market was already well supplied with the choice fish required for European palates. The same was true of what was until then the best-developed market for the timber products of the New England forests; the staves and headings for casks fashioned by farmers in the off-season had only a limited appeal in the Wine Islands of the eastern Atlantic.

The economic salvation for Puritan New England appeared in the timely arrival of sugar cultivation on the island of Barbados. The sugar planters there quickly determined that sugar production was so profitable that it was counterproductive to grow their own provisions. One acre planted in sugar yielded enough to allow them to buy other crops that would have required several acres to grow. Moreover, they needed more than cereals. Low-grade fish would serve as a source of protein for the plantation slaves; wooden barrels were needed to ship the sugar; and other timber products such as lumber and shingles were required for buildings to house the equipment and people on the sugar plantations. There had been some trade with newly settled Barbados in the 1630s, but it grew spectacularly after 1640 as sugar production skyrocketed. An active agent in the process of promoting New England's capturing of this market was the General Court which, for instance, went to the extent of temporarily forbidding the baking of bread in Boston in 1641 in order to insure the completion of a cargo of wheat for Barbados.

Out of these humble beginnings grew the rich maritime history of New England. Demand in the West Indies increased steadily over the next century as other English islands were settled and the French islands later followed suit. To supply this demand, the New Englanders multiplied their fishing fleets, harvested their forests, and developed a sophisticated coastal trade with the other English North American colonies to supply whatever else the Caribbean colonies needed, particularly flour. The complex trade patterns that came into being required considerable mercantile acumen, but could best be done only on a comparatively small scale. Goods for export had to be assembled piecemeal and exported to the West Indies in small, mixed cargoes. Moreover, all of this had to be managed on the spot. This was not the stuff of London merchants; they left it to others. Thus sheltered and promoted by imperial statute and local law, the merchants of the North increased and prospered. Within a half century of its settlement, Boston had already become the "market and staple" of the New World.

Significantly, these words describing Boston's exalted position appeared in a complaint from London merchants to the Board of Trade about the competition offered them by Englishmen across the sea. This was not the last of such complaints, nor was it the only one to assume a tone implying that such competition was not only harmful but even unlawful. Whether or not the New England merchants were generally law-abiding citizens of the British Empire who honored far more of the provisions of the Navigation Acts than they dishonored is not the issue. It should be pointed out, however, that all the activities so far described were well within both the spirit and the letter of those acts, including the trade with the West Indian islands. One can also suggest that petitions complaining to the British government from aggrieved parties, be they London merchants earlier or British West Indian merchants and planters later, might not have presented a balanced picture. The merchants of New England neither bent nor broke the law by carrying on coastwide trade with their near neighbors or overseas with the West Indies. All they did, in fact, was to respond to the promotive measures implicit in the Navigation Acts.

Wartime not only altered the usual commercial relationships but also offered some unusual opportunities. When England went to war with France, as it did periodically during the colonial period, Parliament passed new, temporary trade regulations that forbade commerce with the enemy at home or in the colonies. Some New Englanders found these new rules difficult to obey for a variety of reasons. One reason was, of course, that merchants of Old England continued to trade with the French, or any other enemy. Moreover, the "enemy" in the islands, cut off from the usual markets and sources of supply, actively encouraged such trade. The loopholes in the regulations were too apparent and the possibilities for profit too great to be ignored. Besides, mercantilism argued that trade, so long as the balance was favorable, was a means of weakening a foreign competitor.

Privateering offered another wartime opportunity for colonial merchants, one that had the encouragement of Parliament, if not the French as well. Commercial warfare had an ancient and venerable history by the eighteenth century—and a large practice. Colonial governors were empowered to issue letters of marque that created private vessels of war out of colonial merchant ships. Mounted with a few cannon and augmented with a few extra crew members, a ship that had previously traded with the French in the West Indies turned to prey upon them. The profits for colonial shipowners were considerable. The advantages for the British government were even greater. Colonial privateering in the Anglo-French wars of the eighteenth century weakened the French to a degree contributory to British victory. Not incidentally, many of those involved in the American navy in the Revolutionary War had been privateers fifteen years earlier.[9]

Merchants who were sophisticated enough to engage in the coastwise and West Indian trades, and to take advantage of the changed circumstances of a period of war, were sufficiently perceptive to appreciate that further profits could easily be theirs through a vertical integration of related activities. That is, the merchant who began by exporting goods quickly appreciated the value of owning the ships that carried the goods to be exported. Payments of wharfage fees became a profit to himself if the merchant owned his own wharf. Profits from the sale of return cargoes could be increased if the merchant himself owned part, or all, of the plant that processed a raw commodity into a finished product. Molasses importers became rum distillers and moscovado sugar importers became sugar refiners. With several ships in the carrying trade, one could save money and increase profits by dealing in ship chandlery on the side and, perhaps, investing in a ropewalk. It was then a small jump from the shipping business to at least a part interest in the business of shipbuilding. It is small wonder that, on the eve of the American Revolution, New England was the site of more rum distilleries, more sugar refineries, and more shipbuilding than all the other colonies combined.

New Englanders had built ships from the earliest years of the colony. Integrally related to colonial trade and its changing needs, the shipbuilding industry of New England and the other colonies grew and developed until, by the 1770s, the place of colonial shipping within the empire was of considerable importance. Colonial shipbuilders, preeminently pragmatic, borrowed from the variety of designs that they saw entering and clearing their ports. Over time, they tended to build fewer of the smaller, faster vessels associated with the intercolonial trades and more of the larger, more efficient vessels that could turn a good profit carrying the colonies' products across the Atlantic. By the end of the colonial period, there were roughly a million and a half measured tons of British shipping afloat, including colonial vessels. The best contemporary estimates suggest that colonial shipyards had constructed one-third of that tonnage, or five hundred thousand measured tons, worth roughly £2,500,000 sterling. They did so at a rate of about forty thousand tons per year, roughly half of which was sold abroad (see Appendix B). The vessels sold to colonial merchants, they, of course, used in the colonial carrying trade. The shipbuilding industry of the continental colonies earned credits in the colonial balance of payments both directly and indirectly.[10]

However much of New England's trade might have conformed to both the spirit and the letter of mercantilism, however neatly integrated they were, some colonial economic activities fit less well into the mercantilistic scheme of things. Ideally, it would have been better had West Indian molasses been sent to England, there to be distilled into spirits and exported to North America. The same is true of sugar. Every pound of American refined sugar and every gallon of American distilled rum the colonists consumed was one less of either to have been exported from England to the colonies. Every ton of shipping built in North America was one that might better have been built in England.

Few complained about any of these activities, although the shipbuilders on the Thames and the sugar refiners of London did make their feelings known on more than one occasion. Much more interesting is the response of the British government: there was none. Even when colonial-built ships began to compete directly with British-built vessels, the government still made no attempt to stop shipbuilding in North America. This was as much an incentive, a promotion of colonial shipbuilding, in a particular way, as was the government's failure to disallow a colonial law that erected a protective tariff on imported British refined sugar to protect colonial refiners or to disallow the granting of a distilling monopoly within a colony. Such toleration of competitive activity permitted the enterprise to continue and provoked others to engage in the same or similar economic activities.

To have stopped colonial rum distilling would have seriously disrupted the North American–West Indian trade. This would have undermined the whole of New England's economy and, with it, the capacity of New England to import manufactured goods from London, Bristol, and Liverpool. High levels of exports from Great Britain to the colonies kept manufacturers, laborers, and merchants working productively, and their prosperity rebounded across the rest of England. There was no guarantee that the same level of prosperity would have been achieved by moving the distilling of rum to the mother country. The maintenance of prosperity in Great Britain was one good reason not to interfere with colonial trade and shipping as they had developed by the middle of the eighteenth century.

To have stopped colonial shipbuilding would have cut off the supply of fully one-third of all the British shipping afloat by the time of the American Revolution. There is no guarantee that British shipbuilders would have been able to produce either the quantity or the types of vessels required by the customers of colonial shipbuilders. The lack of adequate shipping would have significantly disrupted the trade of the empire on both sides of the Atlantic.

To have stopped colonial commerce, either by upsetting trading levels with the West Indies—or anywhere else—or by restricting colonial shipbuilding, would have diminished considerably the pool of sailors available to the Royal Navy in wartime. England looked to its maritime and fishing fleets as the nursery of its seamen. Decreased levels of trade put sailors out of work and inhibited young men from going to sea. This meant fewer recruits and slimmer picking for the press gangs when England went to war. A lack of trained seamen could threaten the effectiveness of the navy, and England depended on its navy for its survival. The maintenance of the integrity of Great Britain was another good reason not to interfere with colonial trade and colonial shipping as it had developed by the middle of the eighteenth century.

Policy Consequences

There were, therefore, sound economic, commercial, and even strategic reasons behind British mercantile policy as it affected the colonies. That Parliament did choose during and after the

Seven Years' War to try to change things with regard to the colonies is a matter of record. Why Parliament did so is not part of the present discussion, but some have found answers in the changes in British domestic politics that allowed for new power for some interest groups. Be that as it may, it is surely ironic that the very strengths cultivated in the colonies by British mercantilism became weapons of war in the hands of the colonists which were used effectively to attain their independence. The prosperity of the colonists and the experience in acquiring it provided the revolutionary cause with money to fight the war. The pool of colonial seamen produced sailors to man the naval and privateering vessels that captured substantial quantities of British shipping during the war. The shipyards of the colonies produced merchant ships and naval vessels to be used in the war effort. British mercantile policy, in promoting a colonial merchant marine, had, albeit inadvertently, helped the colonists to fight and win a war of revolution.

The lesson was not lost on the leaders of the revolutionary navy—and, of course, of the new American government. The first American naval vessel was a converted Philadelphia merchant ship previously owned by the largest mercantile house there. After buying it, the Naval Committee of the Continental Congress rechristened it. To the first flagship of the United States Navy, they gave the name of the king of England who was revered as the founder of the Royal Navy and whom we have noted above as the earliest English king to promote a merchant marine: *Alfred*.[11]

Appendix A

A sense of the importance of the colonists' involvement in the carrying trade can be gained by examining a number of the major components of the colonial balance of payments, circa 1770. The following is a reconstruction based on eighteenth-century trade and price data and some modern estimates of their value.

It is known that the colonists were importing goods from Great Britain at an annual average value of about £3,200,000 sterling, including insurance and freight charges. At the same time, they imported sugar, molasses, and rum from the West Indies worth roughly £1,000,000. These were not the only colonial imports, of course, but they do account for the vast majority. The total was probably in the neighborhood of £4,500,000 sterling.

The export value of the five most important colonial commodities came to nearly £2,100,000 sterling, viz.:

Tobacco	920,000
Wheat, bread, and flour	550,000
Rice	305,000
Fish	185,000
Indigo	125,000
	2,085,000

In addition, the colonists exported a large variety of other goods, the total value of which is harder to estimate, but which were worth probably almost as much again. This included about £140,000 earned from ships sold abroad (see Appendix B).

However, none of this accounting of exports includes any credits earned by the shipping industry itself (see Appendix C). A recent study has suggested that such credits—the invisibles in the balance of payments—amounted to nearly as much as credits earned from the export of tobacco, perhaps as much as £700,000 sterling a year. The conclusion can be drawn that the colonists' balance of payments was certainly at par and perhaps somewhat in their favor on the eve of the American Revolution. Colonial shipping and shipbuilding contributed as much as three-quarters of a million pounds sterling per year to this and thereby earned for the colonists almost one-sixth of their foreign credits.[12]

Appendix B

On the average, over the decade before the American Revolution the colonists built about 40,000 measured tons of shipping per year.[13] Of this, nearly half (18,600 tons) was sold abroad, all of it within the British Empire. This earned the colonists roughly £140,000 sterling in credits per year. The rank order with the appropriate estimated number of average measured tons built each year is as follows:

Massachusetts	14,200
New Hampshire	6,900
Rhode Island	3,450
Pennsylvania	3,150
Connecticut	2,800
Maryland	2,800
Virginia	2,500
New York	2,250
South Carolina	850
North Carolina	600
Georgia	400
New Jersey	100
Total	40,000

There are no systematic or reliable data for earlier periods of the colonies, yet there are some points of comparison. In the 1720s, shipbuilders in the Delaware River Valley built an annual average of 1,050 measured tons of shipping or only one-third of the quantity produced fifty years later. The shipbuilding industry of Massachusetts, which already at the beginning of the century was larger than Pennsylvania's some seventy years later, grew during the period at a somewhat slower rate. Over the ten years 1701-10, Massachusetts shipyards launched about 5,550 tons annually; they launched two and a half times that much in the early 1770s.[14]

Appendix C

One way of determining who earned the profits from the carrying trade is to discover who owned the ships. This tells us not only who controlled the vessels, but also to whose favor the moneys earned in the shipping of goods should be credited. A contemporary study supplies the following breakdown of the ownership of shipping tonnages that were engaged in the trade of the several listed colonies, viz.:[15]

	Percentage Owned by Residents of	
Engaged in the Trade of	Continental Colonies	Great Britain
New England	87½	12½
New York and New Jersey	62½	37½
Pennsylvania and Delaware	75	25
Maryland and Virginia	25	75
North Carolina	37½	62½
South Carolina and Georgia	37½	62½

For Massachusetts and Pennsylvania, this represents a considerable increase over the eighteenth century in the proportion of the tonnages owned by, and therefore the shipping earnings accruable to, local residents. Of the shipping registered in Massachusetts between 1666 and 1714, 70 percent was owned by residents of the English colonies and 30 percent by residents of Great Britain. Of the shipping registered in Pennsylvania over the years 1726-29, 64 percent was owned by residents of the English colonies and 36 percent by residents of Great Britain and Ireland. For Massachusetts, the later figures thus represented an increase in the percentage of locally owned tonnage of 25 percent over sixty-plus years; for Pennsylvania, an increase of 17.2 percent over some forty-five years—a roughly comparable increase on an annual rate.[16]

Notes

1. See, for instance, Carter Goodrich, *The Government and the Economy, 1783-1861* (Indianapolis: The Bobbs-Merrill Co., 1967).

2. The literature on the subject is extensive. The classical English expression of mercantilism was Thomas Mun's *England's Treasure by Forraign Trade; or, The Balance of Our Forraign Trade is the Rule of Our Treasure* (London: John Mun, 1664), but the word itself was not popularized until Adam Smith's critique in *An Inquiry into the Nature and Causes of the Wealth of Nations*, 2 vols., (London, 1776). The major works

in the continuing discussion of the subject are Gustav F. von Schmoller, "Das Merkantilsystem in seiner historischen Bedeutung: Stadtische, territoriale und staatliche Wirtschaftspolitik," Part 2 of his "Studien über die wirtschaftsliche Politik Friedrichs der Groszen und Preuszens überhaupt von 1680-1786," *Jahrbuch für Gesetzgebung, Verwaltung und Volkwirtschaft in Deutschen Reich*, VIII (1884), 15-61; and Eli F. Heckscher, *Merkantilismen:* [ett led i den ekonomiska politikens historie], 2d ed., rev.; 2 vols. (Stockholm: P. A. Norstedt [1953]). Both have been translated into English, the first in a variety of editions, the second in an authorized translation by Mendel Shapiro, 2 vols. (London and New York: Macmillan [1955]). A useful survey of the subject is Charles H. Wilson, "Mercantilism: Some Vicissitudes of an Idea," *Economic History Review*, 2nd ser., X (December 1957), 181-88. See also Wilson's *Mercantilism* ([London]: The Historical Association, 1958). Of special interest is J[ames] F. Rees, "Mercantilism and the Colonies," Chapter XX of *The Old Empire from the Beginning to 1783*, ed. J[ohn] Holland Rose, et al., Vol. 1 of *The Cambridge History of the British Empire* (Cambridge: Cambridge University Press, 1929), pp. 561-602. An excellent summary of mercantilistic writings can be found in Joseph A. Schumpeter, *History of Economic Analysis*, ed. Elizabeth Boody Schumpeter (New York: Oxford University Press [1954]), pp. 335-76.

3. The preceding and following two paragraphs are drawn from Lawrence A. Harper, *The English Navigation Laws: A Seventeenth-Century Experiment in Social Engineering* (New York: Columbia University Press, 1939). He drew his reference to King Alfred from Henry C. Hunter, *How England Got Its Merchant Marine, 1066-1776* (New York: National Council of American Shipbuilders, 1935), p. 6.

4. See Ralph Davis, *The Rise of the English Shipping Industry in the Seventeenth and Eighteenth Centuries* (London: Macmillan, 1962); and his *A Commercial Revolution: English Overseas Trade in the Seventeenth and Eighteenth Centuries* (London: The Historical Association, 1967). For colonial attitudes, see E[dgar] A. J. Johnson, "Some Evidence of Mercantilism in the Massachusetts Bay," *New England Quarterly*, I (July 1928), 371-95; and his *American Economic Thought in the Seventeenth Century* (London: P. S. King & Son, 1952). Compare Joseph Dorfman, *The Economic Mind in American Civilization, 1606-1933* (New York: Viking Press, 1946-59).

5. Much of the above is further developed in Curtis P. Nettels, *The Money Supply of the American Colonies before 1720*, University of Wisconsin Studies in the Social Sciences and History, No. 20 (Madison, Wis.: University of Wisconsin Press, 1934). See also James F. Shepherd and Gary M. Walton, *Shipping, Maritime Trade, and the Economic Development of*

Colonial America (Cambridge: Cambridge University Press, 1972).

6. The growth and diversification of the Chesapeake economy must be pieced together from a variety of materials, the most useful of which are: Philip Alexander Bruce, *Economic History of Virginia in the Seventeenth Century: An Inquiry into the Material Condition of the People* (New York: Macmillan, 1896); Arthur Pierce Middleton, *Tobacco Coast: A Maritime History of Chesapeake Bay in the Colonial Era* (Newport News, Va.: The Mariners' Museum, 1953); Jacob M. Price, "The Economic Growth of the Chesapeake and the European Market, 1697-1775," *Journal of Economic History*, XXIV (December 1954), 496-511; Price, *France and the Chesapeake: A History of the French Tobacco Monopoly, 1674-1791, and of Its Relationship to the British and American Tobacco Trades* (Ann Arbor, Mich.: University of Michigan Press, 1973); and James H. Soltow, *The Economic Role of Williamsburg* (Williamsburg, Va.: Colonial Williamsburg, Inc. [1965]). See also Edward C. Papenfuse, *In Pursuit of Profit: The Annapolis Merchants in the Era of the American Revolution* (Baltimore: Johns Hopkins University Press, 1975).

7. Marc Egnal and Joseph A. Ernst, "An Economic Interpretation of the American Revolution," *William and Mary Quarterly*, 3rd ser., XXIX (January 1972), 3-32.

8. New England's economic history as interpreted below is based more especially upon: Marrion H. Gottfried, "The First Depression in Massachusetts," *New England Quarterly*, IX (December 1936), 655-678; Bernard Bailyn, *The New England Merchants in the Seventeenth Century* (Cambridge, Mass.: Harvard University Press, 1955); Richard Pares, *Yankees and Creoles: The Trade between North America and the West Indies before the American Revolution* (London: Longmans, Green & Co., 1956); William B. Weeden, *Economic and Social History of New England, 1620-1789* (Boston and New York: Houghton, Mifflin & Co., 1891).

9. See, among others, James G. Lydon, *Pirates, Privateers, and Profits* (Upper Saddle River, N.J.: Gregg Press, 1971).

10. These estimates are derived from John J. McCusker, "Sources of Investment Capital in the Colonial Philadelphia Shipping Industry," *Jour. Econ. Hist.*, XXXII (March 1972), 146-57. See also Bernard Bailyn and Lotte Bailyn, *Massachusetts Shipping, 1697-1714: A Statistical Study* (Cambridge, Mass.: Harvard University Press, 1959); Simeon J. Crowther, "The Shipbuilding Output of the Delaware Valley, 1722-1776," *Proceedings of the American Philosophical Society*, CXVII (April 1973), 90-104; and Joseph A. Goldenberg, *Shipbuilding in Colonial America* (Charlottesville, Va.: University Press of Virginia, 1976).

11. John J. McCusker, *Alfred: The First Continental Flagship, 1775-1778*, Smithsonian Studies in History and Technology, No. 20 (Washing-

ton D.C.: Smithsonian Institution Press, 1973).

12. See, in part, Lester J. Cappon, et al., eds., *Atlas of Early American History: The Revolutionary Era, 1760-1790* (Princeton, N.J.: Princeton University Press), pp. 26-27, 103-4.

13. Based upon Jacob M. Price, "A Note on the Value of Colonial Exports of Shipping," *Jour. Econ. Hist.*, XXXVI (September 1976), 704-24, and the sources he cites there.

14. Bailyn and Bailyn, *Massachusetts Shipping*, passim; McCusker, "Philadelphia Shipping Industry," 146-57.

15. Reports by Thomas Irving, former Inspector General of Imports and Exports and Register of Shipping in North America, December 1790, Board of Trade Papers, Class 6, Vol. 20, fols. 269r-273v, Public Record Office, London.

16. Bailyn and Bailyn, *Massachusetts Shipping*, passim; McCusker, "Philadelphia Shipping Industry," 146-57.

2
The Golden Age
K. Jack Bauer

America emerged from the triumphs of the Revolution with a moribund merchant marine, shattered trade ties, and few prospects for a major role upon the seas. The loss of British citizenship denied American vessels open entry into the British West Indies and the home islands, which had been the destination of most American deep-sea traders before 1775. It closed the British market to American-built vessels, thereby destroying a major part of the shipbuilders' market. And the departure of the Union Jack removed its protection from American craft sailing the less secure waters of the globe. Nor did the arrival of independence secure for the American worker protection from British competition. No sooner had peace returned than cheaply priced goods from the mother country swamped the American market.

The inability of the young nation, either to protect itself from foreign economic invasion or to break the mercantilistic bands which held shut the ports and colonies of Britain and Spain, helped fuel the drive to establish a stronger form of government in 1789. Under the newly established Constitution, the international and interstate trade of the nation became the responsibility of the central government. Led by a handful of realistic Federalists like George Washington, John Adams, John Jay, and Alexander Hamilton, the new government hastened to establish its maritime role.

The Federalist Period

The new American government commenced in New York at

a propitious moment. Britain and France were too exhausted and too concerned with domestic matters to offer a real threat to the new nation. Three years later, they went to war with one another and remained virtually in constant combat for the next quarter century. Even more important, the political, economic, and intellectual climate into which the new government stepped hastened the nation's growth. The industrial revolution had begun in the 1770s, just as the American Revolution placed the star-speckled flag among those of the sovereign nations of the world.

On July 4, 1789, as one of its earliest acts, the Congress enacted a tariff bill. It stipulated rates to be paid and offered an incentive for goods to move on American vessels by instituting discriminating duties which provided a 10 percent or greater reduction in the fees paid on goods arriving on United States-registered vessels. Within a month, the Congress added a second law standardizing fees for vessels entering U.S. ports. United States-built and owned craft paid six cents per ton annually; American-built but foreign-owned vessels paid five times that on each entry; while foreign-built and owned traders paid fifty cents per ton each time they entered an American port. While the law did not formally close coastal trade to foreign craft, it did effectively eliminate them.[1]

By 1795, the preoccupation of the European shippers with the hostilities of the War of the First Coalition combined with the American protective measures to cause 92 percent of American imports and 86 percent of American exports to travel on American vessels.[2] The impact of this on the shipping industry can be gauged from the experience of Salem, Massachusetts. In 1791, her residents owned 9,031 tons of vessels; in 1800 the fleet had jumped to 24,682 tons, and it nearly doubled in the next seven years to 43,570 tons. The leading shipowner of the north-shore town, Elias Haskett Derby, had full or partial interest in at least forty vessels, and on his death in 1799 he left an estate of over one million dollars. When William Gray left Salem for Boston in 1809, he was reputedly worth three million dollars, all derived from shipping.[3]

The explosion of overseas trade derived little of its force from the reopening of the colonial trade routes. Most of the growth of American trade resulted from the energetic development of new routes. Few bodies of water failed to float an American trader seeking new, and frequently exotic, goods and markets. In 1784, Salem and Beverly, Massachusetts, vessels entered the Baltic.[4] The next year Elias Haskett Derby's famous Eastern trader *Grand Turk* initiated trade with the French privateering base at Mauritius in the Indian Ocean.[5] Derby's fellow townsman, Jonathan Carnes, established the great Salem pepper trade with Sumatra in 1793.[6] But Canton, the entrepôt for the glittering China trade, attracted the greatest attention. Since it fell within the region of the East India Company's monopoly, the China market had been closed to American traders before independence.

The earliest United States-registered vessel to reach China was the *Empress of China,* specially outfitted by a group of New York speculators in 1784. Her 25 percent return on her owners' investment brought a number of imitators. Philadelphia merchants duplicated the voyage later that year, and Salem did the same with Derby's *Grand Turk* in 1785. Salem quickly came to dominate the trade.[7] The exchange with Canton helped place American foreign trade on a profitable basis and set the stage for the fabled China trade of the nineteenth century. Normally, American traders sought tea, procelains, silk, and special cottons like nankeens. Finding exports for Chinese consumption taxed the Americans' ingenuity. Nearly all goods produced by American factories before 1812 were too crude to appeal to Oriental purchasers, and the United States grew few natural products having a Chinese market. Almost alone among the latter was the ginseng root, which the Chinese believed improved potency.

Since sea-otter skins brought a premium on the Canton market, one of the most successful triangular trades in the quarter century before the second war with Britain involved the Pacific Northwest. In 1789-90, Boston investors tested the trade. One of their pioneer craft, the ship *Columbia* under Captain Robert Gray, became the first American vessel to circumnavigate the globe. Two years later, Gray returned to the region in the *Columbia* and discovered the river which bears the name of his vessel. That discovery helped solidify the American claim to the region in the next century. More immediately important was the rapid exploitation of the sea-otter trade by Boston merchants. So decisive was it that the generic term for white men among the northwestern Indians was "Boston man."[8]

John Jacob Astor mounted a serious challenge to the Boston dominance in the years immediately preceding the War of 1812. When an experimental fur shipment to Canton netted him $55,000 in profits, he devised a giant trading venture which would give him command of the fur trade both in North America and China. He envisioned establishing a shipping point on the northwest coast which would draw on the Rocky Mountain fur territory to supply the Canton market. He could undersell the East India Company there, he reasoned, since the British monopoly had to purchase its furs from the Hudson's Bay Company. The result, Astor calculated, would gain him a monopoly of the China market, force the Hudson's Bay Company into bankruptcy, and allow his American Fur Company to acquire its Canadian competitor.[9]

Astor launched his campaign in 1811. The scheme failed, however, because the outbreak of war in 1812 forced Astor to sell his post at Astoria to the Northwest Fur Company of Montreal. The war had a similar effect on the Hawaiian sandalwood monopoly which Jonathan and Nathan Winship secured, along with William H. Davis, in 1812. Sandalwood, the basis of incense and joss sticks, Hindu caste-marking paste, and the source of a fragrant oil, held no special value for the Hawaiians but commanded a high price in the Orient. After the War of 1812, irresponsible harvesting rapidly denuded the islands of sandalwoods.[10]

The competitive advantages of American vessels which were so noticeable in the colonial period continued throughout the Federalist period. For the first decade after the Revolution, American operating costs were lower than European costs, and for many years thereafter the relative cheapness of American construction permitted the nation's shippers to underprice their European competitors. Construction costs remained below European levels, except in Scandinavia, until about 1830. Thereafter, the depletion of the timber stands near the coast and the shift toward larger vessels drove costs up. Below four hundred tons, or one hundred feet in length, American builders continued to turn out inexpensive hulls carrying simple rigs which required small crews, but increasingly they were restricted to coastal trades.[11]

The Revolution had decimated the fishing fleet, and it had recovered very slowly during the Confederation years. In 1792, Congress enacted a direct bounty to fishermen of up to $170 per vessel. This brought about a reconstruction of the fleet. Massachusetts alone increased her fishing tonnage 71 percent in the decade of the 1790s and had 57,500 tons afloat in 1807. The bounty was dropped in 1807, but political pressure ensured its restoration in 1813. In 1818, the Congress further sweetened the take by adding a subsidy of two cents per pound for cod. This caused a jump in the size of the fishing fleet from 37,000 tons in 1815 to a record 163,000 tons in 1860.[12]

The rehabilitation of the fishing fleet coincided with the appearance of a new fishing-vessel design, called the Chebacco boat. These visually distinctive craft with their pinkie stern and schooner or double cat rig were strong enough to work the inshore banks in the Gulf of Maine. About 1820, a new design appeared, the Essex pinkie, a strongly built, sharp-sterned craft, generally schooner rigged and about fifty feet long. A decade later the pinkie began to lose ground to a low-quartered, square-sterned schooner which behaved well in the miserable waters off Georges Bank.[13]

The Neutral Carrier

The nearly constant warfare which racked Europe between 1792 and 1815 offered American merchants, shipowners, and seamen fabulous opportunities and great uncertainties. Although the volatile nature of the regulations promulgated by the belligerents in their economic warfare sometimes caused conditions to change between the start of a voyage and its completion, the profits to be gained overshadowed the risks. Moreover, the restrictions tended to conflict with the now traditional American view, enunciated in the Plan of 1776, that neutral merchantmen should be permitted to carry any noncontraband goods irrespective of their ownership between any ports not under blockade. Contraband, in the American view, meant only munitions clearly consigned to a belligerent power. Needless to say, such a sweeping position drew no acceptance from the major belligerents and would be abandoned by the United States once she became a dominant sea power during the Civil War.

As a result of the profitability of trade, the maritime and commercial investment so dominated the economic life of the nation between 1790 and 1807 that it absorbed most of the risk capital. One effect of this was that prior to 1807 very little capital flowed into manufacturing, and what few efforts did occur were largely financed from the profits of maritime trade. Moses Brown's support of Samuel Slater's cotton-spinning mill at Pawtucket is a prime example.

The vitality of the maritime renaissance appeared in various forms. The merchants indulged themselves with mansions designed by Charles Bulfinch and Samuel MacIntire; started scientific collections like Salem's Peabody Museum; endowed charities; and undertook public works like Boston's Bulfinch-designed New India Wharf or the lifesaving stations erected by the Massachusetts Humane Society. The maritime expansion also gave employment to thousands of new workers. For example, New York, a maritime boom town, grew from 33,000 to 75,000 persons between 1790 and 1805.

Shipyards also blossomed. Shipbuilding during the quarter century after the end of the Revolution changed little from what it had been in colonial times. Vessels generally remained under one hundred feet in length, so they could be constructed by a master builder and a handful of helpers nearly anywhere the ground could support a shipway and the water could float the finished hull. If, as along Massachusetts' North River, the stream would not float a fully outfitted craft, or if the yards lacked the facilities to step masts or rig, the hull was moved to a yard where the work could be accomplished.

Yet concentration on small traders did not rule out the building of larger vessels. The navy contracted for six large frigates in 1794. After an "on again, off again" existence, they finally took to the water in 1797 and 1800 and were followed by six projected 183-foot-long ships of the line. Occasional large six- to seven-hundred-ton merchantmen were built in the 1790s, as were a group of fifteen frigates and sloops of war launched in 1798-1800 in response to the confrontation with France.[14] American builders lacked neither the experience nor the design capability to produce large craft when the needs of their customers demanded.

The reluctance of American shipowners to invest in large vessels and the hesitancy of builders to construct them sprang from the economic organization of trade and from some unfortunate experiences in the late eighteenth century with large craft, notably the six-hundred-ton East Indiaman *Massachusetts,* which was built in her name state in 1789. She was constructed of green wood, and by the time she reached Canton on her maiden voyage she had so deteriorated that she had to be sold. Partially as a result of the experience with the *Massachusetts,* New England operators hesitated to build large craft. As late as 1830, many mariners retained the superstition that no vessel over five hundred tons was safe.

Despite the benefits of the neutral carrying trade to shipowners and to the American economy, Thomas Jefferson chose to strangle it in an abortive fling at economic warfare. Jefferson believed that he could force economic and political concessions from the belligerents by closing the American market to them. His plan harkened back to the apparent success of the embargo following the passage of the Stamp Act and that of the Association. Unfortunately, his recollections endowed those efforts with more success than they achieved and overlooked the differences between the eras. After other efforts failed, Jefferson closed American ports to foreign trade. The embargo caused massive dislocations: shipowners lost their source of income; sailors lost their livelihood; shipbuilders offered an unwanted product; and shipment of exports, largely farm produce, ceased. An estimated fifty-five thousand seagoing jobs evaporated, as did one hundred thousand others in related industries.[15]

Two groups of American vessels continued operating. Those owners who could warn their masters not to return home continued shuttling their vessels between foreign ports, although over $10 million worth were seized by Napoleon when they ventured into French ports. The second group unaffected were the coastal traders, some of whom contrived to be driven off course into the West Indies or Canada. The embargo produced no effect on the belligerents and so was quickly scrapped. But the embargo and its subsequent modifications delayed a general reopening of trade until 1810. The impact was immediate; American deep-sea tonnage jumped to 981,019 tons, the highest per capita ratio it would reach until 1848.[16]

Yet the damage done the maritime industries was great. About $5 million in capital flowed from commerce to industrialization in the first six months after the embargo. This movement of capital started the development of the cotton textile industry, the opening wedge of industrialization. Not only was the capital lost to industry gone forever from the maritime sector, but also it set in motion the complex events which would destroy the attractiveness of the sea as a source of livelihood for most Americans and would offer to investors greater profits and less risk than found in shipping.

Much has been written in American history books about the highly emotional issue of impressment. That pressing of seamen from American vessels was often heavy handed and that British press parties frequently seized Americans is clear. Probably ten thousand Americans served in the British navy. Yet, the British had great difficulty in recruiting seamen for their navy, in which service was not joyous, and twenty thousand of their countrymen sought to evade it by signing on American vessels.[17]

The growth of the coastal trade before the War of 1812 kept pace with that in deep-water craft. Throughout the Federalist and Jeffersonian periods the coastal tonnage hovered at about 40 percent of that involved abroad. It grew after the embargo from 349,000 tons in 1807 to 405,000 tons in 1810.[18]

Americans contributed significantly to the development of steam navigation during the years before the War of 1812. James Rumsey, John Fitch, and Samuel Morey all built steam-powered vessels before 1790, the year in which Fitch inaugurated steam passenger service on the Delaware River. It remained for Robert Fulton, the painter turned engineer, to produce the first truly practical steam-powered vessel in 1807.

It is from the September 17-21, 1807, trip to Albany and back by his *Steam Boat*[19] that the steamboat is commonly dated. It was the first truly successful voyage of a steamer. Fulton's success triggered a rapid spread of steamboats. John Stevens's *Phoenix*, frozen out of New York waters by the monopoly held by Fulton and his financial backer Robert Livingston, fled to the Delaware River in 1809. That year, a primitive craft also breasted the St. Lawrence River, and another braved the chop of Lake Champlain. A steam ferry began service across New York harbor to New Jersey in 1810; in 1811 Nicholas Roosevelt, as an agent of the Fulton-Livingston monopoly, supervised the construction of the first western river steamer, the *New Orleans*, at Pittsburgh.[20]

By 1813, Fulton and his backers had developed a plan for a network of steamboat and stage lines running from Canada to Charleston, South Carolina, and from Pittsburgh to New Orleans. The segments north of Philadelphia already existed, as did that between New Orleans and Natchez.[21] The War of 1812 introduced steam into naval warfare. During 1814 Fulton built a huge thick-skinned catamaran steam battery for the navy which he proposed calling *Demologos* (Word of the People) but to which the navy with less flair assigned the name *Fulton*. That year General Andrew Jackson pressed the two steamers operating on the Mississippi into service to haul supplies to New Orelans for the defense of the port.

The war also marked the coming of age of the navy. Its large frigates like the *Constitution* and the *United States* proved to be the best vessels of their class in the world. American naval officers showed themselves to be skilled single-ship fighters and competent squadron commanders. It was ironic, however, that the critical battles of the war ostensibly fought over maritime rights occurred on fresh water. The naval victories on Lakes Erie and Champlain won for the United States control of the upper Great Lakes basin and frustrated the only serious British invasion attempt. Those two battles demonstrated, as clearly as any action since the battle off the Virginia Capes, the importance of command of the waterways in the era before easy overland transportation.

The Merchant Marine Revives

The close of the War of 1812 loosed a wave of nationalism in the nation—a pride in Americanness that had not existed before the war. The nation had survived the Napoleonic Wars without loss of territory or sovereignty. Its navy, in American eyes at least, had bested the wooden walls of England. American sailors, so ran the national self-delusion, were the world's best and American vessels were excelled by none. But the reality was different. The small deep-water navy could not keep American ports open while the fleet victories had come on fresh water employing vessels hastily thrown together and manned by largely untrained crews. But reality mattered little, since Americans believed in their superiority and in the superiority of their system. We were, in our own eyes, the hope of a world beset with autocracy and the Peace of Vienna.

During the next fifty years the United States sprang from national adolescence to nationhood. The years between the Treaty of Ghent and the election of Abraham Lincoln saw the frontier sweep westward as a waterborne transportation network in the West developed to support the new settlers. Well over five million immigrants, overwhelmingly Irish and German, arrived by 1870 to help swell the nation's population to 31 million. Those years saw the merchant marine rise to its zenith in terms of the percentage of American trade carried. Only in the aftermaths of World Wars I and II would its percentage of world tonnage stand as high.

After the War of 1812, shipbuilding continued to concentrate in the Northeast. While it is indisputable that American construction costs rose after 1830, it is not clear that American owners lost any significant competitive advantage, or, if shrinkage did exist, that it had a major impact before the Civil War.[22]

The shift to larger vessels of over four-hundred-tons burden brought changes in the operation of yards. The builders of the large vessels adopted sophisticated machinery and building techniques which insured that the yards became permanent operations. These new yards required more capital investment and stronger managerial and design skills than traditional plants. They also tended to congregate in a limited number of locations. Moreover, the demand for larger pieces of lumber inexorably pushed up the price of new hulls. Not only did the major yards acquire an industrial patina, but also the vessels they produced tended to become more specialized. In the 1820s, distinct types began to develop to meet the requirements of individual trade routes. Among them were the fast freighter-passenger carriers for the premium, dense traffic routes; the large, slow, bulk carriers or "kettle bottoms" for the cotton trade; the fast, medium-sized brigs and schooners to haul perishables and slaves; and the large, fast, deep-water freighters for the run to Canton.

For small and medium-sized freighters, Maine yards could not be undersold. The Pine Tree State's forests contained plentiful timber in the sizes needed. The resulting lower transportation costs and the unique advantage the state's yards derived from workers who, being subsistence farmers, would work for lower wages than their counterparts elsewhere, gave the Maine builders a five to fifteen dollar per ton price advantage in the early 1800s over their competitors. As a result, more vessels came off the ways in Maine than in any other place.[23] Maine yards often built on speculation, which frequently produced sizable profits as long as the shipping boom lasted. When ship prices fell below costs, as they did in the late 1850s, many of the smaller yards failed or ceased building.

Boston remained a major building center during the period because of its access to the New Hampshire forests by way of the Merrimack River and the Middlesex Canal. Those trees and the large tracts in western New York and elsewhere judiciously acquired by the Bostonians assured the yards an adequate timber supply down to the time of the Civil War.[24] As a result, Samuel Hall, Donald McKay, Paul Curtis, and other Greater Boston builders delivered a series of exceptionally successful clippers and other large sailing craft.

From the Hudson River basin and the areas drained by the Erie Canal flowed the timbers for the New York yards.[25] Prior to 1800, New York had not attracted many shipbuilders. This had begun to change before the War of 1812, but the golden age of New York's yards came in the postwar period. Then a group of notably successful East River shipyards, including those of

William H. Webb, Smith and Dimon, William H. Brown, Brown and Bell, and Jacob Westervelt, turned out a constant stream of large, wooden-hulled packets, clippers, coastal freighters, and steamers, along with an occasional man-of-war for export.

As the local timber gave out, the Delaware River yards began experimenting with iron construction, and by the outbreak of the Civil War nearly all the yards in the country regularly building iron hulls were concentrated along a twenty-five-mile stretch of the Delaware River.[26] Although Baltimore and Norfolk housed a small group of yards, neither threatened those to the north of them in quantity of output.

Until the Civil War, shipbuilding was a highly competitive industry, essentially a handicraft one, demanding only limited capital to enter. Most yards were small, often operated by a master carpenter who designed the vessels, usually relying on the rules published by the classification societies. He also selected the timbers, supervised the construction, and handled the financial matters. The duties were sometimes divided between an operator who handled the financial and nonstructural responsibilities and a hired master carpenter who designed and supervised the construction of the hull. A hull could be built by as few as three men, and normally much of the work was subcontracted to specialized gangs of ship carpenters, caulkers, riggers, sailmakers, etc. Only the largest yards maintained a level of activity high enough to warrant specialization or even a permanent work force. Although the proportion dropped after 1840, about 10 to 20 percent of all vessels came from intermittently operating yards. The average annual production was not high; in 1850, it was slightly above one per yard.[27]

Few iron-hulled craft were built in the three decades before the Civil War. American yards could not produce them at a price competitive with wood or with those built by their European counterparts. Although a handful of experimental craft had been built in the United States earlier, the first major iron craft was the navy's Great Lakes gunboat *Michigan,* which slid into Lake Erie in 1843. She survived for a hundred years before her plates joined a World War II scrap drive. Not until Harlan and Hollingsworth built the *Champion* in 1859, however, did an

American yard produce a truly first-class, seagoing, iron-hulled steamer.[28]

The inability of American iron foundries to produce heavy iron forgings and the high prices for the shapes they could produce also retarded the conversion to steam. American marine engineers developed some excellent engines, such as the rugged and simple walking-beam design and Oliver Evans's half-beam or Grasshopper engine. Western river-steamboat operators very quickly installed the lighter-weight high-pressure engines, but multiple expansion designs, except for a handful of unsuccessful experimental installations, did not appear until after the Civil War. On the other hand, American engineers followed quickly on the heels of Francis P. Smith and John Ericsson in installing screw propulsion, especially after the great success of Ericsson's installations in the Great Lakes steamer *Vandalia* in 1841 and in the navy sloop *Princeton* the following year.

The economic concerns which hastened the shift to larger and more specialized craft brought the demise of the traditional small trading partnership employing its capital and shipping on numerous, diverse routes. This mode of shipping gave way to common carriers concentrating on a single or a handful of routes. The change reflected both the increasing sophistication of trade and the growth of capital in the United States that permitted such a division of labor.[29] Assisting in the change was the provision of the British Navigation Acts before 1849 which forbade the registry of foreign-built vessels. Since British shipbuilding costs rose dramatically after the Napoleonic Wars, her shipowners, like their American counterparts a century and a half later, found themselves priced out of trades unsheltered by the Navigation Acts. The unprotected routes became the domain of American and Scandinavian vessels.

The most visible example of the impact of the common carrier, a shipper who for a fee transported goods owned by others, came on the North Atlantic with the introduction of packets sailing on fixed schedules between fixed ports. These appeared in the coastal trade just prior to the War of 1812 and became common following the close of hostilities. Their success encouraged a group of New York importers to establish a similar transatlantic service in 1818. Within five years competitors appeared, and by 1851 sixteen packet lines crossed the Atlantic to Liverpool alone.

The packets were large for the period, averaging four to five hundred tons in the 1820s and six to seven hundred tons in the 1830s. The singular success of the New York packet lines stemmed from their ability to develop eastbound cargoes. New York merchants assembled mixed cargoes, heavily weighted with grain, flour, and cotton, which produced the eastward freight necessary for financial success which the other East Coast ports lacked. Not until 1844 would Boston, for instance, develop enough business to support a permanent packet service. Philadelphia, on the other hand, operated a line after 1822, but its volume of traffic remained small.[30] None of the cotton ports established direct scheduled sailings until 1851.

In an era when oceanborne passenger service across the North Atlantic no longer exists, it is difficult for Americans to realize how completely vessels flying the Stars and Stripes dominated the "North Atlantic Ferry" during the second quarter of the nineteenth century. Even though after 1840 the transatlantic steamers siphoned off those passengers willing to pay for a speedy crossing, the bulk of the travelers went by sail. As late as 1856, 96.4 percent of all passengers arriving in New York came by sail. Most were immigrants, and nearly all came in American vessels.[31]

The packets were fast and surprisingly consistent in their passages. The eastbound passage time dropped from the 28 days of the pioneer packet *James Monroe* to 15 days, 16 hours in 1824; 14 days in 1846; and 13 days, 8 hours by the famed *Dreadnought* in 1859. Westward voyages were slower because of the adverse winds, the record being 15 days, 12 hours from Belfast in 1830 and from Liverpool in 1846.[32] More normal were three-week passages eastward and a month westward.

Packet crews were pushed as no earlier ones had been, since speed was both the essence and the appeal of the service. Owners paid bonuses to masters and crews making quick passages. For various reasons, but notably the abandonment of the sea by new generations of Americans, the packets relied on the "Liverpool rats" recruited from the scum of the English port's saloons and boardinghouses. When commanded by a nerveless captain backed by strong-armed bucko mates, the Liverpool packet rats were superb sailors, able to endure nearly any hardship afloat.[33]

The Civil War ended the packet era. Most of the lines relied on cotton shipments for the bulk of their eastbound freight, and when those evaporated in the fratricidal holocaust, they collapsed. The handful of stronger lines that survived could not recapture their lost trade following the war and faded into history.

Complementing the packet lines on the North Atlantic Ferry were the immigrant operators. Although the packets usually carried several hundred steerage passengers on their westward crossings, infinitely more traveled on the immigrant lines sailing from Liverpool, Greenock, Hamburg, and Antwerp. The largest of the immigrant lines, the Black Star Line, in 1850 dispatched a ship a week from Liverpool. Conditions on board the immigrant ships were miserable. The travelers received a place to sleep, drinking water, and a place to cook their food in return for their meager passage price. They were stuffed into holds from which emanated an odor of massed bodies, stale food, slop barrels, and vomit which haunted many an immigrant for the remainder of his or her life. Efforts at amelioration began early. Federal law in 1819 placed limits on the numbers which could be carried, and in 1847 legislation was passed which required that each passenger receive at least fourteen square feet of deck space.

The crowded conditions helped spread contagious diseases, especially "ship's fever" (typhus). In an effort to encourage greater enforcement of health standards, in 1855 the Congress enlarged the space to be allotted to each passenger to sixteen square feet; limited the total number to one passenger per two tons of burden; and levied a fine of ten dollars per passenger death against the captain.

Despite the tales of horror and the obvious dangers of the North Atlantic crossing, relatively few people died from illness or shipwreck. As with the packets, the Civil War marked the effective end of the sailing immigrant liner. While 96 percent of the immigrant travelers arrived by sail in 1856, only 68 percent did so six years later.[34] Even that percentage dropped drastically, since the European operators who dominated the trade after the war almost exclusively operated steamships.

The great challenge to the American sailing packets before 1861 came from the steam packets. The first crossing of the Atlantic by a steamship occurred in 1819 when the *Savannah*'s owners sent her to Europe in a vain effort to unload their white elephant. Three naval steamers and a Canadian misfit made single crossings between 1821 and 1833, but none represented an effort to establish service. In April 1838, a pair of British lines initiated the first regular commercial steam passage across the Atlantic. They were followed two years later by Samuel Cunard's British and North American Royal Mail Steam Packet Company, which held a $425,000 per year subsidy to carry mail between Liverpool and Boston.

Steamers rapidly established their reliability and relatively greater speed than the sailing packets. This brought them the bulk of the premium express cargo and first-class passenger trade. They carted very little of the less-valuable bulk cargoes until well after the Civil War, because their primitive engines were expensive to operate. Indeed, in some of the bulk trades, such as timber, coal, nitrate, and grain, where speed of delivery was a secondary consideration, sailing freighters held their own into the twentieth century because of their low operating costs.

In 1845, growing complaints about poor American transatlantic mail service and extensive lobbying by the prospective operators combined to secure congressional authorization for postal contracts with United States lines. The initial contracts provided for service to Southampton, Le Havre, and Bremen. The lines proved short lived and suspended service before the Civil War. More realisitic was the 1848 contract with the New York and Liverpool United States Mail Steam Ship Company organized by the former packet operator Edward K. Collins.

Collins received a subsidy of $385,000, which proved to be inadequate and was raised to $850,000 per year in 1852. His four vessels, the *Atlantic, Arctic, Baltic,* and *Pacific* were the finest steamers of their day, near sisters of about 2,850-tons burden with massive, slow-speed, side-lever engines driving paddle wheels. Their heavy wooden hulls came from the leading yards in New York, and their finish bespoke the quality of their construction. They offered such luxuries as steam-heated cabins, a smoking room, a bathroom, and a barbershop. The Collins liners quickly won a following, carrying 40 percent more passengers than Cunard. They were fast and won the eastbound North Atlantic blue ribbon in 1850 and the westbound ribbon in 1851. Their best times were the *Arctic*'s 9 days, 17 hours, 12 minutes eastbound in 1852 and the *Baltic*'s westbound record of 9 days, 18 hours the previous year.

Yet the Collins vessels were magnificent failures. They averaged an operating loss of $16,928.74 per voyage in the first year alone. Their hulls, wracked by the pounding of the powerful machinery and the strain of driving through North Atlantic storms, required costly repairs which consumed much of the line's revenue. Compounding the problems of the line were the loss of the *Arctic* in a collision off Cape Race, Newfoundland, in 1854 and the disappearance of the *Pacific* two years later.

In 1857 the Congress reduced the subsidy to $385,000 and eliminated it completely the following year. Without government money, Collins could not continue and suspended service. His project died from a multiplicity of ills. The subsidy withdrawal reflected the rampant sectionalism which was inexorably driving the nation toward its flirtation with national suicide. It also revealed the unwillingness of a divided Congress to provide the heavy infusions of national money necessary to make such a service profitable. Other factors were the necessary American reliance on wooden hulls and side wheels, the assaults of the Panic of 1857, and just plain bad luck.[35] A few American owners sought unsuccessfully to challenge Cunard on the North Atlantic after the departure of Collins, but they found little reward for their courage. Except for Commodore Cornelius Vanderbilt's *Vanderbilt*, a huge 3,550-ton wooden side-wheeler, none of the craft were spectacular.[36]

The American steamship operators' problems were intertwined with developments in maritime technology. The 1830s had seen the experimental appearance of large iron-hulled steamers, but even in Britain they remained expensive until into the 1850s, although their strength was well established. In 1856 Cunard adopted iron for his vessels. That permitted him to install larger engines and insured the restoration of the blue ribbon to Britain, as well as larger vessels able to carry more paying cargo and passengers.

Cotton vied with the immigrant trade in its importance to the growth of the merchant marine during the first half of the nineteenth century. It generated a quarter of the country's exports in 1817. After 1830, that figure hovered between 40 percent and 50 percent, reaching as high as 59 percent in 1843. By 1860, over 1.7 million pounds of the white fluff, worth nearly $192 million, were carried overseas annually. Although it is difficult to determine the exact figures, the best estimates are that about equal parts of the crop entered American factories, moved directly to foreign ports, and were transshipped through New York, Boston, Philadelphia, and Baltimore. Whatever its destination, nearly all traveled on American vessels.

The American dominance of the cotton trade grew out of the special characteristics of East Coast economics which dictated a triangular trade pattern. The northeastern ports, except New York, lacked cargoes to counterbalance their imports while the import demands of southern cotton ports did not offset their exports. Therefore vessels from the Northeast either shipped a cargo of manufactured goods or sailed in ballast to a southern port. There they embarked cotton or occasionally another southern export like naval stores or timber for European delivery. From Europe, the freighters returned to northern ports with cargoes of manufactured goods, raw materials, and occasionally immigrants. Since this triangular trade involved a coastal leg, most foreign vessels, except for an occasional British ship which could substitute a Canadian stop for a northeastern port, were excluded.[37]

Coastal craft offered merchants the only means of moving goods in quantity between the North and South until the completion of the railroad systems shortly before the Civil War. Moreover, coastal schooners and brigs offered passengers a pleasant alternative to suffering the jolts of poorly sprung carriages bounding along the rutted trails which still passed for roads in most of the nation. Between 1815 and 1817 an average of 1,282 vessels a year took to the water. The vast majority were licensed for the coastal service alone. (In 1817, the Congress formally closed the coastal trade to foreign craft, but the impact seems to have been negligible.) By then new construction had glutted the market and helped bring on the recession of that year. Aided by the growing demand for cotton to feed the mills of the Northeast, good times returned to the coastal shippers in 1821.[38] By then it was clearly evident to anyone who chose to look at the figures that the growth of the industrialization then under way would cause the coastal trade to supplant foreign trade as the major activity of the merchant marine. It did so in 1831.[39]

Initially, the coastal services were served by sailing vessels alone. Steamers first edged their way into the trade on protected waters like Long Island Sound and Chesapeake Bay. The pioneer steamer appeared on Chesapeake Bay in 1813. Long Island Sound acquired its first one in 1815. Nevertheless, interstate steamers were slow to ply coastal waters. Marine engineering was still in its infancy and had yet to produce engines capable of operating in heavy seas or sufficiently economical in their fuel consumption to make extended voyages. The greatest inhibition, however, was political. Several state legislatures, following the lead of New York, granted monopolies of service within their waters. Until such grants were outlawed by the Supreme Court in *Gibbons v. Ogden* in 1824, interstate steamer travel lagged. After the opening of interstate waters by law, the construction of coastal steamers, even though they were still very fragile craft, spurted. Their use on outside routes, like those from New York or Baltimore to Charleston and Savannah, caught the public fancy until two accidents in 1837-38 took 236 lives. A full decade passed before the steamers once again regained public confidence.

For most of the first three decades following the War of 1812, the coastal steamers, like their ocean-crossing larger sisters, hauled only express freight and premium paying passengers. The bulk of all coastal shipments, and a large portion of the passenger traffic, moved by sail. Large stretches of coastline contained too few settlements to generate enough traffic to support steamer operation. Most of the coastal traffic, moreover, was in bulk goods like timber, lime, stone, fish, cotton, and coal which were unsuited to the small holds of the early steamers and could move easily and cheaply by sail.

The growth of Bangor, Maine, as the lumber center of the

nation is an excellent example of the interrelationship between maritime trade and the development of an area. Between 1832 and 1888 Bangor shipped 8.7 billion feet of lumber. At the height of the trade, 150 vessels loaded at the same time. Not only did the timber move downstream to the sawmills on the Penobscot and her tributaries, but also the finished wood had to move by water. The Maine city was so far from its markets that not until well after the Civil War would it have rail connections with the outside world.[40]

Long Island Sound is another good example. It attracted a large fleet of steamers once *Gibbons v. Ogden* eliminated the monopoly. Although they faced stiff competition from the sailing packets which could make nearly as good speed, the steamers rapidly won the passenger traffic since they were both larger and more palatial. They formed part of a complex transportation system which developed in the region during the 1830s. The earliest rail lines along the north shore of the Sound thrust north to tap the trade of the local river valleys. They relied on steamboats to carry their goods and passengers to New York City. Even when the railroads shifted to east-west service, they offered little competition to the longer steamer runs because they could not compete in luxury with the floating palaces on the Sound before the Civil War. Nor could the railroad generally compete in speed because of the slow construction of bridges across the rivers.

In 1835, Providence became the first Sound port to gain a rail connection to Boston. This reinforced an excellent existing stage service and established the Rhode Island capital as the chief transshipment point for passengers passing between Boston and New York since the land and sea route eliminated the rough passage around Cape Cod. But Providence lost that distinction two years later when the railroad reached Stonington, Connecticut. Embarkation or debarkation at Stonington eliminated the unpleasant passage around Point Judith. This city held the dominant position until the establishment of service through Fall River in 1847. Although beset with numerous competitors, the Fall River Line, through able management and a sound financial base, dominated the Sound throughout the century, continuing to operate until 1937.[41]

The healthy trade on Long Island Sound was one of the factors in the rise of New York City. The Empire City dominated the Hudson River basin, northwestern New Jersey, and most of Connecticut, an area which contained 13 percent of the country's population in 1820 and nearly a third of its economic activity. The opening of the Erie Canal in 1825 added the western grain area to that whose produce flowed onto New York wharves, while the tens of thousands of New Englanders and immigrants who moved westward created an enlarged market for the goods passing through New York. The Erie Canal brought to New York a better selection of export goods, thereby insuring that it maintained the best balance of import and export trade of any major port, North or South.[42] As it established its successful trade balance, New York naturally became the port of deposit for imports, which in turn helped it develop close commercial ties with the cities that depended upon it for those goods. New York's spurt coincided with the boom in cotton production. In 1850 it handled more cotton than any other port in the nation except New Orleans and Mobile.[43]

New York's rise attracted the attention of its rivals. Philadelphia, in particular, had a superb location at the junction of the Schuylkill and Delaware rivers, which between them gave access to the grain, coal, and timber areas of eastern Pennsylvania and central New York. In large part because of its proximity to the coalfields, Philadelphia was the nation's leading industrial center into the 1830s. It very naturally, therefore, developed into the center of the American iron shipbuilding industry, and remained in the lead until the 1890s. It shared with New York prominence in marine engineering, notably in the building of screw propulsion machinery.

Philadelphia's coastal trade after the 1830s concentrated on coal shipping, either through the canals which tied the coalfields to New York City or by deep-water colliers which, down to the Civil War, were almost entirely wind powered.[44] Equally important to the story of Philadelphia are the frustrations of its failure to match the success of the Erie Canal with a series of westward-pointing canals and portage rail lines.

Baltimore had a similar experience.[45] Boston, after flirting with a canal tie to the Erie, also shifted to rails. Nevertheless, all three ports quickly discovered that their western connections were not sufficiently attractive to divert large quantities of goods to their docks. South of Chesapeake Bay, the local efforts to develop canal and river networks to feed the cotton ports, notably Charleston and Savannah, had only modest success because the developers relied on private and state support which was insufficient to develop a major system.[46]

Maritime Routes to Western Settlement

Probably no place in American history illustrates the impact of maritime trade more clearly than in the movement of settlers to new homes west of the Appalachian Mountains. A few pioneers moved into the area around Fort Pitt (modern Pittsburgh), along the tributaries of the Tennessee, and beside the Kentucky River before the Revolution. The Kentucky settlements expanded only slightly during the Revolution, but those in Tennessee, protected from hostile Indians, grew more rapidly. Neither area, however, could attract numerous settlers until cheap transportation became available to carry the products of the frontier farms to market. Since the cost of horse-powered transport was prohibitive, the pioneers had to ship their produce by water.

The first effort, a small scow laden with flour, floated into Natchez in 1784. Its arrival violated Spanish mercantile policy and brought scowls to the local officials who promptly closed the Mississippi River to American goods. The tight enforcement of the regulations reflected the Spanish fear that free use of the river would strengthen the American western settlements and bring in more settlers who would further threaten the weak Bourbon hold on Louisiana. Despite the regulations, a few craft continued to try trading with the Spanish settlements. In 1801, after the Mississippi was opened to American craft, over a million dollars worth of goods, mostly flour, reportedly passed through the customs house at Natchez.[47] Spanish control of the Mississippi did not throttle shipbuilding in the American settlements on the Ohio since vessels could be sent to sea so long as they did not attempt to trade with Spanish colonies along the way. A seagoing sloop took to the water at Pittsburgh in 1789, and a schooner followed about four years later. By 1810 at least thirty-four more oceangoing vessels had been built on the banks of the Ohio. Thereafter, production of large craft slackened as builders found a better market in river vessels.[48]

A small but significant pool of settlers gathered in Kentucky in anticipation of the opening of the land north of the Ohio to settlement. In 1794 General Anthony Wayne crushed the resistance of the local indians in the Battle of Fallen Timbers and in the following spring secured their surrender of southern Ohio and southeastern Indiana. The Pinckney Treaty of 1795 formally opened the Mississippi and granted American traders the right of transshipment at the mouth of the river. The following year the British withdrew from the posts south of the Great Lakes which they had held since the end of the Revolution. These moves broke the shackles which prevented the settlement of southern Ohio.[49] By 1803, enough settlers had paddled across or drifted down the Ohio to win statehood for the area.

Although the Louisiana Purchase that year removed all political hazards to shipment of produce through New Orleans, it did not overcome the near impossibility of moving goods inland against the currents of the great rivers. That was solved by the steamboat, the first of which, appropriately named *New Orleans*, left Pittsburgh in 1811. Until after the War of 1812, too few steamers existed to have any significant effect.

Most historians of western navigation date the true start of steamboat service in 1817 with the completion of a round trip between New Orleans and Louisville by the *Washington*. She proved the real value of steamboats as well as starting the development of the unique western river-steamer design. That development was gradual and would not reach its full expression until the 1830s.[50] Although best known as passenger carriers, the true value of the western river-steamers lay in their role as freighters. Their ability to move with or against the current permitted western farmers greater freedom than ever before in timing shipments to New Orleans in hopes of avoiding the traditional market glut there. Steamers had the additional advantage of so reducing the cost of goods shipped upstream that they no longer needed to be considered luxuries.

Steamboat dominance and development lasted until the

decade before the Civil War. During those years, the value of goods reaching New Orleans from upriver doubled each decade to grow from $12.6 million in 1820 to $185.2 million in 1860. Despite that phenomenal growth, the Mississippi River steamboats faced increased competition from canals and, after 1840, railroads. They drew ever larger amounts of produce into direct east-west movement rather than shipment through the Crescent City. But it more than offset the losses with cotton shipments from the river plantations and upriver transport of West Indian goods.[51] As a result, by 1860 New Orleans had ceased to play a major role in the trade patterns of the upper Mississippi and the Ohio River Valley. That shift was not perceived by many southerners, who counted on the closing of the Mississippi export route in 1861 to force western support of the concessions demanded by the seceding states.

After 1817, St. Louis developed into a major river port. She served as the commercial center for the region further northward along the Mississippi and as the magnet for the furs floating down the Missouri River from the Rocky Mountains. St. Louis also benefited from the flood of German and Irish immigrants who rushed into the country through New Orleans in the decade and a half before the Civil War. In 1860 a million waterborne travelers crossed the St. Louis levee. These patterns began to change during the 1850s. At mid-decade St. Louis gained her first rail connection to the East Coast while in the next few years the rapidly expanding Chicago rail web siphoned off significant portions of the trade traveling along the upper Mississippi.[52]

The shift of trade patterns in the Mississippi basin from north-south to east-west began with the opening of the Erie Canal in 1825. That waterway, built by the state of New York at a cost of $7,143,798, was the largest civil works project yet undertaken in the United States. It fulfilled all the promises of its promoters. Freight rates between Albany at its eastern end and Buffalo at its western fell from $90 per ton to $8.53. Towns along its route blossomed. Rochester bounded from 2,700 to 11,000 people between 1822 and 1828. Buffalo, which became the transshipment point for grain flowing east, had nearly as instantaneous a growth. The key to her growth was the grain elevator built by Joseph Dart in 1842-43 that broke the transshipment bottleneck which threatened to strangle the grain trade. By the end of that decade, Buffalo had passed Rochester in population and could claim 80,000 in 1860. Yet in the long run it was clearly Chicago that benefited most from the new trade route. She developed into the disseminating point for goods arriving from the East via the canal and the Great Lakes and later as a collection point for cargoes bound for the eastern market.[53]

As important as the Erie Canal was to the towns touched by its currents of trade, its political and economic impact on the western states was even greater. The canal opened the Great Lakes basin to settlement. The new inhabitants, largely New Englanders, rapidly came to outnumber the older, predominately southern-born, residents of the Ohio Valley. This shifted the area's political orientation toward the Northeast and away from the South in a complete reversal of the political alliances existing since the beginning of the century. Moreover, the canal, the feeder routes developed by the westerners, and the railroads so tightly tied the West economically to the East that when the great sectional controversy arose in the years following the Mexican War, it found the West siding with the North which caused much of the feeling of frustration and alienation which led to the southern Secession of 1860-61.

Both the eastern seaports like Baltimore, Philadelphia, and Boston, which hoped to tap western markets, and the western states, which viewed canals as an economic panacea, embarked on massive canal programs after 1825. Few were finished and fewer yet were successful. Only Philadelphia completed its western tie, an expensive, state-financed canal and inclined-plane system opened in 1834. The route could not compete with the Erie and in the 1850s gave way to an all-rail line. Ohio suffered an orgy of canal company authorizations which foundered in the Panic of 1837 and nearly bankrupted the state, with no greater success. Canals, experience proved, were too expensive to build, too inflexible in route, and too difficult to maintain to compete with railroads for the bulk cargoes originating away from the rivers. Only the Erie, which continues today as the New York State Barge Canal, developed enough traffic to remain long in operation.[54]

A third area affected by the westward movement was the

Great Lakes. Only a sprinkling of settlements broke the forest landscape along their shores before the War of 1812. The war not only hastened settlement along the Great Lakes but it brought to the area trained shipwrights to build the naval squadrons which contended for control of the inland seas. Maritime trade developed rapidly after the war. In 1818, about 111 American vessels, including a pair of steamers, operated on Lakes Erie and Ontario. Lumber, copper, furs, trade goods, and government stores provided most of their cargoes.[55]

Opening of the Erie Canal drastically altered the economic life of the region. Wheat, heretofore lacking markets, now could be shipped east where it sold for less than locally grown grain. While Ohio naturally shipped the bulk of the grain in the 1830s and 1840s, the western farms whose natural port was Chicago thereafter became dominant. In 1858 the Windy City loaded 20 million bushels of flour and grain, nearly twice that departing Ohio ports. Chicago grew from five thousand to a hundred thousand inhabitants between 1840 and 1860. Houses were built so fast that the city absorbed nearly 300 million board feet of lumber per year after 1850, nearly all arriving by water from the great forests of Michigan and Wisconsin. Thirty years later the Great Lakes lumber mills would surpass even the Maine ones in volume.[56]

Despite its volume, the grain trade suffered from competition after 1850 as the railroads completed their connections with the eastern markets. That decline in waterborne shipment would play a major role in the general shrinkage of total Great Lakes tonnage in the fifteen years following the Civil War.

Copper and iron ore gradually replaced grain as the dominant bulk cargo. The copper trade began after the discovery of the Keweenaw Peninsula copper deposits along the south shore of Lake Superior in 1840 but was limited by the necessity to transship the copper around the falls of the St. Mary's River at Sault Sainte Marie. That bottleneck was eliminated in 1855 by the completion of the first of Sault Sainte Marie locks. The Soo passage, enlarged or supplemented five times in the next century, remains one of the world's busiest waterways. Without it, neither the iron ore of the Mesabi and the other Lake Superior fields, which made possible the post-Civil War development of Pittsburgh into the world's greatest steel center, nor the wheat from the great grain fields of the Canadian and American northern plains could have found the easy waterborne route to market which they needed.

Fishing

After the second decade of the nineteenth century, American-born fishermen became as scarce as any other native seamen. Increasingly, the New England vessels had to be manned either with part-time sailors who also farmed, as was common in Maine, or by foreigners, usually from the Canadian Maritimes or the Portuguese Atlantic islands.

During the 1850s dory fishing became common. Instead of dropping their lines over the sides of the fishing schooner, the crew fished from double-ended dories which spread over the face of the sea in search of the elusive fish. This new "Captains Courageous" method proved itself in 1858 when one schooner boated 900 quintals of fish on Georges Bank in the same time that nearby traditional hand-liners got only 160. Her success was unusual, but the rule of thumb commonly employed was that dory fishing was three times as efficient as the older methods.[57]

Many of the fishing areas developed special craft to fit the unique requirements of their locale. Turned out by traditional handicraft methods by local builders, they have long interested antiquarians and naval architects, but they had at best only limited effect on the direction taken by American vessel design. Their development and occasional interbreeding can be traced in the catalog of the *National Watercraft Collection*.[58]

Whaling is a much overromanticized aspect of American history. The whaler was an unlovely, easily identified vessel. Heavily built and compactly rigged, she could be identified by her weatherbeaten appearance, smoking tryworks, yards of weed trailing from her foul bottom, and the stench of trying blubber, as well as by the graceful double-ended whaleboats slung amidships. The life of the whaling seaman was scarcely more attractive than the vessel on which he served. Pay was meager. Few whalers were experienced sailors, especially after

1830, for captains feared experienced sailors would mutiny against the appalling conditions they found. Therefore, most of the hands were green farm boys or Atlantic islanders. Even under the most humane and considerate of officers, almost a non sequitur among whalers, life was dirty, rough, dangerous, and monotonous. Yet the captains and mates, nearly all of whom were native-born, were superbly skilled technicians with a commanding knowledge of the industry.

The deep-sea sperm whale had been pursued throughout the Atlantic since before the Revolution. Although American whaling recovered slowly from its near destruction during the War for Independence, American Ahabs entered the Indian and Pacific oceans before 1800. Soon after the turn of the century, the Pacific became the major source of whales. Following the War of 1812, New Bedford gradually pulled ahead of Nantucket to become the center of the industry in the United States. The mainland port had the advantages of a good harbor, better market connections, and stronger leadership. The Nantucket-New Bedford struggle coincided with a further expansion of the whaling grounds. In 1818 a Nantucket whaler discovered the "offshore" grounds west of Peru, and two years later another Nantucketer followed some British vessels onto the grounds east of Japan. In 1835 Captain Barzillai T. Folger of Nantucket discovered an area in the Gulf of Alaska teeming with right whales. In 1843 a pair of New Bedford craft located the great bowhead packs which swam of Kamchatka, and five years later a Sag Harbor, Long Island, whaler pushed through the Bering Straits to discover the bowhead fishery in the Bering Sea.

The market for both whale oil and bone boomed in the period 1830-60. Sperm and whale oil provided most of the illuminant used in American and European homes, while whalebone found its way into corsets, whips, and umbrellas. During the great whaling period, American vessels held a near monopoly. The American whaling fleet reached its greatest size, 735 vessels totaling 233,189 tons, in 1846. The value of its products, which reached nearly $2.5 million in 1838, remained about $2 million for thirty-eight of the next forty years. But by the outbreak of the Civil War, decline was under way. Overfishing drove up the costs of catching whales faster than the price of oil rose. More importantly, in the long run, the Pennsylvania and West Virginia oil fields came into production in 1859-60. After the Civil War, kerosene rapidly displaced whale oil as an illuminant, while the lubricants distilled from the heavier fractions of petroleum proved to be both cheaper and superior to sperm oil for most purposes.[59]

The California Connection

During 1846-47 the navy's Pacific Squadron under Commodores John D. Sloat and Robert F. Stockton seized California. A year later the gold discovery on the American River set off the great California gold rush. Its impact on the merchant marine was both immediate and substantial. Any vessel which could float, irrespective of seaworthiness it seemed, could find a charter for California ports. Approximately 775 vessels sailed in the first year. An estimated twenty-five to thirty thousand people reached California in 1849 on 233 vessels; nearly twice that number of vessels were still enroute. Most of the gold seekers landed at San Francisco where one observer counted 300 vessels abandoned off her waterfront.

The gold seekers drove prices in San Francisco to unimaginable levels. As a result of the high price levels, cargoes destined for California could afford to pay premium rates of twenty-five to sixty dollars per ton in order to secure rapid delivery. The high rates caused shippers to order the group of fast, sharp-lined, over-sparred, heavily crewed freighters we call clippers.[60]

The clippers were undoubtedly the nation's most colorful sailing craft. To most Americans they represent the pinnacle of the wooden shipbuilders' art: sleek, flush-decked craft, with gracefully concave cutwaters and towering suits of sails, which made unheard-of speeds through the water. They were fast, although their speed was often equaled by the "Downeasters" of a quarter century later, but they had small capacity and a short life because of the beating they took from captains who drove them through the unforgiving sea in good weather and storm.

The clipper, a term which properly describes a vessel whose hull has a sharp form which cuts through the water rather than pushing it aside, evolved over a considerable period of time. Its origins can be found in the swift privateers of the War of 1812, slavers, opium smugglers, pilot boats, and fruit carriers as well as the big transatlantic packets and fast warships. There is no "first clipper," although some historians for the sake of convenience would accord the honor to John W. Griffith's *Rainbow* design in 1845. The clippers' narrow hull and hollow lines allowed them to stow only limited cargoes, while the large crews necessary to handle their huge expanse of sails made them extremely expensive to operate. But as long as a market existed that would pay a premium for speed, they were profitable. Very few were built after 1856 when the rates on the California run dropped to $12.50, later $11 per ton, well below the break-even point for the clippers.[61]

Clippers came off ways all along the Atlantic coast, but most were built in New York and New England. New York City's yards, the most extensive and productive in the country between 1815 and the Civil War, turned out the greatest number. William H. Webb, who was probably Gotham's most noted builder of the age, constructed more than any other single builder. Boston's yards included that of the most famous of all the clipper builders, Donald McKay, who constructed a series of unbeatable vessels which included the *Staghound, Sovereign of the Seas,* and the best known of the type, the *Flying Cloud.* In 1853 he launched the largest and most innovative merchant vessel yet built in the United States, the four-masted *Great Republic.* She never sailed under her full suit of sails because of damage in a fire while outfitting. North of Boston, the yards of Newburyport and Portsmouth, and especially of Maine, produced notable vessels.

The clippers were fast. In 1854 the *Flying Cloud* sped from New York to San Francisco in 89 days, 8 hours; the *Northern Light* ran from the California port to Boston in 76 days and 6 hours, while the *Comet* lived up to her name by reaching New York in 76 days out of San Francisco. The *Flying Cloud* ran from New York to Canton, via San Francisco, in 126 sailing days and completed her trip around the world in 6 months, 16 days, port to port.[62]

The clippers were not the only craft attempting to secure a

portion of the California trade. In 1848 the Pacific Mail Steamship and U.S. Mail Steamship Companies began steamer service from New York to San Francisco via the Isthmus of Panama. The twelve steamers operating on the Pacific leg of that trade exceeded the number passing between New York and Europe.

The drop in freight prices started the demise of the clipper but other, largely technological, factors also contributed. British builders shifted to composite craft having iron frames and wooden planking. They were stronger and frequently less expensive to build. British insurance firms gave them a cheaper premium on their insurance. This combined to eliminate the American wooden clippers from the China tea trade, to which many had migrated after the collapse of the California boom.[63]

Contributing to the death of the clipper were changes in the California trade pattern in the years preceding the Civil War. The state moved from importing consumer goods to exporting wool and grain, althogh the full impact would not be felt until after 1860.

As the nation moved into the last decade before the Civil War, the impact of foreign trade on the average American diminished. American factories, using American raw materials and technology, provided an increasing proportion of the goods which the nation consumed. Very little flowed overseas from American factories, so few American workers saw foreign trade as a contributor to their job security. Even the cotton, tobacco, and grain farmers who did export large portions of their crops were now more aware of the larger proportion consumed in the United States. It is no surprise, therefore, that the American deep-water marine found few champions among politicians, publicists, or proletariat.

Coincident with the declining awareness of maritime affairs were several other negative developments. Native-born Americans increasingly found the lure of the relatively cheap lands in the West or the wages of a factory more appealing than the cramped quarters, difficult working conditions, and long hours of a seaman. After the War of 1812 the percentage of American-born seamen dropped drastically. By 1830, Americans represented less than half of those manning the vessels. The crews for the great transatlantic packets commonly came from the dives of the Liverpool waterfront; the men who manned the clippers represented many nationalities, but few claimed the United States; the whalers drew on Portugese, Hawaiians, Atlantic islanders, and others who would accept the poor working conditions and low pay. Until the Civil War, however, the deck officers continued to be nearly exclusively American in origin, as were many of the engineers, although there the traditional Scottish engineer made his early appearance.[64] One of the most commonly overlooked aspects of American maritime history is the early abandonment of the sea as a livelihood by Americans. Except in wartime, both the merchant marine and the navy had recruiting problems throughout the last three quarters of the nineteenth century. For the navy they did not entirely disappear until the Great Depression of the 1930s and the post-World War II draft pressures. The movement away from the sea undoubtedly reflects the low pay and unattractive working and living conditions at sea, as well as the necessary long absences from the traditional rhythms of work, rest, and play. Factory work, therefore, despite its drawbacks, appealed more than we recognize today. Nor did men leaving eastern farms find it unappealing to strike out westward in hopes of finding new and richer farmlands.[65]

The 1815 tariff altered the basic principle of American trade by placing it on a reciprocal basis. That same year the new commercial treaty with Britain put the principle into effect by eliminating all discriminatory fees on vessels and goods of the two nations. The elimination of the special tax on foreign vessels reduced the price advantage of American carriers and helped create the conditions that drove American vessels from the carriage of our foreign trade.

The increasing political power of the land-based manufacturing industry fostered a shift in American economic policy from free trade to protectionism. The shipping community, naturally, supported free trade, but when maritime-derived wealth came ashore it normally embraced protection. It was Francis Cabot Lowell and Patrick T. Jackson, both scions of major Boston maritime families, who were instrumental in 1816 in securing a strongly protective tariff to shield their new cotton textile factory.[66] That pattern was repeated throughout the

Northeast as the great textile centers sprang up along the fall line. By 1840, Massachusetts had passed from a commercial to a manufacturing state; New Jersey, Connecticut, and New York followed closely. As a result, by the outbreak of the Civil War the United States had forsaken her maritime orientation.

The years between the establishment of independence and the outbreak of the Civil War give ample evidence of the contributions that the maritime industry can make to a nation as well as the effects on it of changes in governmental policy and national priorities. At the birth of the new nation, enterprising, innovative, and venturesome merchants and mariners developed new trade routes and took advantage of the commercial opportunities of the era to give the new nation a strong merchant marine that dominated her foreign trade. Following a quarter of a century of activity as the leading neutral carrier in a world at war, those merchants and mariners modified their methods to compete in a world at peace. They plunged into new trades like the transatlantic packet, immigrant transport, and cotton export with a gusto which kept the American merchant marine among the world's largest.

Nor did American shipbuilders and marine engineers lag behind their European contemporaries. The successes of the American frigates in the War of 1812 proved that our builders could produce successful large ships when the need arose. The packets, and later the clippers, restated that accomplishment in other forms. The steamboat, even if it had international parentage, was born in America. Unfortunately, the relatively slow American industrial development restricted the utilization of steam power and metal-hulled vessels. As a result, America's ability to compete in the international deep-water trades atrophied as our cheaply built, small- and medium-sized, wooden-hulled sailing freighters ceased to attract business.

More discouraging for the future was the flight of Americans from the sea. Few native-born Americans found the rough, dangerous, and relatively low-paid life at sea, with its unnatural rhythms of work and rest, an appealing alternative to farming in the new West or even to a ten- or twelve-hour stint in a factory. Therefore, by the end of the period, most sailors claiming the shrinking number of berths on American vessels were foreigners. Americans had turned their backs to the sea, but they would soon discover that no nation that totally abandons its maritime role can survive.

Notes

1. Lloyd W. Maxwell, *Discriminating Duties and the American Merchant Marine* (New York: The H. W. Wilson Co., 1926), pp. 17-18; Emory R. Johnson, et al., *History of Domestic and Foreign Commerce of the United States*, 2 vols. (Washington, D.C.: Carnegie Institution, 1915), I, 320.
2. William W. Bates, *American Marine* (Boston: Houghton Mifflin, 1893), p. 96.
3. Johnson, op. cit. I, 186; John G. B. Hutchins, *The American Maritime Industry and Public Policy, 1789-1934* (Cambridge: Harvard University Press, 1941), p. 241.
4. Samuel Eliot Morison, *Maritime History of Massachusetts* (Boston: Houghton Mifflin, 1941), p. 154.
5. Robert G. Albion, William A. Baker, Benjamin W. Labaree, and Marion V. Brewington, *New England and the Sea* (Middletown, Conn.: Wesleyan University Press, 1972), pp. 58-59.
6. Clayton R. Barrow, Jr., ed., *America Spreads Her Sails* (Annapolis, Md.: U.S. Naval Institute, 1973), pp. 57-58.
7. Morison, op. cit., pp. 44-46; Johnson, op. cit., I, 185-86.
8. Ernest S. Dodge, *New England and the South Seas* (Cambridge: Harvard University Press, 1965), pp. 59-62.
9. Walter Barrett, *The Old Merchants of New York*, 5 vols. (New York: Carleton, 1889), I, 420-21.
10. Barrow, op. cit., pp. 41-54.
11. Hutchins, op, cit., p. 173.
12. Johnson, op. cit., II, 161-62; Winthrop L. Marvin, *The American Merchant Marine* (New York: Charles Scribner's Sons, 1902), pp. 303-4.
13. Howard I. Chapelle, *The American Fishing Schooner, 1825-1935* (New York: W. W. Norton & Co., 1973), pp. 36, 114.
14. Hutchins, op. cit., p. 213; K. Jack Bauer, *Ships of the Navy, Combat Vessels* (Troy, N.Y.: Rensselaer Polytechnic Institute, 1970), pp. 13-18, 23.
15. William Hutchinson Rowe, *Maritime History of Maine* (New York: W. W. Norton & Co., 1948), pp. 34-86.
16. Bureau of Census, *Historical Statistics, Colonial Times to 1970*, 2 vols. (Washington, D.C.: Bureau of Census, 1975), II, 750.
17. Samuel Flagg Bemis, *A Diplomatic History of the United States*

The Golden Age

(New York: Henry Holt & Co., 1955), p. 145.

18. Bureau of Census, *Historical Statistics*, II, 750.

19. The *Steam Boat* became the *North River Steam Boat* in 1809 but never carried the name *Clermont*. The latter was her hail port at various times.

20. John H. Morrison, *History of American Steam Navigation* (New York: W. F. Sametz & Co., 1903), pp. 14-19; S. Colum Gilfillan, *Inventing the Ship* (Chicago: Follett Publishing Co., 1935), pp. 82-96; Donald C. Ringwald, "First Steamboat to Albany," *American Neptune*, XXIV (1964), 157-71; Cedric Ridgely-Nevitt, "The Steam Boat, 1807-1811," ibid., XXXVII (January 1967), 16-24.

21. James T. Flexner, *Steamboats Come True* (New York: Viking Press, 1944), p. 346.

22. Hutchins, op. cit., p. 173.

23. Ibid., pp. 281-82.

24. Ibid., p. 101.

25. Ibid.

26. David Budlong Tyler, *The American Clyde*, (Newark, Del.: University of Delaware Press, 1958), p. 5.

27. Hutchins, op. cit., pp. 103-8.

28. Tyler, op. cit., p. 405; Bauer, op. cit., p. 74.

29. Johnson, op. cit., I, 187.

30. Carl C. Cutler, *Queens of the Western Ocean* (Annapolis, Md.: U.S. Naval Institute, 1961), pp. 97-166.

31. Hutchins, op. cit., pp. 262-63.

32. Cutler, op. cit., pp. 563-65.

33. Ralph D. Paine, *The Old Merchant Marine* (New Haven: Yale University Press, 1919), pp. 145-46.

34. Hutchins, op. cit., p. 320; John Malcolm Brinnin, *The Sway of the Grand Saloon* (New York: Delacorte Press, 1971), pp. 6-9; George R. Taylor, *The Transportation Revolution* (New York: Rinehart, 1951), p. 371.

35. David Budlong Tyler, *Steam Conquers the Atlantic* (New York: Appleton-Century, 1939), pp. 6-14.

36. Hutchins, op. cit., pp. 350-53; Paul Maxwell Zeis, *American Shipping Policy* (Princeton: Princeton University Press, 1938), p. 10.

37. Brinnin, op. cit., pp. 206-7; Wheaton J. Lane, *Commodore Vanderbilt* (New York: Alfred A. Knopf, 1942), pp. 143-49.

38. Taylor, op. cit., p. 198.

39. Johnson, op. cit., I, 338.

40. Rowe, op. cit., pp. 65-66, 254-55.

41. William Lennard Taylor, *A Productive Monopoly* (Providence: Brown University Press, 1970), p. 6.

42. Taylor, *Transportation*, op. cit., p. 198.

43. Robert Greenhalgh Albion, *The Rise of the Port of New York* (New York: Charles Scribner's Sons, 1939), pp. 400-401.

44. Edward C. Kirkland, *Men, Cities, and Transportation*, 2 vols. (Cambridge: Harvard University Press, 1948), I, 15.

45. James Weston Livingood, *The Philadelphia-Baltimore Trade Rivalry, 1780-1860* (Harrisburg: Pennsylvania Historical & Museum Commission, 1947), p. 23.

46. Ulrich Bonnell Phillips, *History of Transportation in the Eastern Cotton Belt to 1860* (New York: Columbia University Press, 1908), pp. 84-97, 103, 120.

47. Jonathan Daniels, *The Devil's Backbone* (New York: McGraw-Hill Book Co., 1971), pp. 48-49, 134.

48. Leland D. Baldwin, "Shipbuilding on the Western Waters, 1793-1817," *Mississippi Valley Historical Review*, XX (June 1933), 31-40; *American Neptune*, VII (1947), 317.

49. Charles Henry Ambler, *History of Transportation in the Ohio Valley* (Glendale, Calif.: Arthur H. Clark Co., 1932), p. 73; Henry B. Meyer, et al., *History of Transportation in the United States before 1860* (Washington, D.C.: Carnegie Institution, 1918), p. 101; Archer B. Hurlbut, *The Paths of Inland Commerce* (New Haven: Yale University Press, 1920), p. 67.

50. Louis C. Hunter, "The Invention of the Western Steamboat," *Journal of Economic History*, VII (1943), 212.

51. Taylor, *Transportation*, op. cit., pp. 163-64; Johnson, op. cit., I, 242.

52. Johnson, op. cit., p. 244; Taylor, *Transportation*, op. cit., p. 166; Oscar Osborn Winther, *The Transportation Frontier* (New York: Holt, Rinehart & Winston, 1964), p. 75.

53. Meyer, op. cit., p. 86; Johnson, op. cit., I 234; Taylor, *Transportation*, op. cit., p. 161. The best recent histories of the Erie Canal are Nathan Miller, *The Enterprise of a Free People* (Ithaca: Cornell University Press, 1962), and Ronald E. Shaw, *Erie Water West* (Lexington: Kentucky University Press, 1966).

54. Meyer, op. cit., pp. 128, 247-48; Taylor, *Transportation*, op. cit., pp. 164-65; Julius Rubin, *Canal or Railroad* (Philadelphia: American Philosophical Society, 1961), p. 8; Frank W. Trevorrow, *Ohio's Canals* (Oberlin, Ohio: the author, 1973), p. 3.

55. Meyer, op. cit., pp. 113, 296-97.

56. Johnson, op. cit., I, 230-35, 288.

57. Marvin, op. cit., pp. 303-4.

58. Howard I. Chapelle, *The National Watercraft Collection* (Washington, D.C.: Smithsonian Institution, 1960), 19-76.

59. The standard history of whaling is Alexander Starbuck, *A History of American Whale Fishing* (Waltham: n.p., 1878). More recent but less useful is Edouard A. Stackpole, *The Sea Hunters* (Philadelphia: J. B. Lippincott, 1953).

60. Raymond A. Rydell, *Cape Horn to the Pacific* (Berkeley: University of California Press, 1912), pp. 116, 125; Hutchins, op. cit., p. 317.

61. Paine, op. cit., p. 155.

62. The standard studies of the clipper are Arthur H. Clark, *The Clipper Ship Era* (New York: G. P. Putnam's Sons, 1910), and Carl C. Cutler, *Greyhounds of the Seas* (New York: G. P. Putnam's Sons, 1930).

63. Morison, op. cit., pp. 452-56; Johnson, op. cit., I, 359.

64. Taylor, op. cit., *Transportation*, pp. 125-56.

65. Hutchins, op. cit., pp. 306-7.

66. Morison, op. cit., p. 314.

3
The Civil War and the Period of Decline: 1861-1913

Lawrence C. Allin

The years 1861 to 1913 saw American maritime enterprise, technology, and naval architecture reach unprecedented levels of achievement; yet this is the era commonly called the Period of Decline in the history of the American merchant marine. And, in spite of prodigious advancement in certain areas, the era 1866 to 1890 has been called the Dark Age of American oceanic enterprise. How to resolve these apparently irreconcilable views; how to define enterprise, technology, and naval architecture; how to describe the important components of American activity at sea; and how to describe, with objective balance, the perceptions of the men who were active participants in this marine epoch are the major problems faced in any attempt to understand this crucial half century.

These would be relatively simple tasks if one were to confine himself to discussing the American merchant marine—those men and vessels that engaged in carrying American foreign trade on the high seas. But the simplicity is deceptive. Producers of goods for foreign trade, shipbuilders, the men and vessels in the coasting trade, competing foreign merchant marines and foreign shipbuilders, and the local, state, and national political processes must be considered for their importance to and impact upon the merchant marine during this period. So must the United States Navy, its officers and those who built its ships, and so must competing foreign navies. All of these men, processes, and conditions were factors in shaping or thwarting American seaborne development in the latter decades of the nineteenth century.

Early national legislation had prohibited foreign-built vessels from American registry, enrollment, and license. The American merchant marine had flourished under these laws. By 1855, 72 percent of American foreign trade was carried in American bottoms. This proportion fell off to 66 percent in 1860 and declined to slightly over 42 percent by 1865.[1]

This loss of almost 24 percent of the American carrying trade to other flags during the Civil War occurred for a number of reasons. The most loudly heralded reason—and erroneously quoted—was the depredations of Confederate raiding vessels. The most famous of these, the British-built *Alabama* and *Florida* and their cohorts, practiced the *guerre de course* against Union merchantmen, as the South lacked a fleet with which to engage the North. These raiders were successful in sinking 239 Yankee merchantmen—many of them older whaling vessels.[2]

Less visible and less comprehensible was the Union navy's part in the destruction of the U.S. merchant marine. Totally unprepared to fight a war at sea, even against such a weak naval power as the Confederacy, the Union dragooned hundreds of sailing and steam vessels into wartime service. Often purchased for sums far in excess of their value, these vessels were given hard use during the conflict. Either worn out or outmoded at the end of the war, few returned to commercial service.[3]

The men who received good prices for their craft did not reinvest in new American ship properties. American shipyards were backlogged with war orders, and the Union navy could not protect such investments from the Confederate raiders. Insurance rates also skyrocketed. As a result, many owners "sold foreign"—i.e., sold their vessels into foreign registry and the protection of neutral flags. Many found British buyers for their vessels and thereby strengthened England's merchant marine.[4]

A more subtle, less-visible cause of the decline of American commerce was the war-induced collapse of the cotton trade. Enjoyed predominantly by Maine men and sailing ships before the war, the trade was quickly closed to Union shipping in 1861 and transferred to sleek, iron-hulled, steam-powered British blockade runners. The massive dislocations of the war all but destroyed the South's cotton economy. It did not reach its prewar level until 1879 and, by then, the trade had been engrossed by foreign steamers, mostly British.[5]

Probably the least-understood cause of the decline of the American carrying trade during and after the war was the decision to build monitor-type men-of-war. There were few American shipyards capable of building iron vessels at the outbreak of hostilities. Light-draft monitors were needed to blockade the shallow southern inlets and harbors and to do battle with Confederate ironclads. Boiler plants and machine shops were called upon to do the metal fabricating for the monitors, while shipwrights used to working with wood fashioned their underwater hulls.[6] In the rush to provide monitors to protect the Yankee coast and penetrate southern sounds, little thought was given to building seagoing, ironclad men-of-war. Only one such formidable vessel was built for the Union navy, the *New Ironsides.* As a consequence, neither did the boilermakers learn to bend iron to ships' curves nor did the shipwrights learn to work with metal. An excellent opportunity to master already crucial skills was thus lost to the American shipbuilding industry.[7]

Enactments of various governmental jurisdictions contributed to the merchant marine's decline after the war. One vengeful congressional enactment prohibited the return to American registry of the vessels "sold foreign" during the war.[8] In New York, a 2½ percent tax was levied on vessels. No such tax was collected in England. Rather, owners there paid but 1 percent on their crafts' net profits in taxes. New York also required that vessels be piloted to its docks, and the pilots charged exorbitant fees for their services. Too, American iron founders could not supply much of the material required to build seagoing steamers. Such material had to be imported from England or the Continent if one wished to build in an American yard. Duties were levied on these goods and added substantially to the costs of American-built vessels.[9]

In addition to the problems of war and restrictive legislation, economic impediments hindered the development of the shipbuilding industry which underpinned the merchant marine. There was a shortage of timber in the Northeast. Materials for wooden vessels had to be carried from the South, and this added to their cost. With cheap labor and abundant timber, Quebec and the Canadian Maritime Provinces rivaled the Americans after the war. As a consequence, the Canadians enjoyed a brief heyday as builders of wooden sailing vessels and undercut both American and world markets. Reductions in naval and private orders after the war closed many U.S. yards. Their workmen dispersed to other areas and occupations, depriving the United States of much of its skilled labor pool.

A few builders and owners, too, insisted that American wooden, paddle-wheeled steamers could compete with British iron-hulled, screw-propelled vessels on the sea lanes. The realities of the marketplace soon disabused them of these ideas. The American machine-tool industry could not produce mills, plate benders, and forging appliances for metal vessel construction. The cost of these tools and the generally greater capital requirements for establishing metal building yards retarded their development. Along with these factors, the high wages demanded by American metalworkers made the cost of iron vessels in America prohibitive for all but those employed in the protected coasting trade.[10]

The ensuing chaos of the American marine establishment was surveyed by the *New York Times* in 1866, when its editor wrote that "shipbuilding in this country is already all but completely destroyed." However, one of its readers was less sanguine and commented, "The days of clippers and packetships are numbered and the world is a gainer by the fact."[11]

Most of the crucial problems affecting the merchant marine had been well defined in the press by 1868. The legislative and economic difficulties were clearly spelled out, and it was recognized that England had stolen a march on the Americans when she turned to building iron-hulled, steam-powered, screw-driven merchantmen. So complete was this English triumph on the Atlantic that foreign-built and foreign-owned vessels had to carry American mails across the ocean, there being no native steam vessels to do so.[12]

The postwar commentators argued for the merchant marine's restoration on both economic and political grounds. Some wanted vessel repair, manning payments, stores purchases, and freight earnings to stay in American hands. Others saw that a strong merchant fleet could be an asset in time of war. It would also sustain shipyards in times of peace, augment the navy with its ships, and furnish a pool of trained officers and men for the battle fleet. As importantly, in a European war a sizable merchant fleet would guarantee the carriage of American goods if foreign flag vessels were withdrawn from the nation's trade routes. These arguments would remain prominent throughout the period.[13]

Most of those who debated the problems of the merchant marine at this time accepted these ends as desirable. However, the means of restoring the carrying trade to the flag were bitterly argued. Essentially, three methods of getting ships were advanced: manipulation of the tax structure; the admission of foreign-built vessels to American registry; and subsidizing, either outright or under disguise, American merchant ships.

The inability of American industry to manufacture economic shipfittings in the 1860s produced the initial attempt to manipulate the tax structure. A bill was introduced into the Congress to allow drawbacks (refunds of duties paid), on imported copper, brass, steel, iron, wood, canvas cordage, paint, and tools. It was initially unsuccessful.[14]

Those who argued for "free ships" advocated repeal of the nation's basic Navigation Act of 1798. This allowed only wholly American-owned and American-built vessels to be registered in the American foreign trade. Free-ship advocates claimed that American shipbuilders could not build iron steamers in competition with the British. To attain their avowed goal, equipping the American commercial fleet with competitive vessels, the free-ship advocates demanded the admission of cheap—necessarily British—vessels to American registry. They claimed this would reverse a temporary trend and encourage American shipbuilders to meet the competition.[15]

As to subsidies, it was claimed they would be "nominally for mail service, but really to pay a part of the cost of running expenses." This argument, an argument to compensate owners for high American construction and operating costs, was not developed to its most sophisticated height immediately after the war. But such refinement would not be long in coming.[16]

The difficulty of arguing these questions with clear-sightedness in a period of technological change was demonstrated by one contributor to the *New York Times*. He flatly asserted that American-built, wooden, paddle-wheeled steamers were superior to Britain's iron, screw-type vessels. A more astute observer showed that a wooden vessel would be 30 percent heavier than an iron one of like measure. The iron vessel would have a great weight (hence a freight-earning) advantage. This was the crux of the American problem. The Yankees were the world's premier wooden sailing-ship builders. But efficient, dependable foreign— mostly British-built—steamers were driving windships off the most profitable trade routes.[17]

None of these solutions to the dilemma of the American merchant marine was pursued to its logical conclusion in the 1890s —or the entire era. The progress of technology, changing and expanding patterns of trade, domestic and international politics, and war would all come with the passing of time. These would add new dimensions to the basic problem. With each passing year, the solutions became no clearer nor any easier to adopt.

Early Attempts to Revise the Merchant Marine

The sectional animosities which led to the demise of the subsidized Collins Line before the Civil War were obviated in 1864 when the first attempt to assure the existence of American mail steamship lines was made. This took the form of a contract with the United States and Brazil Steamship Company to carry American mail—with the additional aid of a Brazilian governmental subsidy—through the Caribbean to Rio de Janeiro.[18] Almost concurrently, a subsidy was given to the Pacific Mail Steamship Company to carry U.S. mail to the Orient. This company built four, four-thousand-ton, wooden, paddle-wheeled steamers—manned by beautifully uniformed Chinese crews—to carry out its obligations.[19]

These arrangements encouraged others to seek mail subsidies, a movement which was strong until 1874. One such group was the Commercial Navigation Company. It received authorization to build seven iron steamers to carry the transatlantic mails in 1868. The Postmaster General refused to carry out the agreement. He objected to its monpolistic features and the reduction of mail sailings from four to two a week.[20]

Immigrants who had served as "return cargo" for American sailing ships bound home from Europe quit these obsolete vessels for steamers. This was only one of the many reasons the Congress had to investigate the condition of the merchant marine. It appointed Congressman John Lynch of Maine and a select committee to do so in 1869. After many hearings, Lynch's committee submitted a bill to give almost all things to all concerned. Under its terms "whitewashed" vessels would be readmitted to registry, "free ships" admitted to registry, drawbacks given on building materials, voyaging stores taken out of bond free, exemption from all but federal tonnage taxes granted, and mail-line subsidies enacted. Lynch, his committee, and his bill were attacked, abused, and defeated.[21] The *New York Times* led the attack on the subsidies, and Congressman Washburn of Wisconsin and Secretary of the Treasury George S. Boutwell tried to get subsidies for iron ships in 1870 and 1872. Their attempts were defeated, as were the hopes of those who saw opportunity in the Franco-Prussian War.[22]

Since the Crimean War had caused a shortage of bottoms, some Americans hoped the hostilities between the French and the Germans would do the same. But neither belligerent had the need to move great quantities of men and matériel over long ocean distances, nor was blockading a significant factor in the war. The conditions of the war did not exist to promote a great shipping boom.[23]

The Republican party made the restoration of the merchant marine a national political issue in 1872 when it adopted a platform plank saying, "It is the duty of the General Government to adopt such measures as may tend to encourage and restore American commerce and shipbuilding." Attempts were made to establish lines to Australia and Cuba that year, but they failed. Only a shortsighted bill allowing the duty-free import of materials for building wooden vessels for the foreign trade became effective law.

A second bill of 1872, a subsidy bill, ended in scandal.[24] In 1874, it was discovered that the Pacific Mail Company had spent a million dollars in 1872 to have its mail subsidy contract renewed. A portion of the money was expended in bribes. The contract was abrogated at once. Ironically, the Pacific Mail Line stayed in business, but the scandal squashed consideration of subsidy legislation for years.[25]

Agents of Maritime Change

Two events of 1874 somewhat offset the damage of the Pacific Mail scandal and gave the merchant marine positive support. The first was the establishment of nautical schools in the leading port cities. Such schools for apprentice sailors had long been advocated by Captain Stephen B. Luce, one of the most farsighted officers ever produced by the navy. He saw that early effective training of young Americans to the sea would offset the influx of foreign seamen into the merchant marine, provide competent crewmen, and help reduce the appalling number of groundings, collisions, and fires which plagued American ships. Working with the New York City Board of Education, Luce wrote the enabling congressional legislation which established these schools. He also used his influence to have the sail-powered man-of-war *St. Mary's* and a complement of naval officers assigned for duty to the New York school.[26]

Luce was also a key figure in the establishment of another institution for maritime change. Its roots were in the technologically induced jealousy which existed even before the Civil War between deck and engineering officers of the navy and merchant marine. The line or deck officers—trained as windship sailors—were jealous of the increasing importance of staff, especially engineering, officers who represented all of the changes wrought afloat by steam. The navy's line officers formed the United States Naval Association to protect their positions and interests.

The parochial and regressive nature of the Naval Association hampered its objectives, and it was superseded by the United States Naval Institute in 1874. The Naval Institute was, and still is, an organization dedicated to the professional and scientific examination of naval and maritime problems. Luce was one of its prime movers and read the first paper presented to the organization. It enunciated the officers' continuing concern with the fate of the navy and merchant marine, and dealt with the training of men for both services.[27]

Luce was also instrumental in the creation of the United States Naval War College. It was founded to encourage systematic thinking on naval problems—which perforce included mercantile problems. Like the Naval Institute, Luce's college was influential in the regeneration of American maritime power at the end of this period.[28]

To accomplish this regeneration, Americans had to build new steel ships. No formal training for naval architects was available in the United States, and civilian designers and naval constructors had to take their training overseas. This condition changed in 1894 when the Webb Institute, founded by W. H. Webb, began to admit students.[29]

A host of men and organizations also attempted to influence and affect the condition of the merchant fleet in this period. The New York Shipowners' Association was one of the first and most interested. Like the others, it was represented before congressional committees and in petitions and remonstrances, but achieved little.[30]

The New York Chamber of Commerce attempted to address the problems of the American carrying trade through its regular committee structure, but was also relatively unsuccessful. It became apparent that fragmented local action would produce few congressional enactments and that such enactments were essential for change. In 1880 the New York Board of Trade and Transportation undertook to remedy this condition. It called a National Ship-Owners' Convention which was held not in New York, but in Boston. Little was affected by this meeting in the way of change. But in 1882 a possibly stronger group was assembled in convention. This group met in New York City and included representatives from the New York and Philadelphia Maritime Exchanges; New England Ship-Owners' Association; and the Bath, Maine, and Baltimore, Maryland, Boards of Trade. This convention failed to produce substantial gains; those interested in the survival of the merchant marine resorted to other methods.[31]

The first of these was the creation of a broad-based maritime interest group known as the American Shipping and Industrial League. It was formed in New Orleans in 1886 and held a national convention in Birmingham, Alabama, in November 1887. In later conventions of the association, its leadership attempted to argue that the rehabilitation of the merchant marine was a national and not a political question. Generally speaking, the league was unable to bring about any significant improvement.[32]

An American Merchant Marine Association, with the politically powerful Arthur Sewall of Maine at its head, was also formed. So too was an American Shipping League with Aaron Vanderbilt as its secretary. Perhaps they, too, failed to achieve significant gains for the merchant marine for reasons set out by New York's Reform Club. The Reform Club's essential objection to the league's legislating attempt was "that it is instituted chiefly by those who would receive the Government bounty proposed, on conditions which they themselves have proposed."[33]

The most propitiously founded merchant marine interest group was the Merchant Marine League. Its prime mover was no less than the powerful chairman of the Republican National Committee and United States Senator Marcus Alonzo Hanna. Created in the image of the internationally popular Navy League of the day, Hanna's Merchant Marine League appears to have been tarred with the brush of politics, a great hindrance to the resurgence of the comercial fleet in this period.[34]

Three men loomed large in this period for their concern and action for the merchant marine. They were John Roach, Charles H. Cramp, and John Codman. An illiterate Irish immigrant, Roach rose to be the operator of a steamship line and of a fully integrated shipbuilding plant. Cramp became the leading defender of the shipbuilders and subsidies upon Roach's death. Captain John Codman, a prolific author and perennial free-ship advocate, had been a vessel master. He was consistently chided for being a hireling of British gold. Each of these men was praised, damned, and publicized by his contemporaries.[35]

Constantly aware of these groups, leagues, and associations and of Roach, Cramp, and Codman was Maine's congressional delegation. James G. Blaine, William P. Frye, Eugene Hale, Nelson Dingley, Charles Boutelle, and Thomas Brackett Reed of that delegation all worked assiduously for the mercantile fleet which, with lumber, was a great underpinning of their state. In spite of their enormous influence within the Republican party, and their considerable power in the halls of Congress, these men were unable to revive the carrying and building trades.[36]

These men and groups did realize one of their ambitions in this period, "a governmental Marine Board, a Department of Commerce or a Board of Commerce—similar to the British Board of Trade."[37] It was not an easy realization. By 1882 the merchant marine was so decrepit that naval officers sought to gain control of at least its inspection and licensing. A Naval Institute member, and future Naval War College lecturer, Lieutenant Carlos B. Calkins was the group's spokesman. He wrote a comprehensive report on the American merchant marine, contrasting it with the French and British commercial services. It became a part of the secretary of the navy's *Annual Report for 1882*. Calkins's report urged the establishment of a Bureau of Mercantile Marine within the Department of the Navy which would oversee the commercial fleet.[38]

The Congress chose not to surrender control over this less-than-effective arm of enterprise; rather, it created a Bureau of Navigation within the Treasury Department. This was to oversee the merchant marine and report on commercial conditions. The Bureau of Navigation operated from 1882 to the end of the period, when a cabinet-level Department of Commerce was established.[39]

The Maritime Revolution

The Bureau of Navigation and the Department of Commerce, as political and administrative organs, were but small components of a worldwide commercial and navigational revolution. Iron frames replaced oak and hackmatack in foreign sailing vessels; then iron plates replaced ceiling and skin timbers in the same craft, and steam windlasses replaced human muscle in the working of sails. Maine men built the nation's handful of steel sailing vessels, and another Maine man brought substantial engineering change. This was Charles E. Hyde, who designed the first triple-expansion engine to be built on the Atlantic coast. This was a highly efficient, coal-economizing, three-cylindered propulsion unit. The triple-expansion engine's power-to-weight-to-speed-to-coal consumption ratios were impressive enough to change the nature of marine engineering.[40]

As early as 1876, the Russians were contributing to this revolution by fueling their river vessels with oil. American naval and maritime officers despised (or feared) the fuel for years. The British, ever sensitive to their maritime interests, saw that oil threatened the importance of their globe-girdling system of coaling stations and naval bases. Consequently, little was done to secure the U.S. merchant marine's interest in oil during this period, but its long-range effect would soon become apparent.[41]

With improvement in iron and steel hulls and in engine efficiency—hence in speed and cargo-carrying capacities—came diversification of vessel types. Colliers to carry coal, tank ships for oil, refrigerated vessels for meat, and liners for passengers and mail carriage became important vessel types which supplanted windships on selected sea lanes. The ubiquitous break-bulk "tramp" freight ship carried the world's bulk commerce in competition with sailing ships. More complex and efficient freight terminals were necessitated by these vessels, which were built in increasingly sophisticated shipyards.[42]

Individually, John Roach had built his own integrated shipyard, and Charles Cramp took his place as the nation's leading builder by owning its greatest shipyard. But such men were being supplanted by others trained by organizations and accustomed to functioning in an organizational environment, among them Lewis Nixon and Richard T. Bowles. Both had been trained abroad by the navy as naval constructors. Both had received practical experience in private and government yards building up the American steel navy. Both were lured by private-business interests into the management of shipyards. Nixon's and Bowles's careers were typical of the managerial and financial revolution in shipping and shipbuilding. Corporations able to amass capital were supplanting individual or family-owned building and sailing concerns. For example, Bowles became president of the Fore River Shipyard, and Nixon bought his own yard, became involved with the United States Shipbuilding Company, and suffered some of its losses.[43]

The United States Shipbuilding Company was a part of the

great trust-making activities at the turn of the century. During 1901 and 1902, it acquired Newport News Shipbuilding, Union Iron Works, Bath Iron Works, Hyde Windlass, Nixon's Crescent Shipyard, S. L. Moore and Sons, Canda Manufacturing, and Harlan and Hollingsworth. These properties were purchased at inflated prices as a calculated risk. The corporation did not obtain enough contracts to meet its debts. The profits of trust and monopoly were not forthcoming. Nixon, his friends, and his associates in the venture failed. The American merchant marine was not revived.[44]

What Roach, Cramp, Nixon, and Bowles did learn and practice was that metal shipbuilding was a complex art. Toward the turn of the century, Americans came to build cheap, innovative, construction machinery, such as the rivet gun. The demand for size, a variety of machinery, managerial skill, and capital for metal shipyards changed the building industry.[45]

Despite patriotic pronouncements extolling American genius and ability, the country could not build competitive first-class passenger or war vessels in 1887. There were two reasons for this. First, the nation's ironmongers could sell cheaply in the world market but exercised their tariff-protected ability to charge premium prices at home. This raised the price of vessels and reduced the demand for them. As a result, American builders produced comparatively small metal vessels for the coasting trade. While such orders sustained a relatively lucrative industry, they did not give the builders experience in working the great masses of steel and other intricate metalwork which went into the engines and rudderposts of large oceangoing vessels.

Second, the virtual disappearance of metal ships from the navy—and congressional unwillingness to replace them—deprived the builders of experience. They could not make eight-inch guns or great engine beds, nor could they bend armor-plate in the 1880s, due to a lack of naval orders. This hampered the building of the "new navy" and, indirectly, the revival of the merchant marine.

Henri Schneider of France, the Krupps of Essen, and Vickers of England were the world's quality metalworkers during the period. Their countrymen built many more ships than the

Americans.[46] This presented a curious dilemma. American builders produced enough ships to appear prosperous and develop excellent yards yet were criticized as subsidy hunters because they could not—to the end of the period—build in meaningful competition with foreign yards.[47]

Patterns of World Trade

The period 1865 to 1913 was probably the most dynamic in the development of American trade and industry, and in world commercial and navigational systems. Great amounts of American raw materials and agricultural products were finding their way into world markets, and many products of foreign countries were coming into the United States to feed her industries. Both of these were typified by the development of the guano and wheat trades.

Guano is the excrement of seabirds. The world's greatest supply comes from birds who feed on the fish of the Humboldt Current and nest on the equatorial shores and islands of the rainless west coast of Latin America. The unleached, nitrate-rich deposits on the Chincha Islands were from 100 to 160 feet deep from 1865 to 1879. American vessels took this guano to the agricultural nations of the world. The War of the Pacific between Chile and Peru and Bolivia brought about a disruption of this trade. That war, and inept American diplomacy, resulted in most of the square-rigged wooden American sailing ships being excluded from it.[48]

At about the same time the guano trade was booming, the great bonanza wheat farms of California were reaching their devleopmental apex. Wheat was a slippery and dangerous cargo with a very low per-unit value. It was best transported in tight, dry, economically worked sailing ships. Maine supplied these ships in the form of the great "Downeasters." These wooden square-riggers came out of the low-wage, timber-abundant, capital-rich "middle-coast" of Maine. They left the Kennebec and spent most of their lives rounding either the Cape of Good Hope or Cape Horn, carrying grain to Liverpool and coal and other cargoes from Europe.[49]

But even these vessels, which were run with low-wage,

crimped crews, could not compete with the ubiquitous, usually cheaper, British tramp steamers. As with the cotton and guano trades, the Americans lost much of the grain trade to steamers as the new century was aborning.[50]

The beef trade from Argentina and Australia to Europe was also engrossed by others. British refrigerator ships carried the goods out and back. Americans took lumber to the River Plate in wooden schooners and picked up occasional return cargoes of Brazilian coffee. In the newspapers and the halls of the Congress, great concern was expressed for the South American and Oriental trades, but little was done to put modern American vessels on the lines.[51]

Too, this period was the world's great era of canal building. Ferdinand de Lesseps dug his canal through the Isthmus of Suez in 1869 and revolutionized the trading patterns of the world in two ways. By permitting steamers to enter the Red Sea, he conquered the contrary winds of this backwater and made it an artery of trade. In addition, he eliminated the need to round the Cape of Good Hope on a voyage to Cathay. The British, and in particular Sir Charles Beresford, saw that what de Lesseps had done was the key to empire.[52]

The Greeks cut thorugh the solid rock of the Isthmus of Corinth and revolutionized the trade of the eastern Mediterranean in 1898. Germany's Kaiser Wilhelm authorized the development of the Kiel Canal, which opened in 1895. As much a strategic work as a commercial accomplishment, this canal gave the Germans access to both their Baltic and their North Sea ports through a German artery. The Kiel Canal negated the potentially harmful effects on Germany of Danish control of the Sound while lightening the burden on the German mercantile fleet by eliminating the necessity of paying Sound dues.[53]

Almost immediately after Appomattox, American sailors began agitation for a canal through Central America. The officers connected with the various visions of this "interoceanic canal" were legion in number and produced a great portfolio of canal schemes. Commodore Daniel Ammen organized the surveying expeditions which searched for a suitable canal location in the 1870s. Captain Thomas T. Selfridge explored and advocated a route across the Isthmus of Darien; Commander Edward P. Lull searched out a line across Nicaragua's freshwater lakes; and Commodore Robert W. Shufeldt attempted to find a route across Mexico's Isthmus of Tehuantepec. Lull and Lieutenant Frederick Collins gave a Panamanian canal route only a cursory look.[54]

In 1876, a board appointed to decide the issue voted to recommend the digging of an American ditch across Nicaragua. Momentarily it seemed that such a scheme would contribute to the revival of the merchant marine. But powerful forces—especially the transcontinental railroads—opposed the project, and the Nicaraguan route was still being agitated when Theodore Roosevelt became president. He put an end to the Nicaragua talk, and in a short while put American spades to work in Panama. Not completed until 1915, the Panama Canal gave no stimulus to the merchant marine in this epoch.[55]

The Navy and the Merchant Marine

Officers of the United States Navy were vociferous, sometimes wary, and more than once frightened friends of the merchant marine in this era. The Franco-Prussian War had cast doubt on the efficacy of navies in general, and the United States Navy made a poor showing in the *Virginius* Affair. That incident occurred in 1873 during a Cuban revolution in which numerous British, American, and Cuban crew members of the gunrunning vessel *Virginius* were executed. To prevent further executions, the American fleet had to have the assistance of the Royal Navy. What was worse, or what made the U.S. Navy appear ineffective, was its inability to assemble in force in the Bay of Florida until three months after the danger was past. Then the fleet was restricted in its operations by the four-and-a-half-knot speed of its slower units—its Civil War-era monitors.[56]

Six years after the Virginius Affair, the War of the Pacific broke out. The decrepit navy failed to serve as a makeweight in the diplomatic negotiations concerning the prize of the war, the nitrate fields of the South American coast. Chile, which was victorious in this maritime war, had acquired three ironclads through purchase or capture and was disinclined to listen to the

Americans who had no such craft. In short, the war ruined the American guano trade, exposed the weakness of the United States Navy, and brought on agitation to do something for the fleet.[57]

In response, John Roach published his plan to establish a "militia for the sea." He proposed the building of one hundred fast steamers to carry the mails and to serve as a reserve navy. Roach would have strengthened the vessels to carry heavy guns and nine-inch armor. His merchant cruisers would attack the commerce of any maritime enemy in war or—equally important —carry American commerce when a European war erupted. Roach would have built many of the ships himself—if the government had been willing.[58]

The Navy Department appointed its first Naval Advisory Board in 1881 to determine what should be done about the navy's deteriorated condition. Roach's recommendations frightened the officers, who saw the possibilty of such a militia of the sea supplanting the naval establishment. The board's recommendations appear to have been in response both to Roach's proposal and to the sorry state of the fleet. Its report was responsible for nothing of an immediate concrete nature but did start a debate as to whether the fleet should be a commerce-promoting body or a full-fledged strategic navy.[59]

A number of pertinent events occurred in 1882 to focus national attention on the sea. The Congress held separate hearings on the condition of the navy and the merchant marine and what might be done to revitalize them. Roach's ideas were heard, and articles by naval officers in Lewis Hamersly's journal, the *United Service,* figured in the debates. J. D. J. Kelley and John Grier thoroughly examined the question of permitting the entry of foreign vessels to American registry or of sustaining the shipbuilders' monopoly as methods of strengthening both the naval and mercantile fleets. R. M. G. Brown pointed out the interdependency of the navy and merchant marine, their mutual services and common requirements, and the desperate need for a policy to govern both.[60]

The topic of the United States Naval Institute Prize Essay Contest for 1882 was indicative of the concern for the merchant fleet. It was "Our Merchant Marine: The Causes of Its Decline and the Means to be Taken for Its Revival." The prize-winning essayist, J. D. J. Kelley, with Carlos G. Calkins, French E. Chadwick, Richard Wainwright, and W. G. David, came down overwhelmingly for the admission of foreign-built vessels into the American registry as the best method of revitalizing the merchant marine and building a naval reserve. These articles and Calkins's report to the secretary of the navy seem to indicate that the officers feared that their service might be dismantled, to be supplanted by merchantmen and the privateering policy which the government too often followed.[61]

The officers got neither free ships nor a strong war fleet. Neither was their navy supplanted by merchantmen. They did get a second Naval Advisory Board. It established the inability of American industry to produce steel warships of any large size. The board oversaw the initial efforts to develop such a capacity and started the navy on its path to modern development.[62]

By the end of 1882, it was still obvious that something had to be done for the merchant fleet. To some, a French maritime law of 1881 presented a possible solution. That law resulted from France's ill-fated 1866 admission of foreign vessels to her registry, repealing duties on shipbuilding material, and closing her coasting trade to all but her own vessels. This practically ruined her shipbuilding industry. The law of 1881 tried to revive French maritime fortunes with subsidies to builders and navigating bounties of one franc, fifty centimes, per thousand miles sailed on net tonnage to owners. Foreign-built, French-registered vessels could claim half the bounty. But the builders gouged the owners who bought them, and the owners retaliated by buying "all the rubbish of the foreign fleets." France's steam tonnage increased, but her merchant fleet was not in a truly competitive position.[63]

In 1893, bounties to French shipbuilders were increased, steam navigation bounties were readjusted, and handsome navigating bounties were given French sailing ships. France wished to maintain a fleet of wind-driven ships to train true sailors, but her steam fleet showed no increase, while a great fleet of steel sailing vessels grew under the Tricolor. Shipowners were seriously disturbed; they felt that they had again been sacrificed to the builders.[64]

In 1902, a new law was promulgated giving a greater but progressively reduced bounty to the builders for both steam and sailing vessels. Foreign-built vessels also received an allowance. Unfortunately, a spending limit was placed on these provisions; as a result, the builders rushed to lay down vessels and partake in the largess. Within nine months, enough vessels to absorb all of the appropriated funds were on the stocks and the law of 1902 proved to be a long-term failure.[65]

In 1906, the French tried again. The construction bounty under the law of that year was to give builders a fair profit and owners a fair price for their ships. Bonuses were allowed the owners on a gross-tonnage, knots-sailed, distance-navigated formula. Extra money was paid if a vessel was utilized by the navy. Still, the French merchant marine made no spectacular gains.[66]

Additionally, Denmark, Sweden, Norway, the Netherlands, Portugal, Spain, the Austro-Hungarian Empire, Russia, Italy, Germany, and Great Britain were paying government funds to their respective merchant and fishing fleets to sustain some kind of activity at sea. As an example, Japan began her drive to develop a formidable merchant marine in 1896 after the Sino-Japanese War. She paid navigating and building bounties and encouraged speculative shipbuilding. By 1910, she was subsidizing lines to Europe, North America, South America, and Australia.[67] Russia's approach was considerably different. Her merchant marine was the Volunteer Fleet. It has been created by subscription in 1877 and presented to the tsar. Its vessels were all auxiliaries to the navy and capable of being armed as cruisers. It was a governmental organization and monopoly.[68]

The Germans waited until 1885 to enact legislation to create a merchant marine. Free ships from Britain first sailed under the kaiser's flag, and then a national shipbuilding industry sprang up in Stettin. The North German Lloyd Line was compelled to accept government funds and to maintain service to Asia and Australia, while the German East African Steamship Company was put on the African route. From these efforts the Germans gained an effective merchant marine.[69]

As mistress of the seas, Britannia presented a special problem to the Americans. Some, such as Codman and Kelley, said she was a free trader in all maritime aspects. Others claimed her mercantile power was the sine qua non of her existence and that she nurtured it in every way. Charles Cramp claimed England had used subsidies to ruin the American merchant marine on three occasions. The first, he said, occurred before the Civil War when Samuel Cunard's Cunard Line was heavily subsidized to drive the American Collins Line off the seas. In 1870 and 1871, the British attempted to drive the four steamers of the American Line off the sea by giving heavier subsidies and a Naval Reserve Subvention to its Atlantic lines. The third occurred, according to Cramp, in 1901 when the British gave additional heavy subsidies to Cunard. This was a move to keep Cunard out of J. P. Morgan's shipping trust, the International Mercantile Marine.

As Cramp claimed, the British did subsidize their fast passenger-mail liners on the great transatlantic ferry service. They paid premiums to a number of ships which could be used as auxiliaries in time of war. Their naval reserve was created by paying officers and men of the merchant marine in peace for an obligation to serve in time of war. But, as Codman continually maintained, the British did not subsidize their tramp steamers which carried the Red Duster, the ensign of the British merchantmen, to the ends of the earth.[70]

Nevertheless, it was not subsidies, bounties, or differentials that made the British great on the sea. It was rather their early and continued building of inexpensive metal steamships which they placed in service to every major port in the world. In addition, they laid a web of telegraph cables under the world's seas to gather and disseminate commercial information and orders. Lloyds of London insured and rated the world's vessels —with favorable treatment for British bottoms—and British banks financed all of these efforts with credits which flowed into Threadneedle Street from all over the world. It was the totality of this Victorian heritage which made the British great at sea.[71]

Within five years of their promotion of free ships, American naval officers had to take a different tack. They resignedly accepted the need for subsidies to strengthen the merchant marine. They came to realize that only with subsidies would the United States get the equivalent of the British auxiliary liner-cruisers, a naval reserve to augment the war fleet, and service vessels to support the men-of-war.

Under the leadership of retired Lieutenant J. C. Soley, the Dorchester Yacht Club, and the Massachusetts legislature, the officers took the lead in establishing a naval reserve. Using the principle of a land militia, they induced various state legislatures to create naval militias. Recognizing the fait accompli, the Congress authorized the equipment and training of these organizations with naval vessels and naval officers. Unable to create a merchant marine, the officers were able to "work from without" and create a naval militia.[72] This naval militia movement supplied men who were useful in the Spanish-American War but did not get ships to carry American trade.

The Spanish-American War revealed several inadequacies about both the American navy and the merchant marine. Rear Admiral George Dewey had to take the coal that fueled his passage to glory at Manila Bay from a British collier. Rear Admiral William Sampson had to send vessels from his squadrons to coal at Key West as the Americans had neither the colliers nor the training to permit him to fuel on station. Transports had to be dragooned into the service at exorbitant rates to carry the army to Cuba. Once there, their untrained civilian masters had to be forced to approach the beaches of Daiquiri and Siboney to land their military passengers. And, too, foreign merchant vessels had to be chartered to facilitate American logistical plans during the war.[73]

All of these things revealed the weaknesses of the American maritime position. So too did the argument after the war to bring the Philippines, Puerto Rico, and Cuba into the protected American coasting trades. By 1902, officers of the navy were beginning to understand the extreme difficulty involved in defending the Philippines and using the merchant marine to give logistical support to such a task. The weaknesses of both the navy and the merchant marine then came into clear and comprehensible focus.[74]

Factors in the Revival of the Merchant Marine

The Spanish-American War was but an incident in the late

nineteenth-century expansion of the Atlantic world's cultural, technological, business, and geographic bounds. The war with Spain brought Puerto Rico, Cuba, and the Philippines, their products, people, and markets within American reach. The European Atlantic community sent ships carrying explorers, missionaries, businessmen, goods, and ideas to Africa, India, the Malay Archipelago, Australia, China, Japan, and the coasts of Latin America. This great reaching out of the Europeans served to underscore the reality that maritime commerce is international in scope and is competitive in an international economic framework.

Given the worldwide dimensions of commerce and navigation, competitors in the trades were faced with common economic constants. The journalists, naval officers, shipbuilders, and shipowners, as well as producers of goods for international trade who argued for the revival of the merchant marine, all debated against this background of economic imperatives. Among these were the first costs of vessels, their operating costs, and their manning costs.

The first costs of a vessel are the materials which go into her, the wages of those who fabricate and assemble those materials, and the amortization of the yard in which she is built. These costs must be recovered over the life of a vessel—say twenty years—before she earns a profit. That is, a vessel costing $500,000 would have to earn $25,000 a year to pay her first costs, while a vessel costing $1,000,000 would need to earn $50,000 a year to amortize her first costs in twenty years. John Codman and those who argued for the admission of cheap foreign-built vessels to the American registry reasoned that American-built vessels had high first costs and were at a competitive disadvantage.

The operating costs of the vessel itself included both wages and materials for repairs, fuel, tariffs, taxes and dues of innumerable kinds, and insurance. Some decried the high wages and expensive materials which entered into repairs in American yards and wished to reduce them. Those who wished to change the tax structure affecting American vessels could do little about wages, but wanted changes in the tariff to permit duty-free entry of inexpensive European shipbuilding materials to reduce first costs.

Local, country, and state property taxes on vessels contributed to their operating costs, as did tonnage dues and the admeasurement rules by which they were calculated. Compulsory pilotage charges figured in these costs, as well as fees American consuls charged for their services in foreign ports. In all of these assessments, the English had the advantage of lower exactions.

In addition, it was loudly claimed that Lloyds of London, the world's premier maritime insurer, discriminated against American vessels (and especially American wooden vessels) in its charges for insurance. The differences in a Lloyds' percent on the hull and a percent on the cargo would either divert freights from American vessels or add to their operating costs and undercut their competitive positions.

Wages paid to American officers and seamen were the highest in the world and added very substantially to the operating costs of American craft. Owners of vessels in the foreign trade were disgruntled as the system of boardinghouse crimps which brought them their sailors produced less than able men, most of them of foreign origin. Owners despised the system of laws that demanded the payment of three months' wages to seamen whose voyages were broken in foreign ports. The necessity to transport shipwrecked sailors to American ports from any location in the world for ten dollars also irked the owners. The owners complained of their inability to attract good men to the sea, but the declining opportunities for advancement afloat and more attractive fields ashore worked against shipping good men in American vessels.[75]

Each of these costs injured the competitive position of American vessels, and no single concerted effort was made to reduce most or all of these charges. However, four methods were successfully used to keep Americans owning and operating ships during this era.

The first was to build and run American ships in open, unsubsidized competition with foreign vessels. This was attempted by J. H. Hill, president of the Great Northern Railway. He built two large freighters in the United States and used them as an extension of his railroad across the northern Pacific. The Boer War had hurt his business and the Russo-Japanese War had helped it by causing a withdrawal of British, and then Japanese, vessels from the northern Pacific. But Hill appears to have dipped into his rail profits to keep the vessels running in the face of two subsidized lines—one British and one Japanese.[76]

Second, one could do as Edward Henry Harriman did: control a railroad and a steamship line, in this case the Union Pacific Railroad and the Pacific Mail Line. After the scandal of 1874, the line managed to maintain eighteen vessels in the protected coasting trade to Panama and two to the Orient without a subsidy. In 1892, the Pacific Mail again received a subsidy and carried the mails to the East. Still, the bulk of its income came from activities on the Panama route. The gigantic railroad land grants that subsidized those enterprises, and Harriman's part in the railroad wars at the century's end, did not give him the appearance of a needy shipowner. He and the Pacific Mail were castigated in the press for a number of sins, political and economic. Meanwhile the American merchant marine made no great strides.[77]

The third method of operating American-flag vessels in the foreign trade was to obtain subsidies from foreign governments to carry freights. The New York and Cuba Mail Line did so with Mexican and Cuban subsidies; it ran vessels to Havana, Santiago, and Vera Cruz. Haiti and Santo Domingo subsidized the Clyde Line in the West Indian trade; that line had five vessels on its runs. The Red D Line had a similar arrangement with the government of Venezuela.[78]

The final, most effective, and most utilized method of keeping Americans owning and operating vessels was simply to buy, register, and operate them under foreign flags; the Guion Line was the first to do so. The Chesapeake and Ohio Railroad followed suit as did W. R. Grace and Company, United Fruit Company, John A. Donald, the Anglo-American Oil Company, the New York and Cuba Mail Line, and the International Mercantile Marine Company. In 1894, this American-owned foreign-flag, steam fleet was larger than the American-owned, American-flag, steam fleet. By 1901, this hybrid fleet controlled some 670,000 tons of shipping.[79]

None of these methods of putting American capital to work carrying American goods in American-owned ships contributed to the building of an American merchant marine. These expedients failed to meet what were becoming essential duties of mercantile fleets in the period. They furnished no reserve of trained officers and men for wartime service. They furnished no auxiliary cruisers or logistically important vessels for wartime service. They gave no reserve carrying capacity to meet the contingency of foreign-flag vessels being withdrawn from American routes in time of war. They produced no healthy, competitive shipbuilding industry, and they produced no comprehensive, national mercantile marine policy.

The years 1889 to 1901 were similar to the years 1879 to 1882 in the development of such an American maritime policy. The War of the Pacific of 1879-81 had caused Americans to look at their decrepit navy and begin the search for a naval policy. The years 1889 to 1901 saw Americans looking to define and broaden that impetus further and to push for the development of a national maritime policy.

Leading in this effort were three naval officers, a secretary of the navy, and two members of the United States Senate. The first to write was the cold, almost impenetrable, Captain William T. Sampson. He furnished an "Outline of a Scheme for the Naval Defense of the Coast" which gave a theoretical method of preventing the naval bombardment of American cities and protecting the flourishing coasting trade. Benjamin Franklin Tracy, the secretary of the navy and a sometime jailer of Confederate prisoners of war, followed Sampson's article late in 1889 with his *Annual Report*. In it he emphasized the American need for a navy and a naval reserve of officers, men, and ships to reinforce it in time of war. Drawing on the lessons of history, Captain Stephen B. Luce, the power behind the nautical schools of the 1870s, also published an article "Our Future Navy." In it, he lamented the passing of the merchant marine and emphasized the need for a new navy.[80]

Following their writings came Alfred Thayer Mahan's classic: *The Influence of Sea Power upon History, 1660-1783*. In background Mahan was like many of his influential naval contemporaries. He was a member and vice-president of the Naval Institute, president of the Naval War College, and president of the American Historical Association. His influential work can be read as three treatises reflecting these associations. It can be read first as an historical narrative of the rise of British naval power; second, as an explanation of the factors underlying mercantile greatness at sea; and, third, as a special plea for the enlargement of the United States Navy. Mahan's importance as an original thinker and his influence on oceanic thought are almost immeasurable. After the appearance of this first of his classics, the United States made some progress in developing an oceanic policy.[81]

The task of formulating, articulating, and enacting a national maritime policy was undertaken by Senators Frye of Maine and Hanna of Ohio. Frye was a political subordinate of James G. Blaine, a loyal supporter of the shipbuilders of "hundred-harbored Maine," and a man of moderate circumstances. Hanna owned ships, was wealthy, chaired the Republican National Committee, and made presidents. Both were in powerful positions, both worked ardently to create a sound merchant marine, and neither was able to overcome the political difficulties entailed in the task.[82]

Frye materially assisted in the passage of the Postal Aid Law of 1891, which strengthened the existing American lines by granting them subsidies to offset the lower costs of operation enjoyed by foreigners. This law divided steamers into four classes: (1) vessel weighing 8,000 tons or more and capable of twenty knots were paid four dollars a mile on the outward voyage; (2) vessels weighing 5,000-7,999 tons and capable of sixteen knots were paid two dollars a mile outward; (3) vessels weighing 2,500-4,999 tons and capable of fourteen knots were paid one dollar outward; and (4) vessels weighing 1,500-2,499 tons and capable of twelve knots were paid 66 2/3 cents a mile outward.

The first class was intended for service to Great Britain and to compete with British liners. The second class was to carry the mails to Asia and Latin America. The third and fourth classes were to sail as they could. Vessels of the first three classes were to follow specifications provided by the secretary of the navy and to serve in wartime. One American boy for each thousand tons was to be carried as an apprentice by the vessels. Half of their crews were to be American citizens at the end of five years.

Contracts could be awarded for five- to ten-year periods by

the Postmaster General to American citizens for services between American and foreign ports by American steamers. Only five contracts were initially awarded under this scheme. Three went to the Pacific Mail, one to the Red D Line, and one to J. B. Clarke of Chicago. The New York and Cuba Mail, or Ward Line, received a sixth contract in 1892. Only the Red D Line maintained a long ferry service under Frye's bill.

The passage of this act brought severe criticism from the *New York Times*. It said: "This measure will result simply in bestowing a considerable bounty upon certain established lines of steamers."[83] In its original form, the bill was the child of the American Shipping and Industrial League. The *New York Times* was dead against it, cast it as a purely Republican measure, and sided with the Democratic party as being against all subsidies.[84] The newspaper went out of its way to show that similar Italian subsidies had not been effective.[85]

Too, the *New York Times* pointed out that the Postal Aid Law was a sectional as well as a political issue. It showed that the representatives of midwestern grain farmers opposed the law —a position they would come to regret. The bill was called "a betrayal of the public trust" which fattened the profits of owners "after deducting the expenses of running ships, lobby and Congress."[86] On the basis of its own evidence, the *Times* appears to have been correct.[87]

Later lines established under Frye's bill are interesting. One, the Oceanic Steamship Company, began an Australian service in 1900; it failed in 1907. The company did manage to create and sustain a Tahiti-Marquesas Line which survived to the end of the period.

The International Navigation Company set a precedent which, if followed, might have revived the carrying fleet. With a Belgian subsidy, it began a Philadelphia to Antwerp service in 1873 and later added an Antwerp to New York schedule. It purchased the Pennsylvania Railroad's American Line in 1884 and the British Inman Line in 1886.

American owned, the company expected the British to continue their mail subsidy to the Inman Line. On faith, it ordered Clyde shipbuilders to create the great steamers *City of Paris* and *City of New York*. The British would have none of this and withdrew the subsidy. Adroitly, the company persuaded the Congress to admit these foreign-built vessels to the U.S. registry. In turn, the Congress demanded that the company build two similar vessels in American yards. It did so, laying down the *St. Louis* and *St. Paul* in Cramp's yard.[88]

The enabling act called for the *St. Louis* and *St. Paul* to measure at least eight thousand tons, make twenty knots, and be able to serve as naval auxiliaries. Eugene T. Chamberlain, the commissioner of navigation, thought that the principle of the law offered a method of strengthening the shipping interest and building yards. He would make this act of 1892 generally applicable so all Americans could purchase a foreign vessel for each ship they built in an American yard. Chamberlain thought such a policy would let Americans compete in the "tramp" trades. Though approved by the *New York Times*, his suggestion was not effectively acted upon.[89]

Two other methods were proposed to revive the merchant fleet in 1894. One was Senator Frye's attempt to levy differential duties. He would add an additional 10 percent ad valorem tax on goods imported in foreign vessels. He also sought to restrict the foreign trade to American vessels or ships of the country where the goods originated. His ideas became a plank in the Republican party platform of 1896 even though thirty-five reciprocity treaties stood in the way. John Codman, the perennial free-ship advocate, and Alexander R. Smith, peripatetic lobbyist for the merchant marine, fought the issue in the press. Such an act would raise prices, Codman said, but, worse, would invite similar retaliatory action by other maritime states. The nation did not return to a pre-1828 policy of levying differential duties.[90]

The second act passed the Congress in 1894. It allowed Americans to use an act of 1852 to buy, repair, and register wrecked foreign vessels. The operative requirement was that the repairs equal three-quarters of the vessel's first cost. This act was fought by the shipbuilders but brought 350 craft onto the American lists between 1894 and 1904. Most of these went into the coasting trade, but the act was repealed in 1906.[91]

Another patchwork piece of legislation to aid shipowners was passed in 1897. It allowed Americans to buy back and wholly own vessels that had been built in American yards and "sold foreign." By the end of the period, over one hundred thousand tons of shipping had come into the registry because of this proviso, but one-fourth of the total was represented by only two vessels of the International Mercantile Marine.[92]

In 1898, Marcus Hanna attempted to run a bill for navigation bounties through the Congress; it failed. The next year, Senator Frye revived the idea, which had the hallmarks of the French bounty system. Frye's attempt also failed. He tried a new tack in 1900. This bill offered something more substantial than many other pieces of legislation. It would obtain men and vessels for a naval reserve, demand that vessels carry realistic amounts of cargo, and allow foreign-built vessels into the registry on limited terms. In spite of its concession to free traders, Democrats, and shipowners, this effort by Frye failed. These acts were supported by Alexander Smith but condemned by Codman and midwestern congressmen.[93]

The most heroic effort to keep Americans owning and sailing vessels grew out of the trust-building activities of the era. It began in April 1901 when the financial titan of the age, J. P. Morgan, bought control of the British Leyland Line. Within short order, his "shipping trust" bought up the White Star, Dominion, Atlantic Transport, and International Navigation Company lines. By the end of 1902, Morgan controlled 136 vessels of over a million tons—one-third of the dry-cargo vessels in the American transatlantic trade. It was the largest fleet under private ownership in the world and was larger than the entire French merchant marine.

Morgan only needed control of the Hamburg-America, North German Lloyd, and Cunard lines to raise his own trident over the Atlantic. He struck a bargain with the German lines to pool profits and jointly purchase the Holland-American Line. Only Cunard and Her Majesty's government stood between Morgan and hegemony on the Atlantic. The British were not without experience in the game. They awarded Cunard handsome subsidies for staying under the Union Jack. Morgan was unable to "buy the Atlantic." Nonetheless, Morgan exerted control over vessels which exceeded the total registered American steam and sail tonnage of 1913. By 1915, the overextended combine fell into receivership, and Morgan's heroic scheme ended in the clamor of World War I.[94]

With partisan politics, the trusts, and the opportunities of the newly won insular possessions, the merchant marine was adrift on a sea of conflicting ideas, ideologies, and politics. But in 1902, a book appeared which set the stage for the last great attempt to address the problems of the carrying fleet. This was Winthrop L. Marvin's *The American Merchant Marine*.[95]

Marvin's book led to the creation of a ten-man Merchant Marine Commission. Chaired by Senator Jacob Gallinger of New Hampshire, it was composed of four other senators and five representatives with Marvin as its secretary. Admiral Luce, then retired, assisted the commission and induced it to meet in Newport to hear the views of naval officers on the carrying fleet.[96]

The commission held hearings in nineteen different locations from May 23 to December 12, 1904. About three hundred people gave testimony before the panel—nine-tenths of them pro-subsidy witnesses. The reasons for the commercial marine's failure, methods for its revival, and partisan schemes were brought up in the hearings. The commission digested what it heard and presented a bill in 1905 to "promote the national defense" by creating naval reserve forces and establishing mail lines.[97]

Teddy Roosevelt gave the commission's bill his blessing, but the *New York Times* saw it as a means of putting money into the pockets of Hill and Harriman. And for his part in the affair Alex Smith was upbraided.[98] As the *Times* saw it, the commission and its bill were too much Republican creations and sectional measures. The fatal flaw of the American political process —the adversary two-party system—wrought an unnecessary end. The bill was defeated. What was worse, no alternatives were presented.[99]

The Changing Maritime Order

Despite the seeming inability of the Congress to make maritime policy, it was creating a strong navy during this period. Portugal, Spain, Holland, and France had been, and now England was being, challenged for historic ocean supremacy.

France was attempting to build both carrying and fighting fleets and traditionally quiescent sea powers were building both kinds of hulls. Russia, Japan, and the United States were becoming strong enough to cause concern, while Germany made strides which were truly worrisome to the British.

While Morgan was reaching for the trident of the Atlantic, England was menaced by the kaiser's ships and faced a real war in South Africa. The conflict was extended enough to draw many English bottoms from their normal trade routes. At the same time, and while the American shipbuilding industry was learning to build battleships, the United States Shipbuilding Company presented a potentially dangerous challenge to British maritime craftsmanship.[100]

The Americans and Germans acquired naval bases and coaling stations in the western Pacific and put challenging steamers on its trade lanes. The Manchu Empire was disintegrating and the Sewalls' Maine-built ships of steel were carrying case oil west to light the lamps of China. The British cast about for a makeweight and, in 1902, entered their alliance with Japan. The end of fifty years of a British naval, mercantile, communciations, and financial imperium was being foreshadowed in the faraway anchorages of Sasebo, Port Arthur, and Revel.[101]

In Sasebo, Vice Admiral Heihuchiro Togo was preparing a surprise attack on Russia's great base at Port Arthur. There, in 1904, at the end of a long overland logistical route—and much longer ocean supply lanes—lay seven Russian battleships. In Revel and Libau, the Russian Baltic fleet—stronger than Togo's entire navy—waited supinely.

Togo launched his attack, opening the Russo-Japanese War, and in the ensuing weeks blockaded the harbor while the Japanese Army encircled it from the landward side. Admiral Zinovy P. Rozhdestvenski gathered the vessels in the Baltic into a heterogeneous fleet and set sail to relieve Port Arthur. Rozhdestvenski was embarking on the most remarkable voyage in naval annals. He was taking a great fleet across eighteen thousand miles of water in which he had no bases. At the end of his voyage he would meet an enemy securely based in his home waters.

While Rozhdestvenski's fleet was in poor mechanical repair,

coal was his essential problem. Without bases, he would have no coal at sea. But the Russian Volunteer Fleet—the merchant fleet —could not supply him with coal. The Russian Admiralty had to contract with the Hamburg-American Line to fuel Rozhdestvenski's fleet. Sixty colliers were required to do the job.

Togo met and beat the Russians at Tsushima in the most decisive tactical battle of steam warfare. He was able to do so, in part, because the Russian men-of-war rode so low in the water. This they had to do, to carry immense quantities of extra fuel, as there were no naval auxiliaries or merchant marine to support them in the last crucial phase of their voyage.[102]

Theodore Roosevelt and the Great White Fleet

While Togo was planning his surprise attack on Port Arthur, the problems of trusts and monopolies were interfering with the development of an American deep-water merchant marine. The Senate was attempting to legislate a requirement that military goods, especially those for the Philippines, be carried only in American bottoms. Secretary of War Elihu Root wrote to Senator Frye opposing such a measure. It would again supply too few ships and put the government at the mercy of a few shipowners.[103]

These assertions were being borne out even in the coasting trade. Through his Clyde Steamship Company, another Maine man, Charles W. Morse, had arrived at a predominant position in the Atlantic and Gulf Coast trades. His only rival was the Morgan Line of the Southern Pacific Railroad.

Farmers of the Midwest and their congressmen were suspicious of such commanding power. The fact that the total American merchant marine had recovered and reached the Civil War level of 5,164,000 tons did not tend to make these constituents sympathetic to cries of decline. True, Britain had over 14,000,000 tons of vessels, but the American fleet outweighed the combined bottoms of Germany and France. In fact, the United States had 23,333 documented vessels afloat. Perhaps a campaign of public education was called for as over 80 percent of these vessels were in the coasting trade. Few of them could operate profitably in the deep-sea trades, and a withdrawal of a significant number of them from their usual occupations would wreak havoc with the economies of coastal towns and cities.[104]

Two years after Root saw the ocean monopolies as a problem, he was calling for subsidized American lines to run to South America. He frankly admitted that they would be political, not economic, expedients; for such expediency Senator Jacob Gallinger of New Hampshire introduced a bill in his chamber to create mail lines to South America, Australia, and the Orient. Midwestern Republican congressmen complained, and the *New York Times* noted that the "subsidy hunters" had abandoned the idea of getting money for lines to Europe and Africa as they were already well served by ships. In expressing his disappointment with the defeat of the bill, Theodore Roosevelt alluded to developing problems with Japan in the Pacific.[105]

In a speech before the Navy League, William Gibbs McAdoo, who was to play an important role in shaping Woodrow Wilson's merchant marine policy, told of these Japanese problems. He said, "The Japs have had the presumption to dictate that their children must be taken into our schools because Japan is now a powerful militant nation, as great as any in Europe."[106]

The Japanese were indeed powerful. At the time when the Atlantic world believed it had reached the peak of civilized accomplishments, Togo had taken that world's methods, techniques, and technology and beaten its greatest land empire. The sea states of the Atlantic world were frightened and impressed. So was Theodore Roosevelt. Roosevelt assembled a fleet of sixteen battleships, gave its command to Rear Admiral Robley D. Evans, and sent it off on an around-the-world cruise, as much to impress the rest of the world as to impress the Japanese.[107]

Evans, a member of the Naval Institute, was a minor agent of American maritime change. He worked in the Washington Navy Yard, and for the Baltimore and Ohio Railroad, fabricating steel. Secretary of the Navy W. C. Whitney appointed him chief steel inspector for the building of the new American navy. This brusque sailor helped teach the steel industry its business and how it could fabricate plates for men-of-war.

The Japanese were no strangers to Evans. He had spent time in their country on duty. "The leading characteristic of the

Japanese," he later wrote, "was honesty." But he was about to lead the most powerful fleet ever assembled on a cruise intended to awe the world and the Japanese, who had learned to build men-of-war and subsidized merchantmen.[108]

It would be the longest cruise ever undertaken by a comparable force. It would prove the excellence of the ships of the newly emerged American steel shipbuilding industry. It would bolster the military superiority of the Atlantic world. And it would show, for all of the world to see, the weakness of American maritime policy. This was simply that there were no American ships to carry the fleet's coal. On its epic voyage this Great White Fleet had to be fueled from undependable, foreign-flag, commercial vessels.[109] The point was made.

Taft, Wilson, Conspiracy, and the Lobbies

William Howard Taft attempted to increase the number of American-flag ships to prevent the recurrence of such a problem when he followed Theodore Roosevelt into the White House. He spoke on the problem in Rockland, Maine, and Seattle, Washington. The Philippines needed dependable carriers, and, he implied, Japan threatened American navigation in the Pacific. The Japanese were building all manner of ships. There were few American ships in the Pacific, and other fundamental problems faced the merchant marine.[110]

One was reflected in another attempt by Senator Gallinger to establish ocean mail lines through the legislative process. Politics forced him to avoid the question of a worldwide mail service and reduced him to pleading for lines only to Latin America to take advantage of the Panama Canal then being built. Although Gallinger's bill cleared the Senate by one vote—against strong midwestern Republican opposition—it was never reported out of committee in the House.[111]

In 1912, Taft, Gallinger, and the Republicans who had held power during the American rise to greatness were passing. In seven short words, Woodrow Wilson summarized the Democratic party's congressional and presidential electoral triumphs of that year. "There has been a change of government," he said in his 1913 inaugural address.

There had indeed been a change. Victory in the Spanish-American War, figuring large on the international stage, the voyage of the Great White Fleet, and years of what has been called the Progressive Movement gave Americans the essential confidence that they could bring about change. The Panic of 1907 had shaken the financial establishment of trusts, pools, and combines and had eroded its position of leadership. With that erosion, Taft, the Republicans, and "the money power" had been washed out of office.

The ground swell of change had been rising even before Wilson came to the White House. In 1910, a Texas Democrat asked the Congress to determine "whether or not the House of Representatives is being corrupted by lobbyists on two sides of the ship-subsidy matter."[112]

The Merchant Marine League became the focus of the investigation. Its secretary, John A. Penton, was called to account for an article he had written condemning certain congressmen for fighting ship subsidies. Penton defended himself and his organization against the charges of lobbying but found himself the defendant in a libel suit due to his writings. The hearing dragged on in petty bitterness and acrimony.[113] Testimony by the editor of a New York maritime publication and the ever-present Alex Smith—now with the New York Barge Canal Commission—appeared to clear congressmen of accepting bribes.[114]

The cause of subsidies was further damaged by charges of graft by its supporters. These accusations were made by J. W. and A. W. Dodsworth, brothers and editor and business manager of the *New York Journal of Commerce*. They were unable to identify the two men who had separately offered them (or their father) bribes of forty thousand and one hundred thousand dollars to publish stories favoring subsidies. They also said they had been offered a bribe to print stories backing American purchase of the French Panama Canal Company. Too, the Spanish government had tried to buy their sheet's favor. The evidence makes one question their reliability.[115]

Foreign shipping lines were also accused of working against subsidies—and adversely on congressional ethics. The Hamburg-American Line was said to withhold advertising from American newspapers that favored a strong United States merchant marine. Herr Albert Ballin, the German line's director, complained of the congressional investigation and deprecated the digging of the Panama Canal. The United States Naval Institute also awarded its essay prize for 1910 to T. G. Roberts, NC, USN, who flatly claimed that foreign interests were united in opposing a strong American carrying fleet. The *New York Times* told of a reaction to these events: a bill in the Congress to apply the Sherman Anti-Trust Act against foreign shipping monopolies.[116]

Early in 1912, Missouri's Congressman J. W. Alexander called for an investigation of the Atlantic Shipping Trust, but a number of things transpired before he got it. First, there was the ominous news that the great German lines and Morgan's shipping trust had ended their pooling agreement. Next, there were descriptions of the techniques the Germans used to force immigrants from Russia to use their line rather than the tsar's Volunteer Fleet. With these explanations came a revelation of the techniques the Cunard Line and the Austro-Hungarian government used to divert immigrants in their interests. The *New York Times* ran a full-page review of Paul Overzier's book, *The American-English Shipping Trust—The Morgan Line* which was startling. There followed explanations to the Congress of the use of "fighting ships" by steamship conferences. The conferences were groups of lines that set rates and shared the freights on given lines. If competition developed from an independent, they would put a vessel on the line whose rates were so low it would force the competition out of business. These methods of rationalizing the shipping business were repugnant as they reflected the brute strength of concentrated capital.[117]

In this climate, Congressman Alexander was able to push through a free-ship rider to a Panama Canal bill. Codman, the *New York Times,* and the free-ship Democrats got what they wanted after more than forty years of fighting. It was a hollow victory, as the unsettled nature of American maritime policy frightened the owners. They used neither this nor equally problematical legislation of 1914 to rebuild the merchant marine.[118]

In 1913, as chairman of the House Merchant Marine and Fisheries Committee, Alexander got his investigation of the shipping trust. Through this definite inquiry, the Congress attempted to understand the colossus of the Atlantic which controlled freight, people, and prices on the rails and ships of two continents. By then, legal action under the Sherman Anti-Trust Act had been brought against the Hamburg-America Packet Company and the other members of the North Atlantic Steamship Conference for pooling passenger traffic. Eight lines controlling New York's trade with the Orient were taken to court. They, too, used the shipping conference technique of a pooled monopoly of sailings in the trade. The Hamburg-America Line figured in this pool. The Hamburg-South America Line was a member of another which used deferred rebates to capture and keep the Brazilian coffee trade. Against this background the United Fruit Company, with a fleet of eighty-one foreign-registered vessels, claimed it used no unfair practices to maintain its Caribbean trade.[119]

The Texas Railroad Commission also suspected that there was monopoly in the coasting trade and contributed to the investigation. Morse's Mallory Line and the Southern Pacific's Morgan Line were believed to be the monopolists. Baltimore interests loudly stated their belief that they were victims of a monopoly. The New Haven and Hartford Railroad and New England Navigation Company were charged with exercising this control. Alexander sided with the shippers, saying competition in the coasting trade was dead.[120]

Storm Warnings

American maritime achievements in the years 1865 to 1913 were truly impressive. Americans brought the wooden full-rigged sailing ship and the schooner to perfection. They built schools to train naval architects, admirals, and seamen. They learned to organize capital, make shipbuilding tools, heat steel, and build and sail a navy. They carried business organization almost to perfection, obtaining almost complete control of the trade that mattered, the North Atlantic Ferry service. And finally, as the *New York Times* desired for half a century, they got "free ships" in 1912, thanks to Congressman Alexander. In only one respect did they fail. They failed to build an American merchant marine.

They failed for two major reasons. Despite the efforts of

Roach, Calkins, Kelley, Luce, Cramp, Codman, Mahan, and Smith, they failed to educate themselves in the complexities of international ocean commerce. Reprehensibly, they made the question of the revival of the merchant marine a political question, a sectional question, an ideological question.

Sixteen column inches of type in the January 9, 1912, issue of the *New York Times* could have told the Americans that the question of the revival of the merchant marine was an economic, strategic, and security question. Those column inches foreshadowed coming events. They told of limited cargo space, rising freight rates, and crowded wharves. Drought in Europe demanded bottoms to move American and Russian wheat. A record sixteen-million-bale cotton crop waited to be carried to Europe's spindles. A bumper apple crop was crossing the Atlantic, and European potatoes came West to replace a planting that failed. Prosperity in India, Australia, and South America demanded more bottoms. Copper and steel, the metallic bases of war, were being exported as never before. Not, however, in American ships.[121]

Notes

1. Nelson Dingley, "The Decline of American Shipping," *North American Review*, 138 (1884), 314.

2. *Report of the Commissioner of Navigation, for 1901*, (Washington, D.C., 1901), pp. 494, 586, and passim.

3. John Roach, "A Militia for the Sea," *North American Review*, 133 (1881), 182-85; and John Codman, "Shipbuilding vs. Shipowning," *North American Review*, 142 (1886), 483-84.

4. *New York Times*, April 16, 1870, p. 2; and G. W. Dalzell, *The Flight from the Flag* (Chapel Hill: University of North Carolina Press, 1940), passim.

5. J. G. B. Hutchins, *American Maritime Industries and Public Policy* (Cambridge, Mass.: Harvard University Press, 1969), p. 321.

6. Lieutenant Edward Very, USN, "The Type of (1) Armored Vessel (II) Cruiser Best Suited to the Present Needs of the United States," *Proceedings of the United States Naval Institute*, VII (1881), no. 1, 53-55 and passim (hereafter the journal is referred to as *The Proceedings*).

7. *New York Times*, September 14, p. 4, October 14, p. 2, December

The Civil War and the Period of Decline 103

18, p. 11, 1869; and January 11, 1870, p. 4.

8. W. W. Bates, *American Marine* (Boston: Houghton Mifflin Co., 1897), p. 152.

9. *New York Times*, November 25, 1867; January 2, p. 2, and January 25, p. 2, 1868. Henry Hall, *Report on the Shipbuilding Industry of the United States*, Census Monograph, Tenth Census, Vol. VII (1882), pp. 196-200.

10. B. B. Crowninshield, "Wooden Sailing Ships," *Transactions of the Society of Naval Architects and Marine Engineers*, Vol. XXIV (1907), pp. 68-72; G. S. Wasson and Lincoln Colcord, *Sailing Days on the Penobscot* (Salem, 1932), passim; and John Roach, "Shall Americans Build Ships?" *North American Review*, 132 (1881), 472-73.

11. *New York Times*, January 30, 1866, p. 4, and May 21, 1868, p. 4.

12. *New York Times*, January 29, p. 4, May 24, p. 4, July 16, p. 4, and November 25, p. 2, 1867.

13. *New York Times*, January 2, 1868, p. 2.

14. *New York Times*, May 30, 1868, p. 4; and Hans Keiler, *American Shipping* (Jena: G. Fischer, 1913), pp. 124-27.

15. *New York Times*, May 24, p. 4, and November 25, p. 2, 1867; John Codman, *Free Ships* (New York: G. P. Putnam's Sons, 1881), passim, is the best statement of the case.

16. *New York Times*, May 24, p. 4, and November 25, p. 2, 1867; and January 2, 1868, p. 2. John Roach's "The Decline of American Shipping," *International Review*, XII (1882), 533-71, is a capsule statement of the subsidy case.

17. *New York Times*, January 2, p. 2, and June 27, p. 4, 1868.

18. J. A. Saugstad, *Shipping and Shipbuilding Subsidies* (Washington, D.C.: U.S. Government Printing Office, 1932), pp. 57-58.

19. Hutchins, op. cit., pp. 524-31.

20. *New York Times*, May 22, 1867, p. 4. The Commercial Navigation Company's story is told in the issues of September 6, 1868, p. 4, and February 21, 1969, p. 4.

21. *New York Times*, October 14, p. 4, October 15, p. 6, October 16, p. 7, 1869; October 15, 1868, p. 4; and February 18, 1870, p. 5; and *Report of the Select Committee on the Causes of the Reduction of American Tonnage*, House Report 28, 41st Congress, 2nd session, pp. x-xix (hereafter the Lynch Report).

22. *New York Times*, December 4, p. 6, December 8, p. 4, 1869; January 28, p. 1, and July 15, p. 1, 1870.

23. *New York Times*, July 15, 1870, p. 1.

24. Keiler, op. cit., pp. 79-81, 127-30.

25. *New York Times*, January 21, 1875, pp. 4 and 6; and *Report on*

the *Pacific Mail Steamship Company*, House Report 598, 43rd Congress, 3rd session, passim.

26. J. D. Hayes and J. B. Hattendorf, *The Writings of Stephen B. Luce* (Newport: Naval War College, 1975), pp. 9-10.

27. Peter Karsten, *The Naval Aristocracy* (New York: The Free Press, 1972), pp. 357-58; Captain S. B. Luce, "The Manning of Our Navy and Merchant Marine," *The Proceedings*, 1 (1874), no. 1, 17; and Captain Roy C. Smith III, "The First Hundred Years Are...?" *The Proceedings*, 99 (1973), no. 10, 50-55.

28. Rear Admiral Caspar F. Goodrich, USN, (Memoriam) *Stephen B. Luce* (New York: Naval History Society, 1919).

29. George Rock, "The Education of Naval Architects," *Transactions of the Society of Naval Architects and Marine Engineers*, XL (1932), 196.

30. *New York Times*, June 27, 1868, p. 4; and October 14, p. 6, and October 15, p. 7, 1869.

31. *New York Times*, September 25, p. 4, October 5, p. 4, October 7, p. 2, 1880; and November 11, 1882, p. 3.

32. *New York Times*, January 19, 1888, p. 3; January 31, p. 5, February 1, p. 8, February 15, p. 2, 1889; and Keiler, op. cit., pp. 124-30. There is no substantial account of the American Shipping and Industrial League's activities.

33. *New York Times*, August 13, p. 9, August 27, p. 5, September 21, p. 3, 1896; April 18, 1897, p. 3; January 13, p. 5, January 14, p. 4, 1900; and November 21, 1901, p. 8. There is no substantial account of the American Merchant Marine Association's activities.

34. Herbert Croly, *Marcus Alonzo Hanna* (New York: The Macmillan Co., 1923), pp. 342-54. Croly's work has some shortcomings.

35. Examples are in the *New York Times*, February 13, 1870, p. 3; April 27, 1878, p. 4; and June 7, 1913, p. 17.

36. *New York Times*, June 28, 1881, p. 4; and D. S. Muzzey, *James G. Blaine* (New York: Dodd, Mead and Co., 1934), passim; ties the Maine delegation together.

37. *New York Times*, November 9, 1890, p. 6. This plea was put forward in various forms beginning with the *New York Times*, October 29, 1866, p. 4. Other examples are found in that newspaper July 7, 1866, p. 2; October 9, p. 2, and October 21, p. 4, 1880. Variations of the scheme were advocated throughout the period.

38. Lieutenant Carlos G. Calkins, USN, "The Mercantile Marine," *Report of the Secretary of the Navy*, Executive Document 1, Part 3, Vol. I (1882), 47th Congress, 2nd session, pp. 334-42.

39. The important federal documents for this juncture are: *Report of*

The Civil War and the Period of Decline 105

the House Committee on Commerce on the Causes of the Decadence of Our Merchant Marine: Means for the Extension of Foreign Commerce, House Report 342, 46th Congress, 3rd session, 1881; and *Report of the Joint Select Committee on American Shipbuilding,* House Report, 1827, 47th Congress, 2nd session, 1882.

40. W. A. Baker, *A Maritime History of Bath, Maine* (Bath: Marine Research Society of Bath, 1973), p. 647 and passim.

41. "Professional Notes" in *The Proceedings* for the period reflect the American debate on oil as a fuel.

42. W. A. Baker, *The Engine Propelled Vessel* (New York: Grosset and Dunlap, 1966), passim.

43. *New York Times,* May 2, p. 7, May 5, p. 1, May 8, p. 12, 1901; and August 12, 1902, p. 1; and Lewis Nixon, *Cosmopolitan,* April 1910, in an article entitled, "The Crime of Our Vanished Ships," pp. 605-13.

44. *New York Times,* June 13, p. 6, June 14, p. 1, and June 15, p. 3, 1903. The report of the receiver of the United States Shipbuilding Company is reprinted in W. Z. Ripley, *Trusts, Pools, and Corporation* (Boston: Ginn and Co., 1916), pp. 182-217.

45. *New York Times,* November 21, 1901, p. 2; January 20, 1902, p. 6; March 11, p. 3, and April 25, p. 8, 1912; and D. B. Tyler, *The American Clyde* (Newark, Del.: University of Delaware Press, 1958), passim.

46. *New York Times,* August 23, 1870, p. 8; March 14, p. 4, July 24, p. 4, 1879; March 23, p. 4, March 26, p. 3, March 30, p. 2, 1886; and March 23, 1899, p. 6, treat the iron and steel problems. Rear Admiral Edward Simpson, USN, wrote on these problems under the titles, "Wants of the Navy ..." in *United Service,* II (1880), 137-46, 647-56, 724-37, and III, 41-54; and "The Navy and Its Prospects for Rehabilitation," *The Proceedings,* XII (1886), no. 1, 1-39.

47. *New York Times,* June 15, 1870, p. 5; February 15, 1877, p. 8; October 21, 1880, p. 4; April 21, 1899, p. 4; and November 30, 1900, p. 7.

48. *New York Times,* May 1, p. 4, September 2, p. 4, 1880; and December 29, 1884, p. 2. Herbert Millington, *American Diplomacy and the War of the Pacific* (New York: Columbia University Press, 1948), passim, is the best account.

49. *New York Times,* November 18, 1872, p. 4, and February 7, 1881, p. 4; and Bates, op. cit., p. 162.

50. Basil Lubbock, *The Downeasters* (Boston: Charles E. Lavrait Co., 1929), passim.

51. *New York Times,* November 9, p. 4, November 23, p. 4, 1889; and January 28, 1911, p. 10.

52. A. R. Colquihoun, "An Englishmen's View of the Panama Canal,"

North American Review, 187 (1908), 348-56.
53. Archibald Hurd and Henry Castle, *German Sea Power* (London, 1914), p. 88 and passim.
54. David McCullough, *The Path between the Seas* (New York: Simon and Schuster, 1977), passim.
55. Gerstle Mack, *The Land Divided* (New York: Alfred A. Knopf, 1944), passim.
56. Steamer *Virginius*, House Executive Document 30, 43rd Congress, 1st session, passim; still the best available account.
57. Sir William Lard Clowe, *Four Modern Naval Campaigns* (London: Unit Library, 1902), passim.
58. Roach, "A Militia for the Sea," pp. 188-92.
59. L. A. Swann, Jr., *John Roach: Maritime Entrepreneur* (Annapolis, Md.: United States Naval Institute, 1965), pp. 151-84.
60. Their articles in the *United Service* are Lieutenant R. M. G. Brown, USN, "The Commercial and Naval Policy of the United States," VI (1881), 604-10; John Grier, "Should We Buy or Build Our First-Class Merchant Steamers?" VI (1881), 759-62; and Lieutenant J. D. J. Kelley, USN, "Free Ships and Subsidies," VI (1881), 524-35.
61. The essayists' efforts are found in *The Proceedings*, VIII (1882), no. 1, 1-186.
62. "Report of the Naval Advisory Board" in *Report of the Secretary of the Navy* for both 1883 and 1884, Executive Document 1, Part 3, 48th Congress, 1st session, pp. 52-99, and 48th Congress, 2nd session, pp. 226-33.
63. *New York Times*, February 17, 1885, p. 2, and Achille Viallate, "How France Protects Her Merchant Marine," *North American Review*, 184 (1907), 162 and passim.
64. Alan Villiers and Henri Picard, *The Bounty Ships of France* (New York: Charles Scribner's Sons, 1972), pp. 27-29.
65. Viallate, "How France Protects Her Merchant Marine," pp. 163-65.
66. *Report of the Commissioner of Navigation, 1909* (Washington, D.C., 1909), pp. 102-4.
67. *New York Times*, October 31, 1881, p. 2; March 11, 1907, p. 6; and March 14, 1909, p. 3; and Edwin Maxey, "The Japanese Merchant Marine," *North American Review*, 190 (1909), 67-73.
68. *Report of the Commissioner of Navigation, 1909*, pp. 54-55.
69. *New York Times*, October 16, 1899, p. 8; and *Report of the Commissioner of Navigation for 1909*, pp. 38-39.
70. Charles H. Cramp, "British Subsidies and American Shipping" and "The Steamship Merger and American Shipbuilding," *North American*

Review, 175 (1902), 829-34 and 6-16.
71. *New York Times*, January 22, 1881, p. 4; March 25, 1843, p. 4; March 4, 1894, p. 19; and April 23, 1899, p. 4, offer examples of British adroitness.
72. Kevin Hart, "Towards a Citizen Sailor: The History of the Naval Militia Movement—1885-1898," *American Neptune*, XXXIII (1973), no. 4, 264 and passim. Captain A. P. Cooke, USN, "Our Naval Reserve and the Necessity of Its Organization," *The Proceedings*, XIV (1888), no. 1, 169 and passim, with its discussion, reveals much about this problem.
73. F. E. Chadwick, *The Relations of the United States and Spain*, 2 vols. (New York: Charles Scribner's Sons, 1915), see vol. 2, chapter 34.
74. *New York Times*, June 14, p. 6; October 6, p. 6, and December 20, p. 6, 1898.
75. *New York Times* carried sixteen articles pertinent to these conditions. See, too, Hall, *Report on the Shipbuilding Industry*, pp. 96-105; and the following from *North American Review:* J. W. Garner, "The Merchant Marine Investigation," 180 (1905), 362-67; Philip Hichborn, "Shipbuilding Here and Abroad," 156 (1893), 404-7; S. E. Payne, "Our Merchant Marine," 168 (1899), 243-45; and A. R. Smith, "Our Neglected Shipping," 163 (1896), 473-76.
76. *New York Times*, May 25, p. 5, and May 26, p. 6, 1904; March 3, Part 5, p. 13, and March 11, p. 6, 1907.
77. *New York Times*, October 12, 1905, p. 6; February 28, 1907, p. 5; and January 22, 1908, p. 6; Hutchins, *American Maritime Industries and Public Policy*, pp. 529-32; and F. L. Allen, *The Lords of Creation* (Chicago: Quadrangle Books, 1966), pp. 42-69.
78. *Report on ... the American Merchant Marine in Foreign Trade*, House Document 1210, 51st Congress, 1st session, pp. 26, 39, 151, and passim.
79. *Report of the Commissioner of Navigation, 1901*, pp. 34, 307-9, and 334-41.
80. *Annual Report of the Secretary of the Navy for 1890* (Washington, D.C., 1890), pp. 3-36; Rear Admiral S. B. Luce, USN, "Our Future Navy," *North American Review*, 149 (1889), 53-65; Captain William T. Sampson, USN, "Outline of a Scheme for the Naval Defense of the Coast," *The Proceedings*, XV (1889), 169-217.
81. Robert Seager II, *Alfred Thayer Mahan; The Man and His Letters* (Annapolis, Md.: United States Naval Institute, 1977), passim.
82. Ronald Banks, "The Senatorial Career of William P. Frye" (M.A. thesis, University of Maine, 1958), passim.
83. *New York Times*, March 31, 1891, p. 4.
84. *New York Times*, February 16, 1891, p. 4.

85. *New York Times*, June 29, p. 4, October 27, p. 10, December 16, p. 4, 1891; Keiler, op. cit., pp. 81-87.
86. *New York Times*, March 1, p. 4, and March 2, p. 4, 1891.
87. *New York Times*, January 8, 1891, p. 4; and May 14, 1892, p. 4.
88. *New York Times*, May 21, p. 1, June 30, p. 1, December 4, p. 4, December 21, p. 1, 1892; and February 23, 1893, p. 4; E. Keble Chatterton, *The Merchant Marine* (Boston: Little, Brown, and Co., 1923), pp. 194-196.
89. Austin Cobrin of the Long Island Railroad attempted to use the principle in 1892 but was thwarted. The *New York Times*, May 16, p. 4, May 18, p. 3, and May 19, p. 8, 1892; E. T. Chamberlain, "A Present Chance for American Shipping," *North American Review*, 158 (1894), 277-82.
90. Codman's arguments are in the *New York Times*, April 20, p. 10, and October 20, p. 4, 1896; and "The Folly of Differential Duties," *North American Review*, 164 (1896), 25-80; Smith's are in the *New York Times*, October 29, 1896, p. 7, and "Our Neglected Shipping," *North American Review*, 163 (1897) pp. 470-78.
91. *New York Times*, May 12, 1894, p. 8; and *Report of the Merchant Marine Commission*, Senate Document 2755, 58th Congress, 3rd session, Vol. I, pp. 428-29 and passim.
92. Keiler, op. cit., p. 80.
93. The *New York Times* carried thirty-two articles on these efforts in the period 1898-1901. See, too, Payne, "Our Merchant Marine," pp. 244-45; and E. T. Chamberlain, "Ocean Transportation to Eastern Asia," *North American Review*, 171 (1900), 80-81.
94. *New York Times*, March 14, p. 3, April 2, p. 6, April 29, p. 8, 1902; June 4, 1907, p. 9; and May 10, 1912, p. 7; Cramp, "British Subsidies and American Shipping," passim; and "The Steamship Merger and American Shipbuilding," passim; E. T. Chamberlain, "The New Cunard Steamship Contract," *North American Review*, 177 (1903), 533-43.
95. *New York Times*, January 21, p. 8, and February 2, p. 8, 1904; Winthrop L. Marvin, *The American Merchant Marine* (New York: Charles Scribner's Sons, 1902), passim.
96. Hayes and Hattendorf, op. cit., p. 19.
97. *New York Times*, May 2, 1904, p. 5; January 5, p. 6, and January 13, p. 2, 1905; Garner, "The Merchant Marine Investigation," pp. 359-61.
98. *New York Times*, February 17, p. 8, February 25, p. 2, December 23, p. 9, 1906; and January 16, 1907, p. 3.
99. *New York Times*, December 14, 1905, p. 8; May 18, p. 1, November 24, p. 4, December 5, p. 1, December 6, p. 5, 1906; January 24, p. 5, March 1, p. 3, March 2, p. 1, March 3, Part 1, p. 6, March 4, p. 4, and March 5, p. 8, 1907.

100. *New York Times*, August 21, 1904, p. 3; B. F. Cooling, *Benjamin Franklin Tracy* (Hamden, Conn.: Archon Books, 1973), pp. 46-125.

101. A. J. Marder, *The Road to War, 1904-1914*, Vol. I in his remarkable series *From the Dreadnought to Scapa Flow* (London: Oxford University Press, 1966), pp. 6-14, 40-46, and 105-18; and E. G. Woodward, *Great Britain and the German Navy* (Oxford: The Clarendon Press, 1935), pp. 1-66.

102. C. G. Reynolds, *Command of the Sea* (New York: William Morrow and Co., 1974), pp. 420-30.

103. *New York Times*, January 16, 1904, p. 6.

104. *New York Times*, November 19, 1900, p. 9; November 21, 1901, p. 2; March 11, 1902, p. 2; October 27, p. 6, November 29, p. 8, November 30, p. 1, 1906; September 17, 1909, p. 8; and December 23, 1912, p. 14; A. L. Johnson, "Boston and the Maritimes: A Century of Steam Navigation" (Ph.D. diss., University of Maine, 1971), passim.

105. *New York Times*, November 26, p. 8, December 10, p. 6, December 14, p. 7, 1906; April 21, 1907, p. 2; and January 3, 1908, p. 6.

106. *New York Times*, November 22, 1906, p. 11, and L. C. Allin, "Ill-Timed Initiative—The Ship Purchase Bill of 1915," *American Neptune*, XXXIII (1973), no. 3, 178-98.

107. Robley D. Evans, *An Admiral's Log* (New York: D. Appleton and Co., 1910), pp. 342-449.

108. *New York Times*, January 6, 1907, p. 6; and Evans, *A Sailor's Log* (New York: D. Appleton and Co., 1902), p. 131 and passim.

109. *New York Times*, October 6, 1907, p. 2; May 25, 1908, p. 4; January 24, Part 2, p. 5, and November 29, p. 8, 1909; W. R. Braisted, *The United States Navy in the Pacific, 1897-1909* (New York: Greenwood Press, 1958), pp. 230-32.

110. *New York Times*, October 1, p. 6, October 2, p. 8, 1909; January 5, p. 18, July 27, p. 2, 1910; and October 6, 1912, Part 10, p. 9.

111. *New York Times*, January 12, p. 2, January 22, p. 3, and February 3, p. 3, 1911.

112. *New York Times*, December 8, 1909, p. 10.

113. *New York Times*, April 5, p. 1, April 14, p. 4, May 24, p. 5, and June 6, p. 6, 1910.

114. *New York Times*, November 29, p. 3, and December 1, p. 4, 1910.

115. *New York Times*, January 26, p. 1, January 27, p. 3, and January 31, p. 2, 1911.

116. *New York Times*, April 25, p. 4, May 19, p. 8, June 13, p. 1, 1911; January 17, p. 14, March 27, p. 4, and May 2, p. 7, 1912; Naval Constructor T. G. Roberts, USN, "The Merchant Marine and the Navy,"

The Proceedings, 36 (1910), no. 1, 1-40; and *Investigation of Charges Relating to Ship Subsidy Legislation*, House Report 2297, 61st Congress, 3rd session, passim.

117. *New York Times*, May 10, p. 6, June 21, p. 14, and June 23, Part 5, p. 1, 1912.

118. P. M. Zeis, *American Shipping Policy* (Princeton: Princeton University Press, 1938), p. 66. "The Underwood Tariff" of 1913 also instituted differential duties in favor of American ships. In violation of numerous reciprocity treaties, these were struck down by the Supreme Court. Samuel A. Lawrence, *United States Merchant Shipping Policies and Politics* (Washington, D.C.: The Brookings Institution, 1966), pp. 34-36.

119. *New York Times*, March 31, Part 4, p. 12, May 30, p. 14, July 31, p. 15, 1912; January 8, p. 8, January 11, p. 13, and January 28, p. 28, 1912; and *Investigation of So-Called Shipping Combine—Hearings on House Resolution 587*, 62nd Congress, 3rd session, passim.

120. *New York Times*, January 17, p. 1, February 26, p. 1, 1912; June 14, p. 11, August 31, pp. 2 and 8, 1913.

121. *New York Times*, January 9, 1912, p. 2.

4
World War I Maritime Policy and the National Security: 1914-1919

Jeffrey J. Safford

The main outlines of U.S. maritime policy during World War I were shaped by two critical factors: the policies and perceptions developed over the years prior to the war and the programs brought about by the war experience itself. The former can be understood best if one grasps the broad essence of American foreign policy on the eve of the conflict—first, from the standpoint of generally accepted national objectives; second, from the world view of President Woodrow Wilson.

For 125 years preceding World War I, Americans had made a conscious effort to replace Old World values with uniquely American principles and to reject entanglements with Europe's perennially feuding imperial governments. Following the recommendations of the Founding Fathers, as they perceived them, the policy they adopted to preserve their young republic and its high ideals was one of political and military isolationism. Equally representative of the rejection of European ways was the vital importance given to minimal government. In repudiating the European tradition of ponderous bureaucracies, Americans created a nation in which the role of government in foreign affairs would be held to two basic functions: to provide for the national defense and to assist Americans in pursuing their interests abroad. The former was minimized by the presumed security from attack America's insular character afforded (there would be no need, for example, for a large military establishment), and the latter would function only as a subordinate to the interests of private enterprise. Consequently, during the nineteenth century, private interest groups played the most influential role in shaping American foreign affairs. Government did not take the lead but generally followed the initiatives of the private sector.

Viewed commercially, Americans exalted private enterprise, individuality, and initiative and maintained that overt governmental involvement in any aspect of the economy posed a serious threat to individual freedoms, which were based essentially upon the integrity of laissez-faire, marketplace capitalism. The less fettered the economy, so argued this philosophy, the more it would be democratized. Viewing the merchant marine within this context, it was little wonder that, during its dramatic post-Civil War decline, proponents of government assistance to the shipping and shipbuilding industries consistently had to work against this attitude of noninvolvement. Also, the fact that domestic economic development proved capable of returning profits far exceeding those obtainable in maritime pursuits strengthened the arguments of the free-traders—by virtue of natural law, capital would seek out those investments yielding the largest returns. As shipping was not among the big profit makers, it understandably suffered. And from the standpoint of national security geared to coastal, not global, defense, the rationalization for an overseas merchant marine as an auxiliary to the navy could not be justified. During the late nineteenth century, these imperatives prevailed even as England, with Germany a significant second, increased its oceanic hegemony at America's expense.

Circumstances born of America's remarkable industrialization in the post-Civil War era weakened the arguments of those who sought limited governmental direction of the economy. History records the awesome growth of the late nineteenth-century American economy with its constant agrarian and industrial surpluses. Unable to absorb the nation's productivity, the domestic market found itself beset by depreciating prices, vast unemployment, a periodically depressed economy, and unprecedented social unrest. The nation saw itself facing two basic alternatives—either to redesign the economy so as to eliminate surpluses, or to secure foreign markets for their disposal. The policymakers who grappled with the social and economic realities of their times adopted the second alternative—solving the problems of a surplus-ridden economy through an energetic program of foreign exports. That this expansionist alternative was chosen astounded no one; the first alternative would have required an extraordinary, probably radical, government intervention in a marketplace economy ruled by free enterprise and private property.

Tied always to the determination to increase commercial expansion was the reality of America's sadly inferior overseas transportation system. If American industry hoped to strengthen domestic institutions by generating a prosperous foreign trade, then efficient and competitive means of access to the world's markets would require development. Another factor bearing on maritime matters grew out of the desirability of reducing the industrial waste and inefficiency caused by destructive domestic competition. The regulatory commission movement which commenced to oversee railroads in the 1890s prepared the ground for eventual government involvement on the high seas. The construction of a competitive merchant marine could also be rationalized as a means to correct a glaring fault in the American economy—the absence of a complete, or vertical, trade system. To increasing numbers of observers, it was fundamentally wrong to pay one's competitors to carry American freight. That those competitors, primarily Great Britain and Germany, already possessed extraordinary experience and organization in foreign trade as the result of vigorous governmental initiatives, coordination, and integration promoted interest in the United States for an adoption of similar methods.

In short, general attitudes at the turn of the century were distinguished, on the one hand, by a long tradition of governmental abstinence from economic direction; on the other, by a more recent sentiment desiring an active governmental involvement based upon the need to strengthen the domestic economy by democratizing it at home and by improving its competitive capabilities abroad. In both instances, the argument for a merchant marine as an arm of national security was minimally effective, for belief in a small, defensive, military posture remained a fixture in the American mind.[1]

The Wilsonian Approach

Few could have come to the White House in 1913 better equipped to combine new economic reasoning with the old political and military isolationist tradition than Woodrow Wilson. From the outset, Wilson was determined to employ the government as an active agent in the nation's economy in order to protect and strengthen the free enterprise system. The vitality of the republic—its freedoms, institutions, and prosperity—would depend upon the success of private competitive enterprise. Therefore, Wilson labored to fortify America's economic growth and expansion.[2]

Wilson considered foreign trade as an outlet for the nation's industrial energies and as a safety valve for its social dislocations: America's "great irresistable energy ... is doing more than it can keep within its own shops and limits and therefore has got to be released for the commercial conquest of the world."[3] An equally vital source of Wilson's outward view was his goal of a world commonwealth of nations based on America's liberal capitalistic ideals. As Wilson articulated it, the national purpose was "to enrich the commerce of our own states and of the world with the products of our mines, our farms, and our factories, with the creations of our thought and fruits of our character."[4] On these bases Wilson was convinced the United States would inevitably become the grand arbiter of world affairs, a nation neutral and above world strife. With this force it would reorder and stabilize the entire world. Militarism and its corollary, imperialism, would be forever eradicated: "When an American comes into ... competition he comes without any arms that would enable him to conquer by force, but only with those peaceful influences of intelligence, a desire to serve, a knowledge of what he is about, before which everything softens and yields, and renders itself subject. That is the mission of America."[5]

With militarism rejected as a tactic, Wilson reasoned that, in order to achieve a moral and constitutional world peace, the United States would have to improve materially the bargaining strength it did possess—its growing economic and moral power. To secure these ends, he lobbied for three major reforms. First, he emphasized the need for lower tariffs as a prerequisite to reciprocal trade and the consequent increased release of American surpluses. Second, he sought to democratize the domestic economy by breaking down the inelastic and self-centered power of Wall Street's money and banking trusts as a means of redistributing and utilizing their credit facilities to greater advantage in domestic and foreign trade. Finally, Wilson attacked what he considered a willful neglect of the "arms of commerce," the maritime services that would transport the goods released through tariff and financial reforms.

Statistical evidence supported Wilson's shipping concerns. Between 1870 and 1910, the nation's wealth had increased 600 percent, railroad mileage 400 percent, Lake Superior iron-ore production 600 percent, and coal production 1,000 percent. But the United States foreign trade fleet had *decreased* 50 percent. Whereas in 1870 American vessels carried 37.6 percent of the nation's exports, in 1910 they hauled only 8.7 percent.[6] Such inequities in shipping, Wilson asserted, were self-destructive; a nation could not expect efficiency and profits in foreign trade if its competitors delivered its produce. "Without a great merchant marine," Wilson insisted, "we cannot take our rightful place in the commerce of the world."[7]

Once in office, Wilson set out to achieve his objectives. In nine months the Underwood Tariff and the Federal Reserve Act were passed. But Wilson's concern about remedying the maritime problem was momentarily sidetracked by an issue he inherited from the previous administration, the controversial Panama Canal Act which reserved toll-free use of the nearly completed Isthmian shortcut for the American coastwise trade. It had been passed, however, at the expense of violating the Hay-Pauncefote Treaty of 1901 between the United States and Great Britain, which banned discriminatory rates for canal users. Moreover, President William Howard Taft had signed it into law in disregard of an existing Anglo-American arbitration treaty that provided for the peaceful means of debating and resolving just such issues.

Wilson quickly weighed the situation and set the dilemma aside during the tariff and fiscal reform campaigns. When these had been waged successfully, he moved to secure congressional repeal of the canal-toll rider. For, despite its aid to American shipping, Wilson believed that its violations of treaties compromised the national honor and imperiled the concept of world arbitration; in short, it threatened to weaken immeasurably the moral objectives behind his foreign policy. The whole world, Wilson observed, would judge the integrity of his diplomacy on the outcome of this decision. His argument prevailed; the rider was repealed on June 11, 1914.[8] Clearly, other means would have to be developed for building a competitive merchant marine. These came abruptly and unexpectedly with the outbreak of the Great War just six weeks later.

The Effects of War in Europe

The European war created chaos in the American economy in midsummer 1914. Panic swept the money market (still suffering from the depression of 1913-14), a banking failure was narrowly averted, and the New York Stock Exchange closed its doors for four months. These difficulties were accompanied by a paralysis in ocean services as Great Britain and Germany, carrying the bulk of America's overseas trade, withdrew their merchant fleets from transatlantic service.

These withdrawals revealed the total inability of the American merchant marine to meet the requirements of foreign trade. Although the United States was ostensibly the third largest shipholding nation in tonnage, the great majority of its ships were actually engaged in coastal and Great Lakes trade. On the eve of the war, less than 10 percent of America's exports were being carried in American bottoms, and of all the vessels in the world ocean-carrying trade, only 2 percent were of American registry. To complicate matters, exorbitant freight rates were charged for what little shipping space remained, and insurance rates became virtually prohibitive.[9]

The shutoff also coincided with one of the greatest agricultural harvests in American history. With ocean transportation virtually nonexistent, surpluses built up all along the Atlantic and Gulf coasts and prices fell disastrously. The shipping tie-up and the consequent depression in prices aroused widespread concern, not only among farmers but also on the part of all the commercial agencies involved with agriculture—the railroads, merchants, and bankers. James Farrell of United States Steel remarked that one week's war experience had done more to convince Americans that foreign trade was necessary to the domestic welfare than two years of theoretical debate.[10]

While the European conflict caused Americans extraordinary economic disadvantages, it also offered them unparalleled economic opportunities to secure new outlets, particularly in the former markets of the belligerents. Commercial opportunists envisioned their best markets in Latin America, which had suffered most from the Anglo-German withdrawal. "Europe's tragic extremity becomes ... America's golden opportunity," remarked the *New York Commercial*; "the opportunity not of a lifetime, but of a century of national life ... through the annihilation of Europe's foreign trade."[11] But without ships these opportunities would be seriously circumscribed. The Wilson administration moved rapidly to remedy the problem. Out of the early weeks of American neutrality came three major accomplishments: a Bureau of War Risk Insurance; a "free ships" act (legalizing the registration of foreign ships under the American flag); and the introduction of a bill authorizing government ownership and operation of a national merchant marine.

Responding to the administration and to strong urging by the nation's powerful export trade associations, Congress passed the ship-registry and war-risk insurance bills within weeks. This done, Wilson and his Secretary of the Treasury, William G. McAdoo, moved to introduce a bill granting the government the power to purchase vessels. Their rationalization for taking this giant step toward direct governmental involvement in the economy was prompted by several factors. First, it appeared to most Americans that the war would follow previous European patterns and terminate in a few months, if not in weeks. If the United States desired to capture vacated markets, it would have to do so before the belligerents settled their differences and returned their attention to commerce. Second, Wilson and McAdoo harbored serious doubts whether private enterprise could provide capital sufficient to secure the necessary shipping, in addition to fearing that shipping and business interests would attend only to those trades earning substantial profits and not to the broad-based general welfare of all. Third, the administration saw in the war crisis a propitious opportunity to take governmental action while private enterprise appeared susceptible to such initiatives. As McAdoo outlined it, a government shipping corporation would (1) exercise a regulatory function upon rates, management, policy, and the trade routes of the ships; (2) be profitable to government; (3) be predictably stable and assured of capital on all occasions; (4) guarantee American shipping a position from which to compete successfully with foreign operations; and (5) serve in war as a naval auxiliary and reserve.[12]

While the private sector did not question the efficacy of regulation (this had been revealed in congressional hearings in 1912-13) and sympathized with Wilson's and McAdoo's concerns to strengthen American shipping for foreign competition, it did object vigorously to government direction and expressed little concern for the military connection. The concept of profits for government through commercial enterprise was unacceptable, as was the prospect of a rival corporation largely immune to laws of supply and demand functioning in the private economy. And as America's isolated position led to the assurance that the nation was not in peril of being drawn into the European conflict, the necessity for a naval auxiliary was held to be slight.

The critical issue for many was the spectacle of a nation edging menacingly away from free enterprise. Federal emergency aid granted to private enterprise in support of war risk insurance and lowered barriers to acquiring foreign vessels was compatible with that tradition. But direct governmental entry into shipping was not. The maritime enterprises decried the administration's impetuosity and argued the need for patient and planned growth. The crisis would pass shortly, their arguments read, and private enterprise would be more than up to the task. McAdoo and Wilson were moving so quickly, they protested, that business was being deprived of the opportunity to respond to the crisis on its own initiative.

These arguments were strengthened when a break appeared in the economic crisis toward the end of August. The domestic and international financial picture began to clear, and British naval superiority subdued the military storm at sea. These developments, combined with governmental assistance to private enterprise, broke the impasse and unleased a deluge of business optimism. Wielding these new realities, the shipping enterprises lobbied intensely in Washington and succeeded in persuading Congress to table the controversial ship-purchase bill.[13]

The private sector's resolve had not diminished in the slightest when Congress reconvened in early December 1914. The shipping industries argued that times were good and no longer of the "emergency" nature described by the administration. In five short months, they pointed out, the United States had already cleared its huge indebtedness to Europe. The rewards of high rates, which Wilson had attacked, were considered "just" after years of moderate and even minimal gain. Chartering was active, and vessels long idle were now employed. In fact, vessel shortages and high rates were a great boon to shipping, making it possible for the first time in years for American vessels to engage profitably in foreign trade. Furthermore, commercial interests insisted that all of this would stimulate private maritime investment.

To this, they added their fear of the consequences of government ownership in time of war. Senator Henry Cabot Lodge's contention that "there is all the difference in the world between the dangers to be apprehended from the privately-owned ship getting into trouble, which are insignificant dangers, and the international dangers arising from Government-owned ships," spelled out the opposition's position in another dimension. Although Wilson this time employed strong-arm tactics to force approval, and hinted that government vessels would not be used in the war zone, significant numbers of his own party refused to support the bill, and it fell victim once again to the proponents of limited government and political and military isolation.[14]

The issue might have remained deadlocked had not new war developments brought the need for fresh perspectives. Reconciling themselves to a prolonged military confrontation of trench warfare, the belligerents began to make provisions for a resumption of the commercial rivalries that most Americans believed had initially ignited the war. Responding, Wilson moved in 1915-16 from a position of strict neutrality to one of military and commercial preparedness to safeguard American interests. Within this context, the private sector's opposition to a government merchant marine was broken down.

The Sinking of the Lusitania

Although military preparedness had been discussed in 1914, it was not until the sinking of the *Lusitania* on May 7, 1915, that it was given more than lukewarm consideration. The loss of 1,198 passengers, including 128 Americans, etched the harshness of war on American awareness and brought about increased hostility toward Germany. Advancing these sentiments, Wilson sidestepped private capital's resistance to a government shipping program by adroitly marketing the merchant fleet as an auxiliary force for the navy. It was the expedient thing to do, McAdoo later remarked, since experience had convinced them that "people as a rule are far more interested in fighting, and in preparation for fighting, than they are in any constructive commercial or industrial effort."[15]

Wilson and his treasury head then combined ships and military preparedness with a strategy they considered equally important to the national security—linking war trade opportunities with a program for Pan-American, or hemispheric, solidarity. While Pan-Americanism was an attempt to pioneer business, Wilson and McAdoo had designs far beyond a simple concern for profits. Both saw in the political and economic connections forthcoming from hemispheric unity a potent means by which to strengthen American isolationism and influence Old World affairs. As McAdoo expressed it, Pan-Americanism had the potential of becoming a "powerful agency for world peace." By the simple denial of its assembled resources, by sheer market muscle, it could "exercise a persuasive power of irresistable force upon other nations of the world in the settling of international disputes." All of this depended, however, upon a "wholesome materialism" concerning the basic essentials of trade and communication. No such policy, therefore, could function without the development of hemispheric self-sufficiency in the way of commercial shipping. In sum, the military and commercial strengthening of the United States, including the crucial establishment of ocean shipping services, would fortify the ability of the Americas to remain isolated from the corrosive influence of European affairs.[16]

All of this demonstrated how ships had come to represent the substance of Wilson's foreign policy as it evolved during the months of neutrality. In short, by 1915, the European war had promoted a consensus among Wilsonians demanding a liberal, lawful, and procapitalistic world, secure from the disorders of imperialism and within which, as one historian has aptly put it, "America could serve mankind from a position of political and economic pre-eminence."[17] Hence the emphasis given to shipping, for maritime growth increased the national power by giving the economy greater flexibility, freeing it from former commercial dependencies, and increasing the national wealth through the expansion of foreign trade. Wilson had concluded that the United States could not achieve world influence, nor maintain it, without becoming a major maritime power.

Hence also alarm in Washington over indications in 1915-16 that the belligerents would not accede gracefully to the growth of United States overseas commerce, despite its moral objectives. The Allies in particular had been demonstrably piqued at having lost trade to America on account of the war. While the war handcuffed their efforts to regain that trade at once, they promised to give the United States a real run for its money upon the cessation of hostilities, not only in the Western Hemisphere, but on a worldwide basis. Goaded by the fact that the Allies had intensified the severity of their restrictions governing America's neutral trades during the war, had nationalized their own commercial fleets, and were formulating plans (as were the Central Powers) to coordinate their economic and commercial programs, Americans were spurred into broadening their preparedness to include a strong anti-European commercial arm in 1916.

Marshalling administrative men and agencies, Wilson made commercial preparedness a vigorous public issue. In no time, the matter dominated discussion in business circles. For example, the most powerful trade association of all, the National Foreign Trade Council, devoted its entire January 1916 convention program to the subject and to what it termed the "war after the war," the commercial struggle sure to take place following the war's conclusion.[18] Congressional hearings made it clear that the issue had reached Capitol Hill. Only a strong merchant marine, with a strong navy to protect it, members agreed, could insure the perpetuation of America's commercial and political neutrality.[19] As preparedness sentiment intensified, congressional opposition to the bill steadily eroded; it passed the House on May 20 and went over to the Senate.

Two additional events of significance added weight to the urgency behind commercial preparedness and the passage of the shipping bill. The first concerned the failure of Wilson's second major effort to bring the belligerents together for a negotiated peace. In May 1916 the Allies rebuffed an American mission, making clear that they had no intention of seeking an armistice but had determined to fight it out, in anticipation of winning the war and reaping the rewards, a policy promising to affect American interests severely. Wilson recalled the mission in disgust and doubled his energies on behalf of preparedness measures.[20]

The Paris Economic Conference of June 1916 further disappointed American hopes for the creation of a postwar commonwealth of nations predicated on democratic principles and free trade. The stipulations of the conference indicated that the Allies planned to employ discrimination freely in an effort to recapture their former trade. The Paris resolves, as one Wilsonian observed, were sheer "militarism translated into commercial warfare."[21] When Great Britain preemptorily increased the severity of its restrictions on American trade to Europe, still another argument had been added in favor of American ships.[22] All factors combined, support for the shipping bill crescendoed in midsummer. The measure passed the Senate on August 18, 1916, as part of a comprehensive economic and military preparedness package (army and navy bills were passed in May and August, respectively), and received the president's signature on September 7.

The Shipping Act of 1916 reflected both old and new perspectives. On the one hand it was an emergency measure only. That the act prohibited the new United States Shipping Board

(USSB) from continuing business more than five years after the European war, that cabinet members could not sit on the board, and that the board would be prohibited from purchasing belligerent vessels, pointed out the strengths of the old arguments for the supremacy of private enterprise and the hostility against measures that would endanger America's isolation. The great majority of those who voted for the bill still considered public ownership unacceptable and approved it only as a special case in support of commercial and military preparedness—not as a measure to enhance America's ability to wage war, but as an instrument to enable the United States to strengthen itself economically and militarily in order to resist efforts by the belligerents to compromise its neutrality or to draw it into the conflict.

Nevertheless, the act provided new reforms of considerable importance. Although its designers did not conceive of it as a means by which to provide transportation of soldiers and equipment to the French front, the act was passed for the purpose of "encouraging, developing, and creating a naval auxiliary and naval reserve"—a clear understanding of new realities. The act also provided for the overall development of an efficient, scientifically managed foreign trade program; for the first time, a regulatory agency had been created to oversee maritime affairs. Discrimination by foreign shipping companies against American exporters was forbidden, and the board was given the power to "disapprove, cancel, or modify" any shipping agreements between service lines which could be construed as inimical to the commercial interests of the United States. Finally, the Shipping Act of 1916 authorized the creation of an Emergency Fleet Corporation (EFC) for the purpose of purchasing, constructing, and operating government vessels in time of dire national need.[23]

The United States Enters the War

As the Shipping Act of 1916 had been designed as a peacetime measure and forbade a government shipping operation except during a "national emergency," a functional merchant marine did not exist when the United States declared war on

April 6, 1917. From the start, possibly no agency of government had ever had responsibilities so awesome thrust upon it with so little preparation. The task of building an organization to transport the millions of troops desperately demanded in Europe, providing them with food, munitions, and equipment, in addition to helping replenish the world's appalling losses of tonnage due to submarine destruction, was almost beyond imagination. Unanticipated formative difficulties complicated the effort. At the outset, four crucial months were wasted by a fratricidal conflict between the heads of the EFC and USSB over authority to let contracts and the relative weight to be given wood and steel ship construction. The discovery that every shipway in America was already occupied in building did not lessen the burden; nor did labor unrest, extraordinary overseas demands, continued German submarine devastations, and a monumental coastal freeze during the record cold winter of 1917-18.[24]

Only in early summer 1917 did matters begin to improve. Congress moved to bring shipping operations more directly under Wilson's purview by passing the Urgent Deficiencies Act of June 13 and the Emergency Shipping Act of June 15. Thereafter, presidential authority, rather than the original Shipping Act of 1916, defined most of the powers of the Shipping Board and the EFC. Hence the wartime shipping program was related directly to the White House, an autonomous operation responsible to Wilson—and to Wilson's world view—alone. The importance of this unilateral presidential authority cannot be overemphasized; Congress retained only the purse strings.[25]

One of Wilson's initial moves was to fire the feuding heads of the EFC and the USSB and replace them with Edward N. Hurley, former chairman of the Federal Trade Commission. In August, Hurley commandeered American shipyards and the 3 million tons of vessels they were contracted for; two months later, he requisitioned all American ships afloat in excess of 2,500 tons. In the meantime, 700,000 tons of confiscated German vessels were outfitted for American service. The Shipping and War Trade boards then combined their economic might to lever almost 2 million tons of neutral vessels into United States service. Through similar methods Japan was persuaded to yield

150,000 tons on charters, and both Japan and China were contracted to construct additional tonnage for the board. Still, there were never sufficient ships at any time.[26]

The government's shipbuilding program had been designed to make up the difference and more—15 million tons of vessels were worked out on the drawing board. But these ships did not materialize as quickly as anticipated. Although the Shipping Board began construction of three major shipyards comprising ninety-four ways and commandeered 431 contracts in existing American yards, the enterprise proved so new and so beset by unforeseen predicaments that it was not until the summer of 1918 that ship launchings began in earnest. By September 1918, only 465,454 new tons had been delivered for service. And the first vessel from the EFC's largest shipyard, the mammoth fifty-way facility at Hog Island south of Philadelphia, was not completed until December 3, 1918, almost a full month after the armistice. It has been alleged that for its failure to produce vessels with greater celerity, Wilson's shipbuilding program was the most significant disappointment of America's war effort.[27]

Viewed from a different perspective, however, the Shipping Board's ability to accumulate vast quantities of ships through purchase, seizure, charters, and requisition helped shorten the war to the point where it merely appeared that the construction program had failed. When the Allies first outlined shipping needs with Wilson in 1917, prognostications for the war's end had stretched all the way to 1920; American shipbuilding was planned on that basis. Had the war lasted beyond November 1918, America's construction effort would have played a major role. More important, criticisms of this facet of America's shipping program represented hindsight and obscured the pride with which Americans viewed their record-making accomplishments, despite formative setbacks. It was a fact that by late summer 1918 the United States had not only assembled a massive fleet from foreign and domestic sources in unparalleled time, but was finally producing in its own shipyards, some 158 of them manned by a work force of over 300,000 men, a government fleet of virtually astounding proportions. In October 1918 alone, the yards delivered 391,000 tons, or more than had been produced in virtually any prewar year. By this time, the maximum building program was at its absolute peak, with 17,399,961 tons under contract. Americans were witnessing the production of the greatest profusion of ships the modern world had ever seen.[28]

While the tremendous growth of the fleet had primary significance as a war expedient, Wilsonians always considered it a means by which to bring about an American solution to the postwar peace. No one expressed this better than Edward Hurley. To Hurley, overseas commercial expansion was axiomatic if the nation hoped to dispose of its huge surpluses and avoid economic and social stagnation: "Unless we continue to develop our foreign trade, after the war we can have no enduring prosperity." But, like Wilson, Hurley held the altruistic view that the nation had additional responsibilities beyond the fundamental goal of economic and social equilibrium at home. What was at stake was the liberal mission, he argued, selling America to the rest of the world, selling her ideals and her hopes as well as her goods. Ships, built originally by the Shipping Board as instruments of war, were "designed to serve equally well as instruments of an enduring peace." America's part would be measured by the degree to which its ships brought prosperity to its neighbors as well as to itself. "Our opportunities for service, as well as for trade," he acknowledged to Wilson, "will be found in the markets of the world."[29]

Hurley was never tempted to believe that the European powers would accept these principles with grace. Arguing that in his judgment the European conflict actually represented to the belligerents another phase of the Darwinian struggle for commercial supremacy, and that the United States was "the only nation that has taken a completely unselfish position in the war," Hurley endeavored to add weight to America's call for a liberal peace by increasing its maritime strength. "My whole thought is to get a fleet of large sized ships . . . so that we may be able to compete with Germany and England after the war," he confided at the height of hostilities. For in the same way that big-navy advocates called for a battleship program equaling that of Great Britain, Hurley was certain that, if the United States failed to obtain at least parity levels with its maritime competitors, there could be little hope of eliminating international trade rivalries and of bringing about a universal acceptance of Wilson's benevolent world view.[30]

It is important to recognize these strategies as a part of Wilson's war policy. From the outset, Wilson was not about to dissipate America's energies in a headlong rush to waste materials and men in the criminal conflict brought about by nations with no loftier notions than commercial rapaciousness, the division of postwar spoils, and the strengthening of their imperial systems. Wilson's hopes to serve mankind were based on his belief that world stability and the reconstruction of postwar Europe "rested largely on our ability to keep this country intact."[31] Such reasoning explained Wilson's refusal to allow the amalgamation of American troops into Allied units which, under the command of Allied officers, had been wasted in savage trench warfare. Moreover, Wilson and the War Department were convinced that the Allies were deliberately attempting to force American troops into such Allied units in order to interfere with the development of a strong independent United States Army which might actually win the war and then be used to strengthen Wilson's bargaining position at the postwar peace table. The entire American war strategy based its objectives on maintaining independence in every way; Wilson desired absolute freedom of decision and no identification with what he considered exploitative Allied war aims. Wilson's insistence that the United States declare itself an "associated" rather than an "allied" war power testified to the strength of this commitment.[32]

Wilson forged naval war policies in the same way. The navy's priorities were home and convoy defense, limited participation in the European theater, and a massive growth policy aimed at challenging British naval superiority.[33] American policy was well expressed by the United States Navy Chief of Staff, Admiral William S. Benson. "Don't let the British pull the wool over your eyes," he instructed the head of the American naval mission to Europe: "It is none of our business pulling their chestnuts out of the fire."[34] America would concentrate its growing energies for the fight for a stable postwar world. These attitudes reflected the vast divisions existing between the

United States and the Allies. Cooperation within the coalition was consistently handicapped by antagonistic national aims and ambitions; only when war circumstances became utterly acute were these limitations transcended and agreements secured. Wilson's refusal to name a permanent political delegate to the Allied Supreme War Council and his abiding reluctance to participate in any form of inter-Allied consultation underwrote his determination to keep America strong and accentuated his insistence upon the old tradition of political independence and avoidance of European intrigue.[35]

Like Wilson's, Hurley's developing fear of a European backlash against America's growing financial and commercial power came to dominate his position during the war. After British shipping men visited the United States in the fall of 1917, Hurley concluded that the British were not at all concerned about a democratic world peace, but thought only of postwar economic conditions and the control of commerce. Unless this ceased, he confided, "Instead of being associated with England in the fight against Germany, [he would] watch England to prevent her from gaining some commercial advantage at the present time, and particularly after the war."[36]

The Allies scrutinized the Shipping Board's every move with equal suspicion. From the outset they questioned American shipping assignments. The USSB had placed two of every three ships on the European war run. The remaining third (in excess of two million tons) carried on global foreign trades for the purpose of importing the necessities required for the production in America of munitions, steel, and other war equipment and foodstuffs needed by the American Expeditionary Force (AEF) and the Allies. These trades were also necessary, Washington alleged, in order to replenish goods shipped to Europe that Americans needed for their own domestic well-being. To the Allies, however, it was always an issue as to just how many imports America truly required; in their eyes there was no comparison between the hardships and losses Europeans had suffered and the enviable standard of living prevailing, even in war, in the United States. It went beyond that; America's war policies called for extensive trade with Latin America for nitrates, manganese, sugar, coffee, and beef; New Caledonia and

South Africa for chromium; Australia for wool; the Philippines for hemp; and so forth. These runs, however justified by war, incurred British resentment because they inevitably gave America the inside track to fruitful commercial ties in markets previously dominated by the belligerents.

Such concerns were viewed darkly by Washington; American policymakers thought the Allies, not the United States, blatantly guilty of having failed to utilize shipping exclusively for military ends. Throughout the war, Americans held, the Allies had resisted any form of mutual control and efficiency, actually competing for supplies with one another. When London and Paris put in requests for increased allotments of American vessels, these were considered less than sincere. With minor exceptions, Great Britain possessed the troopships needed to transport the AEF overseas. London could not resist employing this advantage as a negotiating weapon, using it in an effort detrimentally to affect the independence of the American military effort in France. Fears that London would refuse to return the more than one million American soldiers in Europe at the war's end, thereby forcing American ships into passenger rather than commercial services, weighed heavily on the White House throughout the conflict.[37]

Early in 1918, an Allied Maritime Transport Council was created to supervise the coordination of Allied ocean shipping and shipping policy. But the London-sponsored and London-based organization proved to be mostly a British mechanism for pressuring the United States into cutting down its "nonessential" foreign trade fleet for a greater commitment to the European war effort, a policy the Shipping Board interpreted as an attempt to prejudice the trade America had built up during the years of neutrality. Hurley later remarked that "instead of cooperating to the utmost, we found the Allies jealous of one another, other countries suspecting that Great Britain was withholding vitally-needed support, and that one Ally had overreached another. This was particularly true of shipping."[38] As a result, no truly effective integration of shipping policy was ever achieved; there never seemed a moment when the United States and the Allies were not finding some cause to question the justification of each other's shipping programs.

Wilson and Hurley labored over these difficulties: "The feeling of distrust between nations is really unfortunate," the shipping head allowed in August 1918. It was "unthinkable" that America, tied to its Allies in combat, "should, after the war, turn its resources against them for trade conquests of the very kind which were largely instrumental in bringing on the war." Wilson's world mission was so unlike anything that anyone had ever before encountered that most governments doubted its sincerity. The only answer lay in America's ability to persuade her detractors "that for the benefit of government and the world generally, the President's attitude is the only one."[39]

U.S. Shipping in the Postwar World

All told, with the coming of the armistice in November 1918, deeply disturbed by Allied political and economic maneuverings, Wilson determined to maximize his drive for the legal embodiment of these lofty, yet obviously self-interested, goals by employing the new trophy of war, U.S. maritime power, as a bargaining agent at the Versailles peace talks. "I want to go into the Peace Conference armed with as many weapons as my pockets will hold so as to compel justice," the president declared.[40]

The policy chosen was to impress the Allies by three means that American maritime growth and competition was a permanent undertaking: by continuing a very large shipbuilding program (the EFC effort was the only war program not terminated after the armistice); by refusing the Allies use of American shipping and shipbuilding facilities; and by broadly extending the USSB's authority over American maritime services. While Wilson agreed on the ultimate necessity of returning most of the shipping business to private enterprise, he believed that the longer Washington held this in abeyance, the longer the Allies would be pliable at Versailles. In the meantime, this would also provide the United States with more time to bulwark its own bargaining position by broadening its postwar commercial maritime growth. As Hurley summed up, there would be "no arrangement for any part of [American] shipping until there had been at least a tentative agreement on a League of Nations."[41]

To this Hurley added a two-part plan calling for a universal agreement on freight rates and seamen's wages. Noting that, by virtue of the La Follette Seamen's Act of 1915, American maritime working standards were far superior to the rest of the world's, Hurley called for their application on an international basis. He also demanded international uniformity in freight rates in order to free worldwide transportation from the domination of any single power. As Hurley saw it, uniform freight rates and seamen's wages would "solve the problem of trade wars, [and] give reality and force to the 'freedom of the seas.'" Hurley made no argument that the proposal would be received gratefully by European shipping interests. Rather, he concluded that the humanitarian aspects of the proposal, coupled with America's new power in the realm of shipping, would carry the plan over Europe's opposition. It was a perfect monument to Wilsonian commercialism in its liberal garb.[42] Combining all these tactics, Wilson and Hurley had synthesized altruism and tough business talk into a plan to strengthen their hand at the Paris deliberations.

But if the U.S. peace mission believed that its awesome new economic and financial power gave it an irresistible position from which to force an American peace on Europe, such expectations were soon disappointed. Despite the American argument that its mercantile growth was designed as much for the enrichment of the world as of the United States, the Allies maneuvered to compromise American independence by pooling all shipping for postwar European relief, moved to divide Germany's merchant and liner fleet on terms detrimental to the United States, and received with rancor Hurley's plan to create international regularization in freight rates, seamen's wages, and working conditions—increasing your competitor's costs, as the Allies viewed it.[43]

Radical changes in postarmistice requirements for American vessels further complicated matters. Pressure on the USSB to release shipping for foreign trade was enormous and diverse. The shipping sector demanded a return of its war-requisitioned vessels for the resumption of commerce, pressure to allocate ships to military repatriation was extreme, and labor and the shipbuilding industry protested peacetime cancellations of contracts and the moratorium on construction for foreign interests. Simultaneously, the neutrals demanded the immediate restoration of their ships on charter. Moreover, the Allies had tied up Germany's remaining merchant fleet, which, if put to proper use, could have solved many of the Shipping Board's problems. Finally, there was a rousing outcry that unless the board moved quickly, Great Britain would act first and capture the best trade.

These urgencies intensified a crisis situation in which the Shipping Board had been caught in a state of unpreparedness. Despite the administration's talk of the future, the unanticipated armistice had caught the board without a concrete plan for the peacetime utilization of its new fleet. Hurley's long-range plan had always favored "creative" over "competitive" trade as the desirable way to strengthen American commerce. This involved the carefully planned inauguration and development of customers and services on systematized trade routes and included salesmanship, banking, overseas investment, and assistance to the commercial growth of other nations to create markets adding to the wealth of the entire industrialized world. Such a plan required strong central governance and could not evolve overnight. If the shippers were given complete independence, Hurley warned Wilson, they would ship their goods not to the markets where the nation needed them most, but where they would be guaranteed the best prices. Chaos would inevitably ensue.[44]

It was a difficult situation in which the Shipping Board was left with two alternatives: maintain a closed policy for leverage on the peace talks, or respond to the call for aid from private enterprise. Favoring the second alternative, Hurley ordered a cutback on cancellations and began to assign increased numbers of USSB ships to foreign trade in order to relieve congestion at ocean ports. Hurley reasoned that American economic strength at Versailles would carry little weight if, in the adoption of a holding action, the Shipping Board allowed American industry and foreign trade to atrophy for want of jobs and transportation. Hurley also questioned the logic of continuing the prohibition on foreign contracts: "If we keep our fist closed until they open theirs," he cautioned Wilson, "the result may be a delay in the settlement of the larger issues."[45] But Wilson denied Hurley's request. Instead, he ordered the USSB to lower its shipping rates in order to counter Allied maritime competition. Hurley also began to return vessels of under four thousand tons to private control for foreign trade.

These actions demonstrated the animosity growing between British and American representatives over shipping. While the U.S. shipping delegation was greatly distracted by British efforts to hamper American foreign trade expansion, the head of the American naval contingent at Paris, Admiral William S. Benson, was livid over Great Britain's commercial intriguing. So distressed was Benson over what he interpreted as British designs "to block our Naval building program, and also to put every possible obstacle in the way of the development of our merchant marine," that on one tense occasion in January 1919 he very nearly exchanged blows with the First Sea Lord of the British Admiralty. Later that month, Naval Operations summed up for both American shipping groups: Great Britain sought to dominate the world's carrying trades, and unless the Shipping Board organized quickly and efficiently for competition, American foreign trade would be handicapped beyond repair.[46]

While the Shipping Board's evaluation of this need emphasized a non-European solution (by February 1919 the USSB's assignments to that continent had dropped to 18 percent), serious political and social deterioration in Germany and Eastern Europe brought its command back onto the North Atlantic on an important mission. Wilsonians had always agreed on the necessity of getting food relief into Europe to contain revolutionary socialism through support to more moderate political groups. Herbert Hoover, director of relief, was the leading advocate of this effort to combat bolshevism with food. At first, however, French hostility to any program lessening pressure on Germany prior to a peace settlement prevented relief mobilization. But in March 1919, the situation in Germany and the countries of the former Austro-Hungarian Empire worsened dramatically, and the Allied blockade was lifted. Hoover argued that with American food and supplies transported in American ships he could halt the red tide. Wilson agreed and ordered the Shipping Board to reassign large numbers of vessels to the European theater.[47]

Although Hurley complained to Wilson that the food relief program "greatly interfered" with the Shipping Board's plan to strengthen the American economy and the nation's postwar position, his reassignment of ships to relief broke the back of the European crisis. By late April 1919, European economic and political stabilization had been achieved and bolshevism adequately contained as the result of the relief program and Hurley's shipping support, however reluctantly transferred from lucrative non-Continental trades. In fact, while the Shipping Board redirected over 2 million tons of ships into Hoover's program between February and May 1919, in the identical period it increased the nonrelief trade fleet by 900,000 tons. This was accomplished by the nonstop delivery of new bottoms; in May alone, the EFC launched 814,000 tons of cargo-carrying vessels.[48]

Wilson stuck to his three-part nautical power play throughout the Versailles proceedings. Although toned down, the USSB's postarmistice shipbuilding program continued at a scale sufficient to underline Washington's resolve to build a competitive mercantile fleet; during the peace talks not less than 48 percent of all the world's tonnage was building in American yards. All the while, the USSB assigned ships to foreign trades in order to prevent Great Britain from reasserting itself too strongly in the mainstream of world commerce. And Wilson continued the embargo on foreign contracts in United States shipyards. While the Shipping Board began to return vessels of less than four thousand tons to private ownership, Wilson did not authorize it to release all requisitioned ships until peace was made official.

Relatively little came of these tactics. Wilson's refusal to release to the Allies for pro rata apportionment according to actual war losses the 700,000 tons of German ships seized in American waters was conducted outside of his Paris strategy; he already had the vessels and simply declined to relinquish them. The Allies countered by refusing to give up or cooperate in the use of Germany's extensive transoceanic cable system on the grounds that their seizure was no different than Wilson's action.

The Shipping Board did secure temporary use of 200,000 tons of German passenger liners for military repatriation, thereby freeing itself to a degree from dependency upon the British; but this achievement proved somewhat regressive, as Great Britain thereupon freed its own passenger liners for the reconstitution of trade.[49]

Other aspects of America's maritime policy at Versailles clearly failed of their objectives. A primary American concern had been to place Germany's captured merchant fleet in the immediate postwar relief service, but the Allies blocked this for better than half a year. Nor was Wilson able to convince the Allies to grant Germany use of its own merchant fleet to help rebuild and reintegrate its economy into the commercial commonwealth of nations he sought. Furthermore, the principle of the "freedom of the seas," originally publicized as one of Wilson's primary peace goals, was abandoned. Bitterly fought by the British, it suffered a fate similar to most other neutrality issues in Wilson's zealous quest. American efforts at creating universal equalization in seamen's conditions also failed. Conservative shipping interests, notably British, dominated the special Paris Conference on labor legislation and succeeded in maintaining the old and oppressive principles that made seamen subject at all times and places to the law of the flag under which they sailed.[50]

All considered, the American peace delegation agreed with Admiral Benson "that every phase of the treaty of peace while in the making has exposed the commercial ambitions of our Allies."[51] To American maritime proponents, the peace settlement did not reflect the Allies' commitment to a moral, cooperative, and stable internationalism, but testified to their insatiable economic greed. The image of American maritime growth as a benefit to mankind was considerably tarnished during the armistice period, and the ensuing bitterness reflected itself in the remaining months of Wilson's administration.

A major congressional priority in late 1919 concerned the peacetime disposition of Wilson's huge new merchant marine. To the vast majority of the Sixty-sixth Congress, conditions warranting continued federal control and construction no longer existed. Expressing the stipulations of the Shipping Act of 1916 that government was to relinquish its shipping business within five years following the war, the House voted overwhelmingly in November 1919 (240 to 8) to annul the emergency provisions and prevent the Shipping Board from letting additional building contracts. The measure then went to the Senate Committee on Commerce. The committee mirrored House attitudes by determining to provide reorganizational legislation that would promote an American merchant marine operated by private ownership. Yet the experiences of the war had also demonstrated clearly the efficacy of a continual program of strong governmental initiative and support. With the constant specter of fierce British opposition and competition always in the background (an acrimonious debate with London over German tanker ships had just been concluded unsatisfactorily), a bill soon evolved reflecting growing congressional support for protectionist and retaliatory policies.[52]

In order to carry out this program, Wilson appointed the anglophobic Admiral William Benson to the Shipping Board's chairmanship. Benson pushed the Senate committee to produce as tough a measure as possible; he wanted unusually strong discrimination and subsidies and a 100 percent American involvement in all shipping affairs. As the Secretary of War, Newton D. Baker, observed, Benson operated from the standpoint of envisioning the problem as "one of fierce and final competition between the British mercantile marine and the American mercantile marine."[53] Wilson reviewed the pros and cons of the bill with his cabinet on June 1 and sided with the Shipping Board. The president reiterated his old proclivity for the "freedom of the seas," but admitted that his concern with British commercial selfishness and his desire to see the American flag floating over a strong merchant marine took precedence. The president signed the bill into law on June 5, 1920.[54]

The Merchant Marine Act of 1920

The passage of the Merchant Marine Act of 1920, or the Jones Act, accomplished two adminstrative objectives. First, it completed the government's general economic demobilization following the war. The wartime experience had made it clear that major improvements in transportation were necessary and that these could be obtained from federal rationalization. Although Congress was not willing to embark upon a full program of public operation, it agreed that government regulation and encouragement of ships should be retained, strengthened, and expanded. Wilson had already achieved such objectives for the railroads in the Transportation Act of the same year. The Jones Act followed the Transportation Act by arranging ways in which the Shipping Board could turn its fleet over to private business and support, yet regulate its operation and growth. Provision was made for the board to provide funds to American shipping companies for the construction of new vessels, and the act arranged for the systematic sale of government ships at almost ludicrously low rates. Sales to aliens, however, were strictly supervised. The Shipping Act also exempted American shipping companies from corporate income and excess profits taxes, provided that the money saved was invested in the construction of new vessels in American shipyards.[55]

These and other provisions were intended to satisfy the second objective, a major stengthening of the foreign trade apparatus of American commerce. The act created a groundbreaking "essential trade routes" plan and directed the Shipping Board to maintain those designated sea lanes through private management. If private enterprise were unable to provide service, the board was authorized to operate ships until it was. The government was also placed in the business of developing ports and transportation facilities needed for overseas commerce. Additional clauses gave the USSB authority to supervise the rules and regulations of all government departments, bureaus, boards, or agencies directly or indirectly involved with shipping in foreign trade. Further, the act protected American shipping by banning from U.S. ports all vessels and lines resorting to rate cutting (the "fighting ship" tactic), deferred rebates, blacklisting, or discrimination.[56]

An important provision undercut the maritime insurance monopoly of Lloyds of London. Before the war, over two-thirds of the policies issued on American vessels had been foreign. The Shipping Act now exempted American marine insurance companies from the antitrust laws; for the first time,

American underwriters could now syndicate and cover American hulls at liabilities rivaling Lloyds. The Jones Act also created American companies to provide a comprehensive American service plan for shipping surveys and maintenance inspections, services that such companies as Lloyds had previously conducted, often at serious disadvantage to the United States.[57]

Vital as these provisions were, they were subordinated throughout the summer of 1920 to controversies boiling around three other major clauses of the Jones Act, all of which were highly discriminatory. One clause extended to coastal monopoly to the Philippines and other distant American island possessions. A more important clause (Section 28) granted preferential inland railroad rates to American cargoes shipped in American vessels, provided there was a surplus of American tonnage to handle a port's foreign trade. A final clause (Section 34) ordered the president to repeal all treaties conflicting with the right of the United States to employ discrimination.

Debate focused primarily on Section 28, for the preferential rates system of that clause violated no less than thirty-two foreign treaties. Complaints from injured foreign interests and irate domestic parties (fearing foreign counterdiscriminations) reached such proportions that the Shipping Board was obliged to declare a ninety-day moratorium on the execution of this section only four days after the act was passed. This was later extended to January 1, 1921. Protest against the provision extending the coastal monopoly was almost as intense as that directed against Section 28. When the Philippine administration itself alleged that foreign shippers would retaliate by boycotting the port of Manila, the Shipping Board shelved this clause also.

The major question facing the Wilson administration came from the protests of foreign nations that a treaty was "not a scrap of paper" and could not be abrogated except by mutual consent. Moreover, Congress appeared to have exceeded its legislative authority by breaking treaty terms when it inserted abrogation rights into the Merchant Marine Act. Wilson insisted that Congress could not appropriate executive functions, but his cabinet pointed out that he had literally given those privileges away by signing the bill.[58]

Wilson made his decision on September 24, 1920, announcing

that an endorsement of Section 34 would have been totally incompatible with every aspect of the respect America had always given, and would continue to give, to international accords. He had signed the bill under the pressure of time and upon the reasoning that his disavowal of its congressionally mandated discriminations would not affect negatively the operation of the measure which contained a great many "sound and enlightening provisions." Wilson's decision was intended to relieve international commercial and shipping tensions, for he believed that Section 34 had been interpreted globally as a challenge to one of the greatest economic conflicts the world had ever experienced.[59]

Wilson's action to strike down the discriminatory features of the Jones Act clarified an important shift in his attitude toward foreign affairs. In 1919 and early 1920, Wilson's reactions to Allied diplomatic and commercial maneuverings and to the debate over the League of Nations at home had left him a bitter man. The Merchant Marine Act of 1920 had reflected that bitterness; in fact, it had taken the issue a step too far. Recognizing this, Wilson tempered debate over discriminations during the summer and struck out in an old direction—generosity and constructive policy would be the order of the day. The president put it in his own perspective that fall. There were two ways in which the nation could assist the world in creating a pure and spiritual democracy—by applying equality of treatment in domestic matters, and by "standing for right and justice as towards individual nations."[60]

Wilson was also reflecting new realities regarding naval and maritime growth issues. Old threats to build a merchant marine and a navy superior to Great Britain's as the preferable way to create international peace were no longer applicable. For one thing it had become clear that the continuation of an extensive building program in the United States would have been matched ship for ship by the British, thereby neutralizing American efforts. Second, as the emotional pitch of wartime spent itself, the realization that a maritime and naval race would only intensify Anglo-American friction became repugnant to most Americans. Third, Americans had had their fill of wartime expenditures and huge bureaucracies and desired a genuine return to a peacetime economy. Facing two basic alternatives—an armaments and commercial race or an effort at toning down antagonisms—Americans began to comprehend that the risks and expenditures of the first were prohibitive. Instead, they reached for international agreements for the stabilization of relations among the major maritime nations. The most immediate materialization of this came with the Washington Naval Conference of 1921.

Other international factors affecting the Shipping Board's operations in 1920-21 played a part in the administration's decision to move toward the second alternative. The most significant of these was the onset of a worldwide recession in 1920. Despite vast destruction of shipping during the war, the armistice revealed the greatest surplus of merchant ships ever known. As the result of its own Herculean efforts, the United States owned most of the world's surplus. For approximately one and a half years after the war, however, the surplus was effectively concealed, largely because of continued government spending on the foreign trade economy. During this time, the Shipping Board endeavored to market its ships to existing private companies and to promote the foundation of new companies. The board also continued to operate vessels over as many as forty-one separate ocean trade routes. None of these efforts was highly successful. Only a third of the new companies the board sought to establish were ultimately formed, and USSB ships frequently sailed with partial loads. By the beginning of 1920, postwar government spending tapered off greatly, and for the first time since early 1917 the Treasury enjoyed receipts above expenditures. In addition, increased Treasury rediscount rates to harness inflation, the revival of European production, intensified foreign trade competition, and the increased foreign shipment of American, and non-American, goods brought about a serious economic decline in which the United States maritime industry suffered greatly. Beginning in midsummer 1920, cargoes for the world's merchant marines became extremely scarce. The bottom fell out in December. By March 1, 1921, 35 percent of the Shipping Board's vessels were idle; eventually this figure would reach 70 percent. The crisis was not confined to the United States; Great Britain also suffered and Japan possibly more. There were simply too many ships for the business.[61]

The Aftermath of the Wilson Administration

While America's World War I shipping program appeared on a downward beat in 1921, the maritime accomplishments of the Wilson administration generated much pride. In 1917-18, the Shipping Board had put together a monstrous wartime fleet which transported men and equipment to the European front and carried on critical global trades for the materials required to conduct the war. Managed at considerable cost and sacrifice, these accomplishments helped to shorten the conflict. Had the war been prolonged, the EFC's massive shipbuilding program would have come into play with even greater significance. Although the sudden cessation of hostilities reduced the fleet's usefulness, no one could dispute that the administration had put tremendous effort into its construction. In 1921, a special House committee acknowledged that "considering the program as a whole, the accomplishments in the number of ships constructed, the tonnage secured, and the time within which the ships were completed and delivered, constitute the most remarkable achievement in shipbuilding that the world has ever seen."[62]

The armistice period revealed Wilson's diplomatic goals for the shipping program. Contemplating two uses for the new vessels, Wilson attempted to employ their commercial and military potential as a means of forcing an American peace. He also utilized them in a major effort to stabilize the faltering political economies of numerous European states. In the first objective he failed utterly. The prodigious growth of the American merchant marine did not force the Allies to accept Wilson's plan for a pro-American peace, but catalyzed barely disguised wartime rivalries into intense commercial and political competition.

Wilson's second objective produced more significant results; American relief dispatched to Europe in American ships did arrest anarchy and social radicalism in many instances and strengthened Western capitalist economies. This lesson would be put to excellent use during the next world war and its aftermath.

Another lesson came from the failure in war to achieve Allied shipping cooperation; a generation later, shipping men concerned for World War II maritime policy cited this experience as an example to be avoided at all costs. Yet another caveat came from the crises caused by the unequipped state in which the American merchant marine found itself both at the outset of war and at the unexpected armistice; the nation could not afford ever again to allow itself such costly unpreparedness.

From the position of the American post-World War I economy, the USSB's vessels provided valuable initial service. During the unforeseen eighteen-month period of prosperity, the world's maritime nations rushed to place their tonnage in peacetime trades. Had the United States not possessed its new fleet, American commerce would have suffered as it had in 1914, overwhelmed by huge surpluses and lacking the means to transport them abroad. This tonnage also saved the American shipping industry vast sums on freight costs and promoted the establishment of permanent and profitable global trade. Even the Harding administration could look upon this aspect of government control and operation as "an act of courage and vision."[63]

Once the boom reached its end, however, the weaknesses of the government fleet became obvious. The haste with which American ships had been built was reflected in inadequate performance; the wooden ship program was disastrous—most of them could not be employed after the war, and the transition from coal to oil and then to diesel fuel made many vessels obsolete even before they were launched. Most of the fleet should have been scrapped or never built, but it would have been an extremely difficult, if not impossible, policy to enforce in the job-hungry immediate postwar environment. The plethora of American ships added to an existing world surplus and caused a serious depression in the maritime industries. In the meantime, wages and operating expenses skyrocketed. The Merchant Marine Act of 1920 did not remedy these problems; in the hurried effort to meet foreign shipping competition and satisfy congressional deadlines, the measure was written without adequate notice of the impending depression, signs of which were already evident at the time of its passage. Such features as the construction loan fund and exemptions from excess profits taxes proved anachronistic in the crash that shook the shipping industry in 1920. Between that year and 1926, the percentage of American foreign trade carried in American ships declined to less than 25 percent.[64]

Although the Merchant Marine Act of 1920 did not halt the slump in American shipping, in important ways it was the culmination of Wilson's eight-year campaign to strengthen the nation's domestic economy through the governmental promotion and integration of foreign trade. That the work of Wilson's Shipping Board had lasting significance is evidenced by the fact that the provisions and aims of the Jones Act provided the fundamental principles upon which subsequent maritime policy would be based.[65]

Always in the foreground of the crusade to create an efficient oceanic shipping system was the vital emphasis Wilsonians gave to world politics. Although Wilson's ardor slackened on occasion, he never fully abandoned the idea that the achievement of a liberal, pro-American world was possible only if the United States assumed international leadership based upon national power and prestige. It stood to reason that a vigorous shipping program provided the nation with a source of the commercial strength and independence needed to negotiate the just and stable world capitalism Wilson sought through American participation in, and direction of, international commerce. It was a fantastic mission, justified and mobilized by the experience of World War I. And shipping policy played an integral part in it. To Wilsonians, the merchant marine and national security enjoyed inseparable relationships.

Notes

1. The general outlines of American maritime policy between the Civil War and World War I can be followed in congressional debates, hearings, testimony, reports, and documents. See, for example, the final reports of the Industrial Commission of 1899-1902 and the Merchant Marine Commission of 1904. A standard work covering the decline of the shipping industry during this period is John G. B. Hutchins, *The American Maritime*

Industries and Public Policy, 1789-1914 (Cambridge, Mass.: Harvard University Press, 1941). A good study of the politics of shipping is contained in Paul Maxwell Zeis, *American Shipping Policy* (Princeton, N.J.: Princeton University Press, 1938). For analyses of the impact of a surplus economy on foreign policy, see Walter LaFeber, *The New Empire: An Interpretation of American Expansion, 1860-1898* (Ithaca, N.Y.: Cornell University Press, 1963); and William A. Williams, *The Roots of the Modern American Empire: A Study of the Growth and Shaping of Social Consciousness in a Marketplace Society* (New York: Random House, 1969). A fine statement of the isolationist and minimal government traditions is in Morrell Heald and Lawrence S. Kaplan, *Culture and Diplomacy: The American Experience* (Westport, Conn.: Greenwood Press, 1977).

2. The best analysis of the connection between Wilson's domestic and foreign trade policies is Burton I. Kaufman, *Efficiency and Expansion: Foreign Trade Organization in the Wilson Administration, 1913-1921* (Westport, Conn.: Greenwood Press, 1974).

3. Woodrow Wilson, *Selected Literary and Political Papers and Addresses of Woodrow Wilson*, 3 vols. (New York: Grosset and Dunlap, 1925), I, 378-79.

4. Ray Stannard and William E. Dodd, eds., *The Public Papers of Woodrow Wilson*, 6 vols. (New York: Harper and Brothers, 1925-27), III, 227.

5. Ibid., IV, 323. How Wilson combined national interest with international mission is discussed thoroughly in N. Gordon Levin, Jr., *Woodrow Wilson and World Politics: America's Response to War and Revolution* (New York: Oxford University Press, 1968).

6. Jesse A. Saugstad, *Shipping and Shipbuilding Subsidies: A Study of State Aid to the Shipping and Shipbuilding Industries in Various Countries of the World* (Washington, D.C.: Department of Commerce, 1932) p. 18.

7. John Wells Davidson, ed., *A Cross Roads of Freedom: The 1912 Campaign Speeches of Woodrow Wilson* (New Haven, Conn.: Yale University Press, 1956), p. 114. Wilson's eight-year campaign to create a government merchant marine, and the relationship of that effort to World War I, is the subject of Jeffrey J. Safford's *Wilsonian Maritime Diplomacy, 1913-1921* (New Brunswick, N.J.: Rutgers University Press, 1978).

8. The controversy is covered in Arthur S. Link, *Wilson: The New Freedom* (Princeton, N.J.: Princeton University Press, 1956), pp. 304-14.

9. Department of Treasury, *Annual Report on the Finances, Dec. 7, 1914* (Washington, D.C., 1914), p. 203; *Report of the Commissioner of Navigation, 1914* (Washington, D.C., 1914), p. 79; Joan Bentinck-Smith, "The Forcing Period: A Study of the American Merchant Marine, 1914-1917" (Ph.D. diss., Radcliffe College, 1958), pp. 36, 39, 59-60; William G.

McAdoo, *Crowded Years: The Reminiscences of William G. McAdoo* (Boston and New York: Houghton Mifflin, 1931), pp. 194-302.

10. *New York Times*, October 23, 1914.

11. *New York American*, August 8, 1914.

12. Mary Synon, *McAdoo: The Man and His Times, A Panorama in Democracy* (Indianapolis: Bobbs-Merrill Company, 1924), pp. 179-80. See also McAdoo, *Crowded Years*, for his own account.

13. For the government's position, see McAdoo, *Crowded Years*, and the majority report to U.S. Congress, House, Committee on Merchant Marine and Fisheries, *Government Ownership and Operation of Merchant Vessels in the Foreign Trade of the United States*, 63rd Congress, 2nd session. For the shipping industry's opinion, see the minority report to the above and "Effect of the War upon American Foreign Commerce," Report of the Merchant Marine Committee of the National Foreign Trade Council, Sept. 23, 1915, Woodrow Wilson Papers, Library of Congress. Analyses of both are John J. Broesamle, *William Gibbs McAdoo: A Passion for Change, 1863-1917* (Port Washington, N.Y.: Kennikat Press, 1973), chapters 10-11; and Safford, op. cit., pp. 32-51.

14. Lodge to Henry Lee Higginson, Feb. 5, 1915, as cited in John A. Garraty, *Henry Cabot Lodge: A Biography* (New York: Alfred A. Knopf, 1953), p. 310. See also Lawrence C. Allin, "Ill-Timed Initiative: The Ship Purchase Bill of 1915," *American Neptune*, XXXIII (July 1973), 178-98.

15. McAdoo, op. cit., pp. 311-12.

16. McAdoo, "The Pan American Financial Conference," *World's Work*, XXX (August 1915), 393-96. See also McAdoo to William Jennings Bryan, July 31, 1916, William G. McAdoo Papers, Library of Congress.

17. Levin, op. cit., p. 7.

18. National Foreign Trade Council, *Convention Proceedings, 1916* (New York: National Foreign Trade Council, 1916).

19. See, for example, U.S. Congress, House, *Creating a Shipping Board, Naval Auxiliary, and Merchant Marine*, 64th Congress, 1st session, Hearings before the House Committee on Merchant Marine and Fisheries (Washington, D.C.: Government Printing Office, 1916).

20. Lloyd C. Gardner, "A Progressive Foreign Policy, 1900-1921," in William A. Williams, ed., *From Colony to Empire: Essays in the History of American Foreign Relations* (New York: John Wiley and Sons, Inc., 1972), pp. 241-42.

21. William S. Culbertson, *Commercial Policy in War Times and After: A Study of the Application of Democratic Ideas to International Commercial Relations* (New York: D. Appleton Company, 1919), p. 348. See also Carl P. Parrini, *Heir to Empire: United States Economic Diplomacy, 1916-1923* (Pittsburgh: University of Pittsburgh Press, 1969), chapter 2;

and V. W. Rothwell, *British War Aims and Peace Diplomacy, 1914-1918* (Oxford: Clarendon Press, 1971), pp. 266-81.

22. Frank L. Polk to Edward M. House, July 22, 1916 in House, *The Intimate Papers of Colonel House*, ed. by Charles Seymour, 4 vols. (Boston and New York: Houghton Mifflin, 1928-29), I, 312; Wilson to House, July 23, 1916, ibid., I, 313.

23. Arthur E. Cook, ed., *A History of the United States Shipping Board and Merchant Fleet Corporation* (Baltimore: Day Printing Company, 1927), pp. 9-10; Darrell Hevenor Smith and Paul V. Betters, *The United States Shipping Board: Its History, Activities, and Organization* (Washington, D.C.: The Brookings Institution, 1931), pp. 6-8; Zeis, op. cit., pp. 92-94.

24. Edward N. Hurley, *The New Merchant Marine* (New York: The Century Company, 1920), p. 38; Hurley, *The Bridge to France* (New York: J. B. Lippincott, 1927), p. 32; C. Ernest Fayle, *The War and the Shipping Industry* (London: Oxford University Press, 1927), pp. 196, 245, 278-79; Safford, op. cit., pp. 95-108.

25. Hurley, *Bridge to France*, pp. 23-26.

26. Ibid., pp. 39-41; Safford, op. cit., pp. 96, 106-8, 117-40.

27. James G. Randall, "War Tasks and Accomplishments of the Shipping Board," *Historical Outlook*, X (June 1919), 305-10; Cook, op. cit., p. 30. Hurley outlined the "merciless inside facts about tonnage" and the enormous tasks facing the USSB in the fall of 1917 to Secretary of War Newton D. Baker; see Hurley to Baker, October 17, 1917, in Frederick Palmer, *Newton D. Baker: America at War*, 2 vols. (New York: Dodd, Mead, 1931), I, 404-6.

28. Cook, op. cit., p. 27.

29. Hurley, "The War and Foreign Trade," address, New York City, April 24, 1918, Edward N. Hurley Papers, University of Notre Dame; Hurley, address before Latin American diplomats at the Hog Island Shipyard, June 26, 1918, ibid.; Hurley to Wilson, March 2, 1918, ibid.

30. Hurley to Bernard Baruch, May 21, 1918, Wilson Papers; Hurley Diary, August 18, 1918, Hurley Papers.

31. Robert Lansing, *War Memoirs* (Indianapolis and New York: Bobbs Merrill, 1935), p. 212; Levin, op. cit., p. 21.

32. David F. Trask, *The United States in the Supreme War Council* (Middletown, Conn.: Wesleyan University Press, 1961), pp. 11-12, 74-75.

33. Edward M. Coffman, *The War to End All Wars: The American Military Experience in World War I* (New York: Oxford University Press, 1968), chapter 4.

34. Ibid., p. 93. In *Wilsonian Diplomacy: Allied-American Rivalries in War and Peace* (St. Louis: Forum Press, 1978), Edward B. Parsons argues

that Wilson willfully withheld military, financial, and shipping support in order to prevent the Allies from winning an overwhelming victory so that the United States could dictate the peace terms.

35. Daniel R. Beaver, *Newton D. Baker and the American War Effort, 1917-1919* (Lincoln, Nebr.: University of Nebraska Press, 1966), p. 177; Trask, op. cit., pp. 5, 15.

36. Hurley Diary, September 28, November 1, 1917, Hurley Papers.

37. Trask, op. cit., pp. 74-75; L. W. Martin, *Peace Without Victory* (New Haven, Conn.: Yale University Press, 1958), pp. 112, 128-29, 176-77; Safford, op. cit., pp. 159-60.

38. Hurley, *Bridge to France*, p. 197.

39. United States Shipping Board, News Release, August 23, 1918, Hurley Papers.

40. Josephus Daniels, *The Cabinet Diaries of Josephus Daniels, 1913-1920*, ed. by E. David Cronin (Lincoln, Nebr.: University of Nebraska Press, 1963), October 17, 1918, p. 342.

41. Hurley Diary, December 9, 1918, Hurley Papers.

42. Hurley to Wilson, November 9, 1918, Wilson Papers.

43. Hurley to Wilson, November 28, 1919, Hurley Papers; Hurley Diary, November 23, December 9, 1918, ibid.; Andrew Furuseth to Thomas A. Hanson, January 8, 1919, William B. Wilson Papers, Pennsylvania Historical Society.

44. Hurley to Wilson, November 9, 1918, Wilson Papers.

45. Hurley to Wilson, December 20, 1918, ibid.

46. Admiral William S. Benson memorandum, May 16, 1921, Naval Records Collection of the Office of Naval Records and Library, National Archives, Record Group No. 45, Subject File, 1911-1927, Case File VM (hereafter cited as RG 45 plus file number, NA); "Memorandum for Chief of Naval Operations," January 30, 1919, RG 45/UB, NA.

47. Wilson to Hurley and Baker, March 24, 1919, as quoted in Herbert Hoover, *An American Epic*, 2 vols. (Chicago: Henry Regnery, 1960), II, 398-99.

48. Hurley to Wilson, March 3, 1919, Wilson Papers; USSB, *Second Annual Report, 1919* (Washington, D.C., 1919), pp. 10-11, 15, 18-19; "Report of the War Trade Board" (Washington, D.C., June 20, 1919), p. 182; Cook, op. cit., p. 27.

49. Safford, op. cit., pp. 193-94.

50. Ibid., pp. 194-95.

51. Benson to Josephus Daniels, May 29, 1919, Admiral William S. Benson Papers, Library of Congress.

52. Zeis, op. cit., p. 115.

53. Baker to Wilson, May 13, 1920, Newton D. Baker Papers, Library

of Congress.

54. Daniels, op. cit., June 1, 1920, p. 536.

55. Cook, op. cit., pp. 10-13; Zeis, op. cit., pp. 116-19; Burl Noggle, *Into the Twenties: The United States from Armistice to Normalcy* (Urbana, Ill.: University of Illinois Press, 1974), pp. 82-83.

56. Noggle, loc. cit.

57. *New York Times*, July 1, 1920. For maritime insurance conditions before and during the war, see Hurley's remarks, July 9, 1919, U.S. Congress, House, *Hearings before Subcommittee on the Merchant Marine and Fisheries*, 66th Congress, 1st session, pp. 8-11.

58. Daniels, op. cit., August 26, 1920, p. 552. See also Bainbridge Colby, *The Close of Woodrow Wilson's Administration and the Final Years* (New York: Kennerley, 1930), pp. 18-21.

59. *New York Times*, September 25 and 30, 1920.

60. United States, State Department, *Papers Relating to the Foreign Relations of the United States*, "Foreign Relations 1920," I, vii-xii. This was Wilson's annual message, December 7, 1920.

61. USSB, *Annual Report, 1921* (Washington, D.C.: Government Printing Office, 1921), pp. 79-80, 118; John D. Hicks, *Rehearsal for Disaster: The Boom and Collapse of 1919-1920* (Jacksonville, Fla.: University of Florida Press, 1961), pp. 24-27; William S. Benson, *The New Merchant Marine* (New York: The Macmillan Co., 1923), p. 116.

62. *New York Times*, March 3, 1921. Army Chief of Staff General John J. Pershing conducted his own study of the war effort in 1923. His aide, George C. Marshall, examined the War Department records and concluded that considering the "inevitable confusion" connected with coordinating training, shelter and shipping, that it "was surprising that the demands from the AEF were met to the extent they were"; see Coffman, op. cit., p. 186.

63. Statement of Albert D. Lasker (chairman of the USSB), U.S. Congress, House and Senate, *To Amend Merchant Marine Act of 1920*, Joint Hearings before the Committee on Commerce and Committee on Merchant Marine and Fisheries, 67th Congress, 2nd session, I, 9.

64. Ibid., pp. 5-9; Saugstad, op. cit., p. 30; Abraham Berglund, "The War and the World's Mercantile Marine," *American Economic Review*, X (June 1920), 227-58; E. S. Gregg, "Failure of the Merchant Marine Act of 1920," *American Economic Review*, XI (December 1921), 610-16.

65. Samuel A. Lawrence, *United States Merchant Shipping Policies and Politics* (Washington, D.C.: The Brookings Institution, 1966), p. 41.

5
The Years between the Wars: 1919-1939
John H. Kemble and Lane C. Kendall

The two decades of uneasy peace between World Wars I and II witnessed a succession of efforts to place the American merchant marine in a commanding position on the sea lanes of the world. Three major pieces of legislation during these years were aimed at enunciating and implementing a long-range merchant marine policy for the United States. American shipyards turned out a number of admirable vessels to serve oceanic and coastal routes, although general economic conditions were far from favorable during most of the period. Organized seagoing and longshore labor came to exert an unprecedented influence on maritime activity under the American flag. Finally, any orderly growth of the merchant marine was completely upset by the outbreak of general war in Europe in 1939, and the United States once again found itself bending every effort to meet emergency conditions. Altogether, it was a period of flux, important in both policy and practice for the future of American shipping.

The Legacy of World War I

At the time of the armistice, the Shipping Board owned 455 newly built vessels of 2,468,892 deadweight tons. Shipbuilding could not be halted at once; the laying of keels of new vessels went on until the summer of 1919. By June 1920, the government owned 1,502 merchant ships totaling 9,358,421 deadweight tons. Of these, 270 were wooden, composite, or concrete cargo steamers which were ultimately of little value. Of the steel cargo and passenger cargo steamers, however, many proved to be valuable carriers for years to come. The 23 passenger cargo steamers of the "535" and "502" classes (so designated because of their length), mostly named for presidents of the United States, served well on a variety of ocean routes until the coming of World War II, when they finally saw the service as transports and naval auxiliaries for which they had been originally intended. Steel cargo steamers of standardized design which came from the yards at Hog Island on the Delaware River and from shipbuilders on the Pacific Coast, as well as some which were built to the order of the Shipping Board in Japan, likewise formed important units in the interwar merchant fleet. A number of German ships which had been interned in American ports upon the outbreak of war in 1914 continued as part of the American merchant marine; among them was the *Leviathan* (ex-*Vaterland*), the largest ship in the world.

Postwar Policy

The Shipping Act of 1916 provided for the ownership and operation of ships by the Shipping Board for the duration of the war and not longer than five years thereafter. Hence, new and more comprehensive legislation was needed if the wartime fleet was to be used effectively under peacetime conditions. This need was met by the Merchant Marine Act of 1920, which was significant as the first written expression of public policy concerning the merchant fleet.[1] Except for relatively minor changes and updating in 1928 and 1936, it was retained as the basic position of the government on the subject. Viewed in this light, it is worth quoting the opening declaration of policy.

> It is necessary for the national defense and for the proper growth of its foreign and domestic commerce that the United States shall have a merchant marine of the best equipped and most suitable vessels sufficient to carry the greater portion of its commerce and serve as a naval or military auxiliary in time of war or national emergency, ultimately to be owned and operated privately by citizens of the United States, and it is hereby declared to be the policy of the United States to do whatever may be necessary to develop and

encourage the maintenance of such a merchant marine, and in so far as may not be inconsistent with the express provisions of this act, the United States Shipping Board shall, in the disposition of vessels and shipping property as hereinafter provided, in the making of rules and regulations, and in the administration of the shipping laws keep always in view this purpose and object as the primary end to be attained.[2]

The act went on in a subsequent section to authorize and direct the Shipping Board "to investigate and determine ... what steamship lines should be established and put in operation from ports in the United States ... to such world and domestic markets as ... are desirable for the promotion, development, expansion, and maintenance of the foreign and coastwise trade of the United States" and to determine the character of ships and the nature of schedules necessary to achieve the ends of the act.[3] This concept of essential foreign trade routes was the basis for the structure of operating differential subsidies which was preserved, confirmed, and reconfirmed by the laws of 1928 and 1936.

The Postwar Depression in Shipping

It was the clear intent of Congress in the 1920 act to transfer the merchant fleet to private ownership as soon as practicable. Only if satisfactory sales could not be made were the ships to be placed in the hands of approved managing operators, or, only if no citizen could offer a needed service, was the board itself authorized to "Operate vessels on such line [or lines] until the business is developed so that such vessels can be sold ... and the service maintained."[4]

The success of this policy was almost fatally threatened by a worldwide shipping depression which began at the end of 1920 and reached full force in 1922. Ships which had cost $200 to $250 per ton to build were selling for $150 to $175 per ton in 1921, and were being offered for $30 per ton in 1922.[5] By the end of 1920, time charters were to be had at about one-third of the rate prevailing six months earlier. In 1922, liner cargo rates had declined to pre-1914 levels, and ten million tons (17 percent) of the world's shipping was laid up.

Beginning with incredible optimism, the Shipping Board had placed 1,530 ships in service on 209 different routes to all parts of the world by the end of June 1921. There was no economic justification for activity on such a scale, and within the next twelve months the fleet had been reduced to 359 government-owned ships assigned to 76 routes. As the program of selling ships for operation or for scrap proceeded, the number of government-owned ships was gradually cut during the next eleven years to 38 vessels under management contracts. In addition to meeting all losses, the government assumed the full cost of repairs and upkeep on these vessels so that for the twelve-year period ending in 1934, the cost to the Treasury for ships under management contracts, as well as those directly operated, amounted to about $247,000,000.

Not only did the postwar merchant marine move toward new operating conditions with a potentially immense fleet, but there were also new problems related to manning the ships. At the war's end in 1918, there were three elements in the American maritime labor picture: the International Seamen's Union, which had grown to a membership of 117,000 during the war years; the Shipping Board, with its dominant influence on the whole American shipping industry; and, finally, the American Steamship Owners' Association, which represented the industry's private sector.

During the war, the Seamen's Union was successful for the first time in American maritime history in negotiating an agreement with the Shipping Board and the owners which raised wages, improved working conditions, permitted union representatives to board ships on union business, and gained at least de facto recognition as the voice of the seafarers. That the union hoped to preserve these significant achievements in peacetime was understandable, and therefore, in the early days of 1919 it requested the board and the owners to continue to pay wartime wages and bonuses; to improve certain working conditions such as reducing the number of furnaces tended by a single fireman; and to adopt the three-watch system for all deck seamen, i.e., that such seamen would stand only two four-hour watches separated by eight hours of free time in one day. The owners refused these requests, thus precipitating a brief strike by the union.[6] In the settlement, the terms of which were announced on July 26, 1919, the basic wage for an able-bodied seaman was raised from sixty to eighty-five dollars a month, but bonuses were eliminated. The access of union representatives to ships was continued, and the eight-hour day, with some qualifications, was granted to deck seamen.

This precedent-setting agreement was followed by a second signed on May 1, 1920, which continued all the benefits gained in 1919 and added the establishment of grievance committees. The trend of benefits represented by this achievement was soon halted by the harsh realities of a depressed industry.

As the worldwide recession began to affect the American shipping industry, the Steamship Owners' Association, claiming that costs must be lowered in the interests of survival, asked the union to accept a reduction in wages. This idea was rejected by the union, which instead submitted a counterproposal.[7] The stalemate was broken by the Shipping Board's announcement of a new scale of wages and modified working conditions, effective May 1, 1921. The board action set wages 15 percent below the prevailing level, abolished overtime pay, and trimmed the subsistence allowance of seamen required to live ashore while their ships were in port. Significantly, there was no mention of the three-watch system for deck seamen.[8] In response, the union called a strike and received the support of the Marine Engineers' Beneficial Association, which represented the licensed engineers. By May 10, 1921, the strike appeared to be fully effective; the sailings of American ships had ceased; marine schedules were suspended; and the tie-up was complete. The shipowners were able to assemble some nonunion crews, however, and, after some weeks of violence, injunctions and restraining orders were issued at various ports. By the middle of June, the solid front of the strike had collapsed, and by the end of the month the strike was over. Crews of union members returned to Shipping Board vessels on the same terms that had existed before the strike, and the Steamship Owners' Association took advantage of the union's weakened position to set its own scale of wages, which was noticeably lower than that approved by the board.[9]

By January 1922, the recession had become a major depression, and the Steamship Owners' Association again moved to reduce wages. Able-bodied seamen on Atlantic and Gulf ships were to receive a uniform wage of $47.50 a month. In February, the Shipping Board followed suit with a wage of $55.[10] It may be questioned whether such drastic cuts were really necessary for survival, but there is little doubt that the employers were seeking to nullify all the gains achieved by the International Seamen's Union. In this effort they were successful. Membership in the union declined, as did much of its prestige. From 1921 to 1934 there was no collective bargaining in the American maritime industry. Wages were low, and living and working conditions aboard ship were often poor. There is also no doubt that a tide of resentment and ill will toward the owners was built up during these years. These experiences subsequently affected the attitude and position of the seamen and longshore workers in the mid-1930s.[11]

The postwar maritime depression together with the glut of war-built ships meant that American shipyards faced hard times. Most of the yards which the Bethlehem Steel Corporation had acquired in the years before the war survived largely by repair jobs and by diversifying their operations. The Bethlehem establishments at Baltimore, Maryland; Quincy, Massachusetts; Sparrow's Point, Maryland; San Francisco and Alameda, California; and San Pedro, California, survived in this manner until new merchant marine and navy orders materialized in the late 1920s. Bethlehem's Wilmington, Delaware, plant, formerly Harlan & Hollingsworth, discontinued shipbuilding in 1926. At the Newport News Shipbuilding and Dry Dock Company in Virginia there was likewise a dearth of work, but the plant management succeeded in holding its basic work force together. The Bath Iron Works in Maine suspended operations in 1924, and the yard of William Cramp & Sons at Philadelphia gave up shipbuilding in 1927. Both the New York Shipbuilding Corporation in Camden, New Jersey, and the Sun Shipbuilding & Dry Dock Company at Chester, Pennsylvania, survived the lean period, the latter largely because of its specialization in tanker construction. Dozens of wartime yards disappeared in the discouraging years after 1919.

The gross tonnage of merchant ships built and documented

in the United States fell from 3,880,639 in 1920 to 199,846 in 1925 and to 128,976 in 1929. In 1920, the tonnage of American merchant vessels in the foreign trade was about 10,000,000 as compared to some 6,350,000 tons in the coastwise and internal trades. By 1925, the foreign trade figure had declined to some 8,000,000 tons, and the coastwise figure had risen to 9,000,000 tons. In 1929, the tonnage in foreign trades was about 6,900,000, and that in the coastwise trade amounted to some 9,500,000. A comparison of the amount of foreign trade carried by American- and foreign-flag vessels shows in 1921 about 47,000,000 tons in American ships compared with some 44,800,000 in foreign-flag vessels; the comparison in 1925 was 41,363,000 to 62,575,000; and in 1929 it was 48,330,000 to 73,195,000.[12]

Achievement and Equilibrium

Although the 1920s were not prosperous years on the ocean routes, the combination of Shipping Board managing operator contracts, the availability of the better wartime-designed ships at bargain prices, and the possibility of obtaining some funds at low interest rates for new construction gave the United States a more active peacetime merchant marine than it had known before in the century. The Shipping Board succeeded in terminating most of its managing operator contracts by the sale of the ships involved to private owners, often to the same firms that had previously operated them. By the end of June 1927, all the passenger lines had been disposed of except for the United States Lines and the American Merchant Lines which were engaged in the transatlantic trade. The Dollar Steamship Line first purchased seven of the 502s in 1923 which it placed in a service around the world, sailing westward from San Francisco. Two years later, in 1925, the Dollar interests succeeded in buying the five 535s which the long-established Pacific Mail Steamship Company had been operating for the Shipping Board in the San Francisco-Japan-China-Manila trade, and the same year they acquired five more of the same class of vessel which had been operating from Seattle to the Orient under the house flag of the Admiral Oriental/American Mail Line. At about the same time, the Munson Line purchased four 535s which it had previously been operating from New York to the east coast of South America, and proceeded to maintain them in the same service.

Tourist trade to Hawaii began to assume considerable proportions in the 1920s. The Los Angeles Steamship Company, using reconditioned former German and British liners, inaugurated service from Los Angeles to Hilo and Honolulu in 1922, and gained considerable popularity. Its success may have stimulated the San Francisco-based Matson Navigation Company, which had previously been mainly a cargo carrier with relatively small passenger accommodations on its steamers, to order from Cramp the magnificent steamer *Malolo* (later *Matsonia* [II]) which brought a new standard of speed and luxury to the Hawaiian service.

Notable in the middle 1920s was the appearance of a considerable number of splendid liners in the Atlantic coastwise services. The Eastern Steamship Company, the Clyde Line, the Savannah Line, the Merchants and Miners Transportation Company, the Southern Pacific Steamship Lines, the New York and Porto Rico Steamship Company, and the New York and Cuba Mail Steamship Company (Ward Line), all added new vessels. These ships were, of course, built in American yards, and their construction provided welcome contracts for a number of Atlantic Coast shipbuilders. Of the passenger-carrying lines, only the Fall River Line, the Colonial Line, and the Mallory Line did not reequip their fleets. From Nova Scotia to Texas it was possible to travel in modern, well-designed, comfortable steamers, and coastwise passenger liner service remained available until the eve of World War II.

In addition to the coastwise passenger liners, from 200 to 281 cargo carriers were active during the "long armistice." The Seatrain Line, which entered the trade between New York, Havana, and New Orleans in 1932 with two ships designed to carry loaded railroad cars—thus becoming the precursor of the containership—was the most innovative and the most profitable of the cargo services.

On the Pacific Coast, the dominant Pacific Steamship Company was equipped mainly by secondhand ships. This company, which offered service from Alaska to Baja California, together with the Los Angeles Steamship Company's coastwise liners *Yale* and *Harvard* plying between San Francisco, Los Angeles, and San Diego, provided good service, albeit without the new ships of the Atlantic and Gulf coasts. Only one new steamer, *Alaska* of the Alaska Steamship Company, was built specifically for Pacific coastwise service after World War I. Otherwise the Alaska Steamship Company, which operated year-round from Seattle to the ice-free ports of Alaska, and in summer to Nome and Bering Sea ports, had a collection of marine antiques including the *Victoria*, which had been built in 1870 as the Cunarder *Parthia* and was conceded to be the oldest working steamship on the ocean routes of the world. (She made her last commercial voyage in 1952.)

A new trade was created for American ships when the Panama Canal was fully opened to commercial traffic in 1919. It became possible to offer rapid all-water transportation from one coast of the United States to the other, a trade which was restricted by the cabotage laws to American-flag vessels. This intercoastal operation quickly attracted a number of steamship companies, and by 1923 employed 7 passenger-cargo ships and 154 cargo carriers. The zenith, insofar as the size of the fleet was concerned, was attained in 1927 when 170 cargo and 6 passenger-cargo ships were in operation between the coasts. Seven years later, in 1934, there were only 92 cargo ships in the trade although the number of passenger-cargo ships had risen to 7, all built since 1928 and representing a high standard of design and equipment. Competition with the transcontinental railroads was always keen, and freight rates were therefore kept at low levels, which left little in the way of profit.

Another segment of the domestic merchant marine was the tanker fleet, which grew erratically from 94 vessels in coastwise operation in 1923 to 277 ships in 1939. The statistics for tankers on the intercoastal run were exactly the opposite, showing a rapid decline from 113 tankers in 1923 to 9 in 1938 and 22 in 1939.

Beyond the advantages steamship operators gained from the bargain prices of ships purchased from the Shipping Board, small payments from the Post Office Department for the transportation of mail, and the protection provided ships in the coastwise trades by the cabotage laws, the American merchant marine operated without support from the public treasury. This was in accord with long-standing tradition. The word "subsidy" was exceedingly unpopular with the American politician and the American public, and subsidies for American ships which suffered from real or fancied disadvantages in competition with foreign-flag vessels had proven virtually impossible to provide. Payment for mail transportation, sometimes at high rates, had been criticized again and again in the nineteenth century. Provision of funds to compensate owners for adding features to their ships which would enhance their value as naval auxiliaries was hard to manage. American registry was largely reserved for American-built ships, and vessels built abroad were only admitted under severe restrictions. This was an encouragement to American shipbuilders, but had limited value if unsubsidized operation under the American flag proved unprofitable.

International Maritime Agreements

Meanwhile, vessel safety became an issue once again for the international community. Following the sinking of the *Titanic* in 1912, the first international conference on safety had been convened by the major maritime nations in 1913. A convention was drafted, known as the first Safety of Life at Sea Convention (SOLAS 1913), but was never adopted because of the outbreak of World War I.

It was not until 1928 that the maritime nations again assembled under the auspices of the League of Nations and, in 1929, produced SOLAS 1929. This dealt with, among other things, ship stability and subdivision based on the length of the vessel and the number of its passengers. The convention did not deal with vessel stability during and after damage and flooding, nor with fire protection.

On September 8, 1934, the New York and Cuba Mail Steamship Company's liner, *Morro Castle,* burned, with substantial loss of life, in sight of land off the east coast of New Jersey during the process of Senate ratification of SOLAS 1929. Confidence in the competence of American seamen and in the supervisory bureaus of the government was shaken. The subsequent investigation of the tragedy led the United States Senate Commerce Committee to examine SOLAS 1929 critically and to develop its 1937 Report No. 184, "Rules and Regulations of the Construction and Inspection of Merchant Vessels." The regulations, with few changes, were adopted by the U.S. Maritime Commission as the minimum requirement for all subsidized ships and are (with few exceptions) incorporated today in the published rules of the U.S. Coast Guard. The major changes in design arising out of this incident marks one of the first times that U.S. legislation imposed substantially higher standards on its ships than were required of competing merchant ships. Provision of one compartment standard of subdivision, damage stability under conditions of unsymmetrical flooding, and higher standards of bulkhead spacing and of fire protection were included in U.S. regulations thereafter.

Revival of the Subsidy Question

In the early 1920s, members of the Shipping Board, influential congressmen, and the American shipping community came to the conclusion that subsidies were a necessity if the operation of American-flag lines was to continue. In a special message to Congress on February 28, 1922, President Harding urged approval of a program proposed by the Shipping Board to aid the merchant fleet. A fund was to be created from 10 percent of all tariff revenues in addition to the proceeds from various tonnage and navigation taxes. From this, all American vessels in the foreign trade would receive a bounty of at least one-half cent per gross ton per hundred miles operated. Payments would increase with the size and speed of a ship, a twenty-three-knot vessel receiving as much as 2.6 cents per gross ton per hundred miles. The Shipping Board would administer the fund. Government losses on the operation of the fleet which it then owned were estimated at $192 million per year, and the president stated that the cost of the subsidy would not exceed $30 million annually.[13]

The bill aroused considerable opposition, and, although it finally passed the House, it never came to a vote in the Senate, thus ending for six years the enactment of any kind of direct aid program for the American merchant marine.

In 1928, a proposal was laid before the Congress to encourage American shipping through liberal payments for the transportation of mail on foreign routes and by generous construction loans. In contrast to the reception given the subsidy bill, this legislation passed the House without a recorded vote, the Senate by a vote of fifty-one to twenty, and was signed into law by President Coolidge as the Merchant Marine Act of 1928 (Jones-White Act). It provided for the certification of overseas mail routes by the Postmaster General to the lowest bidder with maximum payments ranging from $1.50 per mile on the outward voyage for vessels of not less than 2,500 tons gross capable of ten knots, to $12 per mile for ships of over 20,000 tons and rated at twenty-four knots. In addition, a revolving fund of $250 million was established to provide low-interest loans of up to three-quarters of the construction cost of a ship.[14]

The Postmaster General promptly negotiated contracts with thirty operators serving forty-five foreign trade routes. These contracts remained in effect for nine years and were terminated with the adoption of a new subsidy system in 1937. During these years, the total government expenditure was $176 million, which worked out to $650,000 per year per route. In almost every instance, the mail contracts were awarded to lines which were already in operation, for service along previously established routes, and at the maximum amount permitted by the law. The routes covered were mostly the essential trade routes provided for in the 1920 act. Some of the contracts provided for service where there was virtually no mail to be carried. It should be recalled, however, that the fundamental purpose of the Jones-White Act was to provide needed construction and operating subsidies in a politically viable guise. No new operators were attracted into the business by this legislation, but even the generous provisions of the act were hardly sufficient to justify the great expense of establishing and equipping completely new lines.

During the lifetime of the 1928 act some sixty-four new ships were built with its support, and sixty-one older vessels were rebuilt or brought up to higher standards of performance for foreign trades. The ships built under the 1928 act were an unusually fine lot. They incorporated the most progressive ideas in marine engineering and naval architecture, and it was notable that at least three of them were still in service, albeit under foreign flags, forty-five years after they were built. The 1928 act was often criticized for the high cost to the government of the ships built and operated under its disguised subsidies, but the fact remained that the ships which it produced held their own on the seas or bested foreign-flag competition, and during World War II they provided admirable service as naval auxiliaries and transports.

The largest ships built under that act were the *Manhattan* and the *Washington* of the United States Lines. Both were turbine-driven steamers of 24,289 tons gross, 705 feet long and 86.3 feet in beam, capable of 22.7 knots speed. Their passenger accommodations set new standards for excellence, especially among cabin-class vessels on the North Atlantic. On the Pacific, the Matson Navigation Company placed three new ships in service, the *Mariposa* and the *Monterey*, built at the Fore River Yard and entering service between San Francisco and Sydney in 1932 under the house flag of the Oceanic Steamship Company, a wholly owned subsidiary of Matson, and a third sister ship, the *Lurline*, designed for the California-Hawaii trade. All three measured just over 18,000 tons gross, were 632 feet long and 79.4 feet in beam, and their twin screws driven by geared turbines gave them speeds of over 22 knots. Other notable liners appearing at this time were the *President Coolidge* and *President Hoover* of the Dollar Steamship Lines; the Four Aces—*Excalibur, Excambion, Exeter,* and *Exochorda*—of the American Export Line; and six ships of the *Talamanca* class of the United Fruit Company. The Panama Pacific Line, a subsidiary of the International Mercantile Marine Company, built three new vessels, *California, Pennsylvania,* and *Virginia,* for its intercoastal service, while the Grace Line countered with four ships of the *Santa Elena* class for the intercoastal trade. Vessels ranged on down to the *Acadia* and the *Saint John*, 6,000-odd-ton liners designed for the Eastern Steamship Company's Boston–Nova Scotia run.

Of the ships built under the 1928 act, thirteen had turbo-electric propulsion, a comparatively new system for merchant vessels but one which had been used successfully in the largest naval vessels. The *City of New York,* of the American South African Line, was the only one to have diesel engines, at that time a radical departure for American ships. Efficient and dependable geared turbines using high-pressure steam from the most effective marine boilers in existence were installed in the other ships.

The Grace Line commissioned William Francis Gibbs to design its *Santa Elenas.* Operating through the tropics for the greater part of every voyage when air conditioning at sea was unknown, the owners determined that every cabin should have portholes to afford natural ventilation and that a private bath should be provided for every room. The dining saloon and galley were located on the promenade deck, assuring travelers of sea breezes as well as an outlook to the horizon, and the dome of the saloon could be rolled back to afford dining under the stars when the weather was good. Considered by many steamship men to be recklessly extravagant, the ship proved to be unusually attractive to passengers and set precedents which were widely followed in years to come.

Of all the sales of Shipping Board vessels, probably the most controversial was that of the eleven-ship fleet of the United States Lines, which had been under direct government operation between the U.S. and English Channel ports. The successful bidder at the auction of Jan. 22, 1929, was Paul W. Chapman, a Chicago banker who offered $16,300,000 for the fleet.[15] He paid $4,000,000 in cash and gave notes for the remainder. As part of the obligation, Chapman agreed to replace the aging ex-German liners *America, George Washington,* and *Republic* by two new ships. He contracted in 1930 with the New York Shipbuilding Corp. for the building of these ships: the *Manhattan* and the *Washington.* He was also interested in two 45,000-ton, 28-knot ships to challenge the finest and fastest on the North Atlantic, and he commissioned the distinguished naval architect Theodore E. Ferris to design them. Unfortunately for Chapman, financial problems made it impossible for him to carry out his plan, which might have placed ships on the North Atlantic Ferry that could compete on equal terms with the best that the European lines could offer.

The Impact of the Great Depression

As it was, the onset of the great depression in October 1929 forced Chapman to default on payments due the government. The Shipping Board refused to grant him any concessions and repossessed the fleet in 1931. A second auction was arranged, and the United States Lines fleet, now reduced to eight ships, was purchased by the International Mercantile Marine Company, a holding company operating both American- and foreign-flag ships and headed by Philip A. S. Franklin.[16] Under the new ownership, the *Manhattan* and the *Washington* were completed and placed in service, and in 1938 the 26,500 ton *America* was laid down for the company at Newport News Shipbuilding and Dry Dock Company.

While the Shipping Board was disposing of ships and the Merchant Marine Act of 1928 was being implemented, maritime labor acquiesced, albeit grudgingly, on the subjects of wages and working conditions which did not improve after the period of strikes in the early 1920s. Serving a struggling industry, many seafarers and longshoremen felt fortunate to have jobs and were not ready to take action that might imperil them. Change came with the Roosevelt administration in 1933, and the years 1934 to 1938 witnessed tumultuous and generally successful organization and action on the part of men who earned their livings serving aboard American ships.

Early in 1934, encouraged by the Roosevelt administration's support of negotiation through elected union representatives and the accompanying assurance that employers would not retaliate for union activity, militant seamen and longshoremen on the Pacific Coast presented their employers with demands for higher wages, improved working conditions, and union recognition. Employers of both groups were adamant in their refusal to consider these proposals.

When the longshoremen's request that only union members be hired to work cargo was rejected, a strike was called for March 23, 1934. Intervention by President Roosevelt delayed the strike, but during the waiting period the seamen decided to join the longshoremen on the assumption that a united front was more likely to gain concessions. The International Seamen's

Union sought recognition as the collective bargaining agent, higher wages, an end to the "blacklisting" of individual seamen, union control of hiring halls, and improved working conditions. All these demands were rejected by the Steamship Owners' Association, just as the longshoremen's had been rejected. The longshoremen reacted by going on strike on May 9, and the seamen followed suit six days later.[17]

To the surprise of the employers, the combined strike was very effective. Scores of ships were immobilized from Seattle to San Diego. There was considerable sporadic violence, but picket lines were maintained and no ships were either worked or permitted to sail. The situation became sufficiently critical for President Roosevelt to appoint a special board to seek a solution.

A tense situation erupted into violence when, on July 5, 1934, the waterfront employers attempted to reopen the port of San Francisco by using nonunion labor to work the ships.[18] This resulted in widespread disorder along the Embarcadero and the death of several longshoremen. In a showing of support for the waterfront unions, a city-wide general strike lasting two days stopped virtually all commercial activity on July 17 and 18. The presidential board's report was published on July 19. It recommended that all parties submit their demands to arbitration and, pending a final decision, return to work. Following some days of deliberation, both longshoremen and seamen resumed their jobs on July 31.[19]

The settlement of the seamen's grievances was delayed until April 10, 1935, partly because an election to choose a union as bargaining agent had to be conducted among seamen employed in the offshore trades. This required three months before the last ballot was received. The International Seamen's Union was found to be the favored representative for the entire Pacific Coast.[20]

While these events were in progress, the Seamen's Union attempted to open negotiations with Atlantic and Gulf Coast shipowners. Pressure from the National Labor Relations Board and the threat of a strike forced the owners to reverse their decisions not to enter into such discussions. On December 21, 1934, an agreement was signed which became effective ten days later and ushered in a new era in maritime labor relations, marking the first major gains on the part of unions since 1920. It established preference in employment for union members, recognized the three-watch system at sea for unlicensed deck personnel, accepted the eight-hour day in port, authorized union representatives to go aboard ships in American ports, and appreciably increased wages.

The Pacific award in April 1935 contained all the same elements but was more specific in its terms—very definite as to what constituted acceptable working conditions—and fixed wage levels for certain ratings somewhat higher than did the Atlantic agreement.

Maritime labor strife in the 1930s was characterized not only by controversy between employers and employees but also by friction within the union organizations themselves. Under the seemingly placid surface of conditions on the waterfront through 1935, there was intense criticism of the leadership of the International Seamen's Union for permitting the Atlantic agreement of 1934 to be less favorable to the working seaman than the Pacific accord.[21] A dramatic "sit-down" strike by the crew of the Panama Pacific intercoastal liner *California* in March 1936 preceded an outlaw strike in New York directed primarily against the "old line" union officials. The dissenters were expelled from membership, and the effectiveness of the strike was thereby thwarted. Despite these attempts to assert control, dissidence continued.

The Pacific agreement was due to expire on September 30, 1936, and both employers and seamen sought changes before a new one was approved. It proved impossible to agree on a compromise, however, and a strike was called for September 30. It was postponed by the intervention of the newly appointed United States Maritime Commission (whose establishment will be described more fully later), but by the middle of October it was obvious that no concessions were to be obtained and the seamen "hit the bricks," again tying up shipping along the entire Pacific Coast.[22] Unlike the 1934 strike, there was practically no violence. After three months of negotiations, the shipowners acknowledged the power of the union by agreeing to terms which gave preference in hiring to union members, provided that unlicensed deck personnel would be hired through union offices, promised that there would be no retaliation for legitimate union activity, and established that a union delegate would be a part of each ship's company. All disputes were to be submitted to joint committees or to referees for adjudication, and there were to be no strikes or lockouts. Conditions and hours of work and regulations as to meals and living quarters were carefully stated and defined. A basic wage of $72.50 per month for able-bodied seamen was established, and overtime was fixed at $.70 an hour.[23]

Much of the success of this strike must be attributed to the Maritime Federation, a working combination of the Sailors' Union of the Pacific (an affiliate of the International Seamen's Union) and the International Longshoremen's Association. Capitalizing on the lessons of the 1934 strike, these two organizations understood that only by uniting their forces could they hope to achieve the goals they sought. The advantages of joint action had been clearly demonstrated.

While the Pacific Coast strike was in progress, the leadership of the International Seamen's Union on the Atlantic Coast exerted pressure on its membership to prevent strike action. For the most part, this tactic was successful and only a few minor work stoppages occurred. On February 3, 1937, the union was able to amend its agreement with Atlantic and Gulf shipowners to make it more nearly equal with the Pacific accord. This action, however, did not placate the dissident elements because the record showed that union leaders, in their eagerness to prove to the shipowners that they controlled their members, actually had prevented strikes, had furnished substitutes for striking seamen, and had ordered seamen back to work.

In May 1937, a number of the more dissatisfied members withdrew from the International Seamen's Union, which was affiliated with the American Federation of Labor, and formed the National Maritime Union.[24] This new union was accepted immediately as a member of the recently established and less-sedate Congress for Industrial Organization. Pursuant to the National Labor Relations Act, the National Maritime Union demanded that Atlantic Coast steamship companies conduct elections among their seamen to select an exclusive bargaining agent. Fifty-two companies were polled, and the new union won overwhelmingly.

The National Maritime Union immediately began negotiations for new agreements, and these were brought to a conclusion favorable to the union on April 27, 1938. The union was recognized as the exclusive bargaining agent, preference in hiring was granted to its members who also obtained paid vacations, and hours and conditions of work were defined in detail. Wage scales were to remain unchanged at least until September 30, 1938.

The American Federation of Labor, reacting to the challenge of the National Maritime Union, removed all the officers of the International Seamen's Union and withdrew the charter of the organization. To fill the void thus created, the Seafarers' International Union was chartered and authorized to enroll seamen, engineers, and stewards.[25] At the same time the Sailors' Union of the Pacific, which was composed exclusively of deck seamen, was designated as the Pacific counterpart of the Atlantic-based Seafarers' International Union. Although it was a somewhat unbalanced team, it did give the American Federation of Labor representation on both coasts, an important factor in competing with the active National Maritime Union.

The ultimate result of these efforts and counterefforts in 1938 was the thorough organization of maritime labor. This assured that the movement would be heard at national levels. While the National Maritime Union gained the support of seamen in the larger companies, the employees of a significant number of smaller companies based in Atlantic ports and several of the largest domiciled in the Gulf chose the Seafarers' International Union as their bargaining agent. Rivalry between the American Federation of Labor and the Congress for Industrial Organization militated against any possible merger in those early days of revived unionism in maritime circles.

The combination of generally depressed economic conditions with disruption of service due to strikes and increased costs of operation spelled doom for important parts of the American maritime industry. The coastwise lines suffered especially because, although they were protected from foreign-flag competition by the cabotage laws, they were increasingly subject to competition from automobile and truck traffic and were not eligible for the subsidies which were now available to offshore lines. The strike of 1936 marked the end of coastwise passenger and cargo liner service on the Pacific south of Seattle while on the Atlantic and Gulf coasts a number of long-established lines withdrew from business.

The Roosevelt Administration

Important changes in the government's policy regarding the merchant marine were inaugurated during the Hundred Days, the initial phase of the Roosevelt administration in 1933. Congress authorized the president to modify or cancel any mail contract that he found not to be in the public interest, provided for a select committee to investigate air and ocean mail contracts, and reduced the Shipping Board to the status of a bureau in the Department of Commerce.

The select committee, which was chaired by Senator Hugo L. Black of Alabama, took extensive testimony between 1933 and 1935 when it issued a voluminous report calling for the repeal of the act of 1928 and the cancellation of any further aid to ship operations. The committee laid bare a sordid picture of collusion, favoritism, unaggressive management, and financial practices which ensured that losses would always be paid by the government and profits invariably be retained by the operators. It should be remembered, however, that political considerations were not entirely absent from the report of the committee which was, of course, dominated by Democrats but was studying the maritime policies of a series of Republican administrations. It was Black's position that unless substantial private capital could be drawn into the merchant marine, and the shipping of the United States be conducted without subsidy, government ownership and operation would best serve the public interest.[26]

The Post Office Department concurrently conducted its own inquiry, and, although it took the position that there had been no improprieties, it recommended that the law be administered more stringently. In addition, the Department of Commerce created an interdepartmental committee to examine these troubled areas. The committee concluded that there had been poor administration of the law but that continued support of the merchant marine was in the national interest. It urged that existing rules be enforced strictly and that federal financial aid be limited to the differentials in construction and operating costs of American ships as compared with their foreign rivals.[27]

Still another approach to the problem came from the hearings held from 1934 until 1936 by the Special Committee on Investigation of the Munitions Industry of the United States Senate under the chairmanship of Senator Gerald P. Nye. These bore heavily on the impact of banking, manufacturing, and shipbuilding interests on foreign policy and on the cost of munitions and naval vessels to the United States government. In a report dated February 24, 1936, the majority of the members of the committee recommended that the government assume ownership of facilities adequate for the construction of all warships required by the navy as well as for the production of ammunition and other munitions. To this end, a bill was introduced into the Senate on June 8, 1937, to provide for government ownership and operation of shipyards as well as ordnance plants. Although the Nye committee's investigations and recommendations related only to shipbuilding for naval purposes, their adoption would have meant the effective nationalization of the entire industry. As it was, the bill was referred to the Committee on Naval Affairs and never came to a vote in either house of Congress.[28]

President Roosevelt sent the various reports and recommendations then available to Congress in the first days of 1935. He appended a brief statement which raised the question of whether the United States should have an "adequate" merchant marine. His comments represented a new approach to the problem, noting that:

> In many instances in our history, the Congress has provided for various kinds of disguised subsidies to American shipping.... I propose that we end this subterfuge. If the Congress decides that it will maintain a reasonably adequate merchant marine, I believe that we can well afford honestly to call a subsidy by its right name....
> An American merchant marine is one of our most firmly estab-

lished traditions. It was, during the first half of our national existence, a great and growing asset. Since then, it has declined in importance and value. The time has come to square this traditional ideal with effective performance.[29]

Beyond this broad statement, Roosevelt laid down general specifications for a new subsidy policy which would apply differentials to the cost of building and operating ships, and would take cognizance of the subsidies paid by other nations. He urged the prompt termination of existing ocean mail contracts and adequate annual appropriations by Congress to support a subsidy program.

The New Deal

Partly as a result of strong White House backing, Congress gave attention to legislation along the lines proposed. Debate was long and often heated. Generalities and details often became confused. Since the bill was discussed at a time when the nation was in the midst of a major economic depression, the potential of such legislation for providing employment in shipyards, aboard ships, and in a host of supportive industries took almost equal importance in the eyes of members of Congress with the long-range policies for a merchant marine. Finally, when the bill came to a vote in June 1936, its passage in the Senate was partly the result of a shift of Democrats from a tradition of opposition to government subsidies to industry as well as the support of Republicans in that body.

Although in many ways a jerry-built piece of legislation, the Merchant Marine Act of 1936 (the Bland-Copeland Act) joined the laws of 1916, 1920, and 1928 as a landmark in American mercantile marine policy. Its broad declaration of goals was adopted directly from the 1920 act with only one substantive change: instead of stating the aim of providing a merchant fleet capable of carrying "the greater portion" of the waterborne foreign commerce of the United States, it now settled for "a substantial portion."

The heart of the 1936 act, the so-called scientific law, was the concept that a national flag fleet of some definite size and composition must be maintained in the foreign trade of the United States. To achieve this end, a five-member bipartisan Maritime Commission was to be appointed by the president. The commission was to be an independent regulatory agency vested with broad promotional, quasi-judicial, administrative, and operating functions. The act was not specific as to what would constitute "an adequate and well balanced merchant fleet including vessels of all types," and the definition of this as well as of much else generally included in the legislation was left to the Maritime Commission. It was to determine what were the essential trade routes on which United States-flag vessels were to be subsidized for operation in competition with foreign lines. A basic concept of the act was that subsidized lines in foreign trades were to be placed on a parity, as to operating costs, with foreign competition.

Two types of subsidy were adopted as the means of arriving at the goal of the 1936 act. One was to provide subsidies that would enable lines operating on essential trade routes to compete with foreign lines. The other type was to pay construction subsidies which would make it possible to build ships in American yards, the government paying the difference between American and foreign costs. In addition, there was a provision to continue, under stringent limitations, the construction loan funds which had been part of the 1920 and 1928 acts, but these were now restricted to ships to be operated without subsidy. The act further provided for the forgiveness of income taxes on profits from operation sequestered in capital reserves to finance future construction. This aspect of the act was to assume greater importance in future years when corporate tax rates increased.

Other parts of the 1936 act empowered the Maritime Commission to build ships for government account if private enterprise failed to respond, and provided that the commission pay the entire cost of any "national defense" features incorporated into new construction as a result of navy recommendation. The advancement of safety at sea and the caliber of American seamen were important aims of the legislation, and the commission was assigned responsibilities for improving the position of seamen serving aboard subsidized ships.[30]

One immediate task faced by the Maritime Commission was the termination of all ocean mail contracts by June 30, 1937. In many instances, service was continued under new operating differential subsidies, but there were some major changes. A complex controversy developed between the commission and the Dollar Steamship Lines over payments for canceled mail contracts and the servicing of debts on the new steamers *President Coolidge* and *President Hoover*. Eventually, in August 1938, 92 percent of the stock of the line was placed in the custody of the Maritime Commission which thus gained control of the company. Later in the same year, the name was changed to American President Lines. The three turbo-electric liners of the Panama Pacific Line were sold to the Maritime Commission as a result of the cancellation of its mail contract. The line continued service with five Baltimore Mail Line vessels. When the Maritime Commission foreclosed mortgages on the Munson Line's New York–Buenos Aires ships, the route was designated Essential Foreign Trade Route No. One, and the former Panama Pacific Line vessels were rehabilitated, modernized, and placed in this service under the names *Argentina*, *Brazil*, and *Uruguay*.

Operating differential contracts were negotiated with fifteen lines, all of which agreed to build new ships. The Maritime Commission concluded that at least fifty new ships would be required annually for the next decade to revitalize the American merchant fleet. To aid this program, the commission directed its own design staff to produce plans and specifications for basic types of cargo carriers. Three plans were developed, labeled (*C* for cargo) C-1, C-2, and C-3. The C-2s were to be 459 feet 6 inches long, and the C-3s 492 feet long. The C-1s had a length of 417 feet 9 inches, with a cargo capacity of 451,624 cubic feet, and proved to be too small for all but local routes. The C-2s and C-3s, with capacities of 537,189 cubic feet and 695,770 cubic feet respectively, were eminently satisfactory and could be adapted to many trade routes. The first of the new ships actually to enter service was the *Donald McKay* (C-2), delivered in 1939 for the Scandinavian service of the Moore-McCormack Lines. The provisions of the 1936 act, by which construction costs in American shipyards were equalized with those in competing foreign yards through construction subsidies, resulted in the building of a succession of splendid merchant ships. Had World War II not interrupted the orderly operation of the 1936 act, the achievement of a balanced, viable U.S. merchant fleet was a real possibility.

Although the 1936 act had not taken full effect by the advent of World War II, an upturn was apparent by 1939. From a "low" of 62,929 gross tons of merchant vessels built and documented in the United States in 1935, the figure rose to 339,899 tons in 1939. The ratio of tonnage employed in foreign and coastwise trade did not vary greatly: 4,500,000 tons to 10,000,000 tons in 1935 and 3,300,000 to 11,290,000 in 1939.[31]

The combination of new and efficient cargo ship designs, a systematic basis for bringing American costs down to levels that made competition on world trade routes possible, and constant pressure from the Maritime Commission to require subsidized owners to commit their profits to the construction of new ships began to produce results by the end of 1939. The new operating differential subsidy contracts obligated the shipowners to replace sea-weary veterans of the 1917-18 war, and there were strong indications that the goal of fifty new ships a year soon would be attained. The launch on the last day of August 1939 of the United States Line's *America* seemed to usher in a new era of U.S. participation in the prestigious North Atlantic trade. Before the next month was out, however, German forces had invaded Poland and World War II was on, dramatically changing the course of the American merchant marine.

Notes

1. Merchant Marine Act, June 5, 1920, 41 Stat. L., p. 988.
2. Ibid., Sec. 1.
3. Ibid., Sec. 7
4. Ibid.
5. Samuel A. Lawrence, *United States Merchant Shipping Policies and Politics* (Washington, D.C.: The Brookings Institution, 1966), p. 42.
6. Joseph Philip Goldberg, *The Maritime Story; A Study in Labor-Management Relations* (Cambridge: Harvard University Press, 1958), pp. 89-90.

7. Ibid., pp. 97-103.
8. *New York Times,* May 1, 1921.
9. Ibid., May 1, 2, 3, 5, 8, 10, 12, 13, June 14, 15, 22, 24, 1921.
10. Goldberg, op. cit., pp. 111-12.
11. Ibid., pp. 104-29.
12. U.S. Bureau of the Census, *Historical Statistics of the United States, Colonial Times to 1970* (Washington, D.C.: Government Printing Office, 1975), part 2, pp. 749, 751, 762.
13. *New York Times,* February 28, March 1, 1922. Paul Maxwell Zeis, *American Shipping Policy* (Princeton, N.J.: Princeton University Press, 1938), pp. 126-34.
14. Act of May 22, 1928, 45 Stat. L. 689, 698.
15. *New York Times,* January 23, 1929.
16. Ibid., October 31, 1931.
17. Ibid., June 3, 1934, sec. 4, p. 6.
18. Ibid., July 4, 5, 6, 1934.
19. Ibid., July 31, 1934; Elmo Paul Hohman, *History of American Merchant Seamen* (Hamden, Conn.: Shoe String Press, 1956).
20. *New York Times,* April 11, 1935.
21. Hohman, op. cit., pp. 58-61.
22. *New York Times,* October 14, 1936.
23. Ibid., February 15, 1937.
24. Ibid., May 6, 1937.
25. Ibid., October 15, 1938.
26. *Investigation of Air Mail and Ocean Mail Contracts,* S. Rept. 898, 74th Congress, 1st session, 1935.
27. *Report of the Interdepartmental Committee on Shipping Policy,* H. Doc. 118, 74th Congress, 1st session, 1935.
28. *Report of the Special Committee on Investigation of the Munitions Industry,* U.S. Senate, S. Rept. 944, pt. 3, 74th Congress, 2nd session, 1936; *Congressional Record,* 75th Congress, 1st session, p. 5408.
29. *Message from the President of the United States,* D. Doc. 118, 74th Congress, 1st session, 1935, p. 1; *New York Times,* March 3, 1935.
30. Act of June 29, 1936, 49 Stat. L., pp. 1985, 2001.
31. *Historical Statistics,* part 2, pp. 749, 751.

6
The Contribution of U.S. Shipbuilding and the Merchant Marine to the Second World War

Daniel Levine and Sara Ann Platt

The Merchant Marine on the Eve of War

The history of commercial shipbuilding in the Second World War is the history of the Maritime Commission which planned the entire effort and saw it through to the end. The commission, the forerunner of the present Maritime Administration, was created by Congress to administer the Merchant Marine Act of 1936. As described in the previous chapter, this act stated that the major goals of the U.S. merchant marine were to carry our "domestic water-borne commerce and a substantial portion of the water-borne export and import foreign commerce... [and to be] capable of serving as a naval and military auxiliary in time of war."

Shortly after its creation, the commission sponsored a study to determine whether it would be possible at that time to realize the second goal. Its subsequent 1937 "Economic Survey of the American Merchant Marine," found that the merchant marine was on the verge of obsolescence and probably unequal to emergency wartime needs should they arise.[1] Few ships had been built since the 1918-22 building boom; as a result, almost 92 percent of U.S. merchant ships over two thousand gross tons in size[2] were twenty years old or older.[3]

To remedy a near-critical lack of ships, the commission recommended an expanded construction program of fifty ships per year over a period of ten years.[4] The recommendation was accepted in December 1938 by Vice Admiral Emory S. Land, USN (Ret.), who had been appointed chairman of the commission in February 1938. This long-range program was accelerated in August 1940, thanks to the ever-increasing likelihood of war, wih the decision to contract for two hundred ships prior to July 1941.[5] Before the program had gotten under way, however, events in Europe led to the first of five major emergency expansion programs.

The first occurred in October 1940, when a British mission met in New York to request United States assistance in building sixty dry-cargo ships for British use.[6] That request was related to the high losses their ships were suffering at the hands of the German U-boats. Of the 17.8 million gross tons of ships in the inventory of the British Commonwealth when Hitler marched into Poland on September 1, 1939, 2.9 million gross tons (16 percent of the total) had been lost to enemy action by the end of 1940, and the rate of loss was still climbing.[7]

Several months later, on January 3, 1941, President Roosevelt announced that 200 similar ships were to be built for our own use.[8] This was the start of what came to be known as the Emergency Program. By the time the expansion was announced, it was anticipated that these 260 ships would not be the end of the emergency building program. The decision was thus made that the U.S. ships should be of a standard design, so as to achieve the cost benefits of series production. Since there was no time to construct an entirely new design, an existing one had to be chosen—and modified, if necessary to meet current needs.

In this context, the Maritime Commission based its considerations on the sixty ships requested by the British,[9] which had a length of about 440 feet, a speed of eleven knots, and a cargo capacity of about ten thousand deadweight tons. The commission considered two specific proposals with these characteristics: the British design itself and a modification of the "Los Angeles" design which had a slightly smaller cargo capacity.

The commission's design team was joined on January 8 by William Francis Gibbs of Gibbs and Cox, naval architects for the sixty British ships. Gibbs argued for the British design. Although the "Los Angeles" design could be built more quickly, there was recognition that delays attributable to design changes, adaptation of drawings, and other factors could be likely.[10] Admiral Land therefore decided to adopt the British design, and the commission set to work on modifications to reduce problems in construction. The ship became known as an Emergency Ship, to distinguish it from the "standard" dry-cargo ships (C-1s, C-2s, and C-3s). It was given the special designation EC2-S-C1. The *E* stood for Emergency, *C2* meant that it had the same general size as a standard C-2, *S* was for steam propulsion, and *C1* indicated the specific design variation.

The administration sought to popularize the construction program of Emergency Ships. As early as December 1940, a year before Pearl Harbor, President Roosevelt had spoken publicly about the growing need to build up the U.S. fleet.[11] The term Liberty Ship was chosen to inspire American enthusiasm for the "defense effort"; another year would pass before the term "war effort" was appropriate.

The capacity of private U.S. shipyards thus came into sharp focus. In July 1940 the navy had received authorization to expand its fleet from about 1.7 million displacement tons to 3 million tons.[12] The resulting ship orders had almost completely filled up the long-established Big Five yards: Newport News Shipbuilding and Dry Dock Company (SBDD); Federal Shipbuilding and Dry Dock Company; New York Shipbuilding Corporation; Sun Shipbuilding and Dry Dock Company; and Bethlehem Shipbuilding Corporation. In order to build the 260 new freighters, new shipbuilding berths were clearly needed. In January 1941, the Maritime Commission received approval to construct nine new shipyards which were to have a total of sixty-five shipbuilding berths.[13]

On December 20, 1940, the British signed contracts for their sixty ships, thirty to be built at the new Todd-Bath yard on the East Coast and the remaining thirty at the new Todd-California Shipbuilding Corporation yard on the West Coast.[14] The first of these "ocean" class ships was launched on October 15, 1941, less than a year later.[15] Because turbines were in short supply, due to the increase in naval ship construction, the "ocean" ships were powered by oil-fired steam reciprocating engines. They were welded rather than riveted, except for joining the shell to the frames.

The two hundred U.S. Liberty Ships were built in the seven other new shipyards: Bethlehem-Fairfield near Baltimore, the

North Carolina Shipbuilding Company at Wilmington, Alabama Drydock and Shipbuilding Company at Mobile, Delta Shipbuilding at New Orleans, Houston Shipbuilding, California Shipbuilding Corporation at Terminal Island (Los Angeles), and the Oregon Shipbuilding Corporation at Portland.[16]

Reference to the nine shipyards (two building the British, and seven the U.S., ships) as "new yards" is something of a misnomer. The acreage was new, most of the equipment was new, but four of them were managed by established companies. Bethlehem-Fairfield was run by Bethlehem Steel Corporation, and the North Carolina Shipbuilding yard was run by Newport News. Both of these were old-line shipbuilders. Alabama Drydock was manged by a ship repair company, and the Delta yard was managed by the American Ship Building Company, which had been located on the Great Lakes. The remaining five yards, Houston, California, Oregon, Todd-Bath, and Todd-California, were managed by a team of new people directed by the Todd Shipyards Corporation. Prominent among the newcomers was Henry J. Kaiser. He had headed a group of construction companies that had built the Hoover, Bonneville, and Grand Coulee dams, as well as the Bay Bridge from San Francisco to Oakland. But, prior to his association with Todd, he had had no experience whatever with shipbuilding or ship repairing. Eventually, he acquired full ownership of two West Coast yards originally under the Todd combines and built and operated additional yards on his own. During the period 1941-45, Kaiser management was responsible for building 1,552 ships totaling 6.3 million displacement tons.[17] Total production by the Maritime Commission during this period aggregated 5,695 ships and 21.8 million displacement tons.[18] Kaiser was thus responsible for 27 percent of the ships and 29 percent of the displacement tonnage constructed in those years.

Admiral Land had cautioned in early 1941 against a too rapid expansion of U.S. shipyards. After the fact, however, Admiral Vickery (vice-chairman of the Maritime Commission after February 1942) noted that "In this type of shipbuilding, which is ship manufacturing, shipbuilding experience has not been necessary, and those people who have not had shipbuilding experience have done a better job than the people who have had it, with the exception of the North Carolina yard, which has done the best job of the old shipbuilders."[19]

After the orders had been placed in early 1941 for the 260 Liberty Ships that marked the first wave of expansion, shipbuiding goals were twice revised upward before U.S. entry into the war. In April 1941, the Maritime Commission received approval to build an additional 306 ships. Included were 112 of the Emergency Liberty Ships, 122 other freighters (C-1s, C-2s, and C-3s), and 72 tankers.[20] This increase was in part a result of the recent passage of the Defense Aid Supplemental Appropriations Act in March 1941, which authorized the Lend-Lease Program under which the United States would transfer a certain number of ships to the British and the Russians without immediate compensation.

Admiral Land, fearful of spreading our existing shipbuilding talent too thin, stated that the new production facilities could only be built with some managerial contribution from the old yards. It was agreed at a conference attended by President Roosevelt that the navy would no longer use the large Sun Shipbuilding yard at Chester, Pennsylvania, for its construction program, thus releasing that facility for the Maritime Commission's program.[21]

The final pre-Pearl Harbor expansion occurred in mid-1941. It chiefly involved acceleration of the schedule for those ships already under contract. The number of Liberty vessels scheduled for delivery in 1941 was increased from 1 to 19, and those for 1942 delivery, from 234 to 267.[22] Construction of the C types was speeded up as well.

The stimulus for this third wave was the high rate at which mechant ships were being sunk by German U-boats. During 1940 and the first quarter of 1941, total losses of dry-cargo ships owned by the British Commonwealth and the other Allied and neutral nations amounted to 6.3 million deadweight tons, far outnumbering the 1.8 million tons which had been built during the same period.[23] Moreover, the loss rate was increasing rapidly. Losses of dry-cargo vessels through the first quarter of 1941 amounted to 420,000 tons per month, on average; for the second quarter of 1941, the average jumped to 680,000 tons monthly.[24]

The United States Prepares for War

Before U.S. entry into the war, and during a period when many believed that we would be able to avoid involvement altogether, the Maritime Commission had increased the rate at which we were building merchant ships far beyond that of the mid-1930s. By the end of 1941, immediately prior to Pearl Harbor, the commission had embarked on a program to produce five million deadweight tons of ships during 1942 and seven million during 1943.[25] By contrast, total deliveries during 1939 had amounted to only 341,219 deadweight tons.[26]

Nor were the new goals set without consideration of the means to implement them. A standardized freighter design had been adopted, one which could be mass-produced in the interests of series production. A method of propulsion (reciprocating steam) had been chosen to avoid competition with the construction of naval ships, which were using turbines to gain higher speed. Additional shipyards had been created and existing yards were expanded. New managerial talent had been obtained in order to complement the existing reservoir of experienced shipbuilders.

Ultimately, of course, the entire process resulted from the farsightedness of the administration. President Roosevelt had announced the first emergency expansion almost a year before Pearl Harbor. Moreover, he had installed as chairman of the Maritime Commission someone who shared his views with respect to the importance of sea power in the conflict that was likely to follow. Emory S. Land had been a lieutenant commander in the Bureau of Construction and Repair when he first met FDR while he was assistant secretary of the navy (1913 to 1920). In 1933, FDR had nominated Land to be chief constructor of the navy and chief of the Bureau of Construction and Repair. Shortly after Land had retired from the navy as an admiral in 1937, FDR selected him (February 1938) as chairman of the Maritime Commission, replacing Joseph P. Kennedy who had been sent as U.S. ambassador to London.

Although there were five members of the Maritime Commission, Chairman Land had the final authority, and he used it with skill and determination. He retained FDR's confidence throughout the war, and gained his support in the inevitable conflict that ensued between the several civilian and military agencies that had a voice in setting overall policy for our wartime construction program.

The record of the Maritime Commission can be summed up in a single sentence: during the Second World War, the United States built far more merchant ships than anyone had thought possible. As mentioned, the commission's goals just prior to Pearl Harbor were for deliveries of 5 million deadweight tons in 1942 and 7 million in 1943. On January 1, 1942, three weeks after our entrance into the war, these goals were increased to 6.2 and 8.1 million deadweight tons, respectively.

The prodigious record of production could not have been accomplished without an equally dramatic rise in the basic inputs of production: labor, capital, raw materials, and technology. Shipyard workers had to be attracted, recruited, and trained. Large quantities of steel, a basic resource in the war effort, had to be diverted for use in building ships. Even the tremendous enlargement in these inputs was not enough by itself to produce the remarkable rise in production. Ways had to be found of increasing the output which could be achieved with given quantities of labor, facilities, and raw materials. In other words, major improvements in technology were essential.

There was fear during the early part of the mobilization that the shortage of skilled labor would prove a bottleneck in the production of ships. This did not occur. Shipyards were able to increase their work forces at a rapid rate, and ways were found to give them the required skills. The number of all employees in private shipyards was 80,100 in June 1939. By the peak, which occurred in November 1943, the level had soared to 1,459,100. This represented an average rate of increase of 5.6 percent *monthly* (92.9 percent on a yearly basis).

How did the shipbuilding industry manage to provide all these new workers with the requisite skills? Shipbuilding is a relatively skilled occupation; in peacetime, for example, many years of apprenticeship are required to train a man as a firstclass mechanic. Many of the new workers had not come from other construction industries and lacked any construction skill whatever. They had to start from scratch. An important part of the answer is that with the shift toward prefabricated subassemblies, in which each worker performed only a few basic tasks, a man could become productive with much less training than in the days of custom shipbuilding. A worker could be taught simple welding, for example, in about a month.[27] Further training in other tasks could proceed as the flow of work permitted. Moreover, a worker could quickly become proficient at a simple job and do it in less time.

At the start of mobilization, there was serious concern within the Roosevelt administration that the anticipated rate of buildup of shipyard labor and the changing patterns of training could lead to disruption. The new shipyards and those undergoing expansion would all be bidding against each other for scarce labor. The resulting escalation in wages, it was said, would help to frustrate the government's anti-inflation policy, and an uneven expansion might lead to fluctuations in the labor force of the individual shipyards and to labor strikes in those whose wages might lag. Many people, FDR among them, remembered the World War I shipbuilding experience when wages rose by 150 percent during 1915-18 and there was substantial labor unrest (101 strikes in 1917 alone).[28]

The use of government coercion, it was argued, was one way to avoid these problems. Men and women could be drafted to work in those shipyards and at those wages chosen by the government. This extreme measure, however, was viewed as unnecessary during prewar mobilization and the early years of the war. President Roosevelt eventually recommended it in January 1944, when the supply of labor had become tight under competing demands by the shipyards, the other expanding industries, and the armed forces. But committees of the Congress were still hesitant in passing the measure; bills were finally reported out in 1945, but the end of the war resulted in the matter being dropped.[29]

In the absence of a labor draft, the Roosevelt administration had to work with the established union structure. The first step was taken by Sidney Hillman, president of a national union within the CIO, who had been appointed to top positions in the National Defense Advisory Commission and the Office of Production Management. In November of 1940, Hillman was auhorized to organize the Shipbuilding Stabilization Committee. Two national unions, the shipyard industry, and the administration were all represented.

Executives of the old established shipbuilding corporations such as Bethlehem, Sun, and Newport News chose not to join the committee. Those yards had been organized by "independent," i.e., nonnational, unions, and management did not wish to negotiate with unions that had not been given representation on the Shipbuilding Stabilization Committee. Such representation had not been given to the independent unions because Hillman felt that it was the leaders of the large national unions who had the power to prevent strikes and to assure a high level of production, while at the same time not giving up such worker benefits as the recently established forty-hour week.

The Shipbuilding Stabilization Committee took two actions designed to avoid the World War I problems of strikes and "scamping." To ensure that there was no interruption of production by either employers or employees, it adopted a resolution containing "no strike" and "no lockout" provisions.[30] Second, the committee established standardized wage rates within each of four geographical "zones"; one for each of the three coasts and one for the Great Lakes.[31] Shipyards within each zone were therefore unable to use wages in competing with each other for labor. Moreover, competition between the zones could be reduced by providing wage adjustments (zone "differentials") with a view to the variation in the cost of living among the various parts of the country.

The actual rate structure for a given zone was to be negotiated at a collective bargaining conference in that zone. The standard "agreements" would have no effect, however, unless they were incorporated into actual wage contracts arising out of collective bargaining between management and unions at each individual shipyard: the zonal conference system was not intended to replace collective bargaining at the local level. Despite the fact that the independent unions and the shipyards they were associated with were not represented at the zonal conferences, the standard wages negotiated at these conferences were in fact accepted by all the yards.[32] Additionally, the agreements included a no-strike and a no-lockout clause, a provision against limitations on production, a clause outlining grievance and arbitration machinery, and a two-year contract duration clause with allowance for cost-of-living wage adjustments.[33] These provisions, too, were accepted by labor and management at all the individual shipyards.

Once the contracts were signed, the Maritime Commission realized that escalation clauses were going to contribute to that inflation of prices which the government was intent on avoiding. The shipbuilding unions agreed, however, during the start of the second year, to a smaller increase than they were entitled to under the contract.[34] The agreement on overtime wages was also a problem. If workers were to receive time and a half for Saturdays and double time for Sundays, it would prove costly to keep yards in continuous production. The problem was solved by keying overtime wages to the *sixth* and *seventh* days worked during the week, whether they fell on the weekend or not.[35] (A worker would get straight-time wages for working Saturday through Wednesday, for example, with Thursdays and Fridays off.)

What were the results of this method of managing shipyard labor during World War II? In terms of total wages, shipyard workers fared better than those in other industries. In 1943, for example, weekly earnings in the maritime shipyards averaged about sixty dollars, compared with only forty-eight dollars for workers in private building construction and forty-nine dollars for those in all durable-goods industries.[36]

It is difficult to measure the effect that standardizing wages by zones had on stabilizing the supply of labor to the shipyards. Wage inflation was certainly less in World War II than in World War I: whereas wages rose by roughly 150 percent during the four years from 1914-18, the increase during the five-year period from 1940-45 was only 57 percent in gross hourly earnings and under 100 percent measured in weekly take-home pay.[37] It would be difficult to determine exactly how much of the relative wage stability in the Second World War was due to reducing competition between shipyards and how much to the national policy of controlling wages in all industries.

When President Roosevelt announced the emergency expansion program of two hundred Liberty Ships in January 1941, U.S. shipbuilding resources consisted of eight navy yards, which had been doing much of the repair and some of the new construction of naval vessels, and nineteen private shipyards, at which the bulk of the naval construction and all of the merchant building had been carried out. (This section deals only with the Class I yards, those capable of building oceangoing ships over four hundred feet in length.)

The expansion programs brought two kinds of changes. Additional shipbuilding ways were created in almost all of the private yards, with funding in many cases provided by the Maritime Commission. In addition, the Maritime Commission built twenty-one new emergency shipyards, the ownership of which remained in government hands but which were operated by private corporations. The choice of the term "emergency" to describe both new shipyards and new cargo ships selected for mass production was not a coincidence. Except for 20 ships built by the Alabama Drydock and Shipbuilding company, the entire stock of 2,708 emergency cargo (Liberty) ships were built in the emergency yards funded during or after January 1941.[38]

The expansion of the private yards and the creation of the new emergency yards represented a more than fourfold increase in shipbuilding capacity. On average, it took about six months to construct a new building berth for the Maritime Commission's program, but this rate was exceeded in particular cases. The Bethlehem-Fairfield yard in a suburb of Baltimore provides a graphic illustration. Sixteen new building ways were built, making it the second largest non-navy yard in the country (the private Sun Shipbuilding yard was expanded to twenty-eight ways). The Bethlehem-Fairfield yard was built during the twenty-one-month period between March 1941 and December 1942, an average of less than one and a half months per way. The fabricating plant was separated from the erecting plant by two miles. Materials arrived at the rate of one hundred carloads per day. Ship sections up to ten tons in weight were fabricated in the shops, and the assemblies were combined outdoors in units weighing up to twenty-five tons. Transportation within the plant and to the building ways required ten locomotives, two hundred rail cars, fifty locomotive cranes, ten mobile cranes, forty-two tower cranes, and thirty bridge cranes.

Steel proved a major bottleneck to ship production. Some overall statistics show how heavily the shipbuilding industry came to depend on this scarce commodity. Total U.S. consumption of steel for all purposes rose from 39 million tons in 1939 to over 64 million tons in 1943, an increase of 13 percent yearly. During the same period, however, the consumption for shipbuilding and ship repair rose by a factor of over 25, a yearly increase of 125 percent. As a result, the fraction of total consumption of steel that went for shipbuilding rose from 1.3 percent in 1939 to over 20 percent by 1943, the year of peak merchant ship construction.

The shortage of steel ingots, basic to all forms of finished products, was not the only problem. About 77 percent of the steel used in ship hulls is in the form of plates, and the mills capable of rolling steel into plates were in short supply. Steel plate production during the war increased by a factor of three—from 4 to 13.2 million tons per year—but the consumption of plate by all shipyards (including naval) rose by a factor of almost seventeen—from .5 million to 8.4 million tons per year. As a result, shipbuilding's share of plate rose from 12.5 percent to 63.6 percent in the four years from 1940 to late 1943–early 1944.

One reason for the limited availability of steel was the unexpected high rate of production of merchant ships mentioned earlier. As early as June 25, 1942, Donald Nelson, chairman of the War Production Board, testified before the Truman committee that demands for steel plate were running three hundred thousand tons over production.[39] The Maritime Commission, one month later, had to cancel a contract with Andrew Higgins to build a large shipyard in New Orleans for the purpose of constructing two hundred Liberty Ships.

What had not been anticipated, was how productive the expanded shipbuilding industry was going to become. The Liberty Ship program provides an excellent example. The six ships delivered in January 1942 took an average of 158 days each on the building ways. The ships delivered in July, only six months later, required only 81 days, about half as long. By December of that year, the time was down to 40 days, another 50-percent reduction. This meant that each building berth was producing Liberty Ships four times as fast, within about a year after the first delivery, and it took four times as much steel to keep it fully occupied. This remarkable and unanticipated increase in productivity greatly explains why U.S. shipbuilding capacity outstripped the availability of steel.[40]

Productivity

In the peacetime years preceding World War II, ships were custom built. Steel plates and shapes were fabricated into small units in an assembly yard. These subassemblies, along with the components ordered from subcontractors, were then transported to the building way and riveted to the structural members already in place. The space in the ship became tight as more subassemblies and components were added, so that such tasks as riveting, wiring, and plumbing had to be done in sequence. This lengthened the time the ship had to stay on the building way.

Custom building of one or, at most, several ships of a kind had its effect on the training of the work force. It was more productive to have each worker skilled in many kinds of tasks. These traditional practices changed dramatically with expanded wartime production. The 2,580 basic Liberty cargo ships (EC2-S-C1 design), for example, were built in only eighteen yards, an average of 143 per yard.[41] It became profitable to view the construction of a ship as thousands of individual tasks. There was enough work to keep one or more men constantly at work on each. If all of these tasks could be carried on at the same time, the total time to build the ship could be greatly reduced.

Work accordingly had to be spread out over a large area. Rather than bringing small subassemblies to the construction way for erection, they were welded into larger assemblies, and these into still larger assemblies. A ship thus had to tie up a place on a building way only long enough to weld or rivet the large units to the main structure. The new emergency yards thus required large areas for fabrication and assembly shops. Brunswick, for example, had a 496-acre yard; Alabama Drydock and Shipbuilding had 306, and the Kaiser yard at Swan Island had 270 acres. Large cranes and rail transportation were also needed to move the huge assemblies from the fabrication assembly areas to the building way, as is indicated by the facilities described earlier at the Bethlehem-Fairfield yard, in which the fabricating plant was two miles from the erecting plant.

Prefabrication of larger and larger assemblies was permitted by the technological advances in arc welding that had been made since World War I. In so doing, individual plates were fashioned into large units in the fabrication and assembly areas. Riveting was only practical in joining units to major structural members that were already in place on the building way. In welding the plates and subassemblies together, moreover, the units could be rotated to increase the amount of down-hand welding. Vertical and overhead welding required more training and was more time consuming, even when carried out by experienced welders.

Series production of a single type of ship led to other kinds of economies in addition to the reduction in construction time that was associated with prefabrication. A single agency—Gibbs and Cox, in the case of the Liberty Ship—could produce a single set of drawings which could then be replicated for all those yards participating in the program. Moreover, the procurement of steel plate and components could be centralized, and the Maritime Commission took over this responsibility in the interests of tighter inventory control. Otherwise, some yards could have had a surplus and other yards a shortage of some item, causing a delay until the imbalance could be removed.

Incentives

Merchant ships were generally procured in World War I by "cost-plus" contracts. The builder was paid a price for his ship equal to what it cost him to build it plus a fee, or profit, equal to a fixed percentage of the cost. Although the fact that profit was guaranteed encouraged shipbuilders to seek contracts, the formula provided perverse incentives during construction: inefficiency led to higher costs, and thus higher profits.

The Merchant Marine Act of 1936 attempted to remedy this

situation. Under Title V of the act, the Maritime Commission would choose a ship design which it thought would interest owners and put it out for competitive bids. The commission then signed a modified fixed-price contract with the lowest bidder, and subsequently sold the ships to interested owners for their estimated cost if built in a foreign yard. Because profit automatically declines as cost rises under a fixed-price contract, the builder was encouraged to economize. His reward for efficiency was limited, however, by Section 505(b) of the act, which allowed the Maritime Commission to recapture any profit the shipbuilder made over 10 percent. Other modifications to the fixed-price contract included allowances for design changes made after the contract was awarded and for escalation in the costs of labor and materials.

With the start of mobilization in early 1941, the Maritime Commission feared that modified fixed-price contracts would not provide enough incentive to assure the desired increase in construction. First, uncertainties had increased on the cost side. Machinery prices had started to rise quickly, and the fact that the navy had obtained priorities for critical items made delivery of these to yards producing merchant ships more uncertain than before. Second, as we have previously indicated, "new blood" had to be brought into the shipbuilding industry. The Maritime Commission thus had to attract people with managerial ability in other construction trades. Because these outsiders lacked experience in estimating the costs of building ships, it was feared that some might be dissuaded from entering the industry. Others, with a more adventurous spirit, might bid too low, to capture some of the new business, and then be unable to deliver at that price. Litigation to reach financial settlements would require time.

The problem, therefore, was to devise a type of contract that would guarantee builders a large enough profit to attract their services but still provide some incentive to economize, in order that more ships could be built with increasingly scarce resources. The "man-hour" contract proved workable and was used for all Liberty Ships. Based on their experience at the time, the commission set production "targets" of 510,000 man-hours of labor and 150 days of construction time to build the ship. A builder who met these targets exactly would receive a price equal to his cost plus a $110,000 fee, or profit. Given an estimated cost of around $1,750,000 to build a Liberty Ship in January 1941, this represented a profit of about 6 percent.

The builder's fee was increased, however, by $400 for every day he was able to cut off the target delivery time, and by $0.50 for each man-hour he was able to save. He was penalized $400 for every day he was late, and $0.33 for every man-hour over the target. The extra reward was not allowed to exceed $30,000, giving a total fee of $140,000 (8 percent of the $1,750,000 target cost). And the penalty was never allowed to exceed $50,000, assuring a profit of at least $60,000 (a 3.4 percent return on the target cost). The costs of building Liberty Ships decreased so rapidly as more ships were built that, by April 1943, the commission was able to reduce the "target" fee from $110,000 to $45,000. The maximum fee was lowered to $60,000 and the minimum to $20,000.

Labor man-hours were used as the proxy for total cost in these contracts because it was easy for the builder to measure them as construction proceeded. Given that steel proved to be the major bottleneck, there might have been some reason to provide an incentive in the Liberty Ship contracts to economize on steel as well as labor. The fact that the ship's design was fixed limited the possibilities for major materials trade-offs: more smaller ships versus fewer large ones. The proper incentives could have helped lower the large inventories of in-process steel which some of the yards had maintained, and perhaps led to reductions in waste as well.

The second major kind of contract, called "price minus," was used both for the tankers that had become scarce because of high losses to German U-boats and for the standard cargo ships. These contracts did aim directly at the goal of reducing total cost. If the builder was able to reduce his cost by a million dollars, for example, his profit would increase by half that amount, or $500,000.[42]

The incentives provided in the "man-hour" contract had a dramatic effect in bringing about the savings in labor input and delivery time that were made technically possible by series production. It took an average of 1,257,000 man-hours and six months on the construction way to build each of the Liberty Ships (EC2-S-C1) in the first "round" (the first to be constructed on each building way). By the time that these ways were each building their fifth Liberty Ship, the man-hours had fallen to 727,000—a decrease of 42 percent—and the time on way had fallen to a month and a half. These dramatic improvements in performance continued as more and more ships were built. By the time the thirtieth ship was built on the same way, the labor inputs had fallen to about *one-third* of those for the first ship, and production time was only *one-tenth* as large. (These reductions are not apparent in measurements of man-hours and delivery time by *month*. Some yards built their first Liberty Ship relatively late in the war, and the higher man-hours and longer delivery times associated with early "rounds" increased the monthly averages).

There were equally dramatic reductions in the time to outfit these ships, once their basic construction had been completed on the building way and they had been launched. From the beginning to the end of the program, the outfitting times fell from about ninety days to only ten days.[43] The total time from keel laying to delivery thus decreased from about nine months to only one. In fact, one of the yards completed a ship in less than a week during a demonstration project staged for morale purposes, but this feat could not be accomplished on a regular basis.

Appraisal of Shipbuilding

One measure of the contribution which U.S. merchant shipbuilding made to the Allied war effort is the increase in the total numbers of ships constructed. How the U.S. ships were employed—the amount and kinds of cargoes they carried—is taken up in a later section. The subject here, however, is the numerical size of the inventory as measured in gross tons.

The number of ships available to the Allied war effort when the United States entered the war in 1941 was considerably higher than it otherwise would have been, thanks to the government's foresight in instituting the emergency expansion programs under Admiral Land. Whereas U.S. production amounted to only 30 percent of total Allied and neutral yearly construction in 1940, it rose to about 85 percent by 1943 (Figure 1). As a result, our share of the total Allied inventory rose from under 20 percent to around 50 percent by the war's end (Figure 2).

Measured in total capacity,[44] the inventory of U.S. plus British ships[45] decreased from 26 million gross tons at the start of the war to 23 million tons by January 1942, due to the heavy losses from German attacks on shipping and to the fact that new ships begun during the emergency expansion programs required time to deliver. By early 1943, the reductions in losses and increases in deliveries led to a rise in total gross tonnage.[46] By the end of the war, the U.S. plus British inventory had risen to over 53 million gross tons, twice the inventory available at the start of the war.

What would the inventory of ships have been had the United States pursued a different shipping policy in the premobilization period? In the analysis of such questions, it is useful to separate U.S. sealift resources into three major elements: ships, shipyards, and industrial mobilization base. It is instructive to make a short digression to relate these elements to subsidy policy, and then return to the main issue.

Operating differential subsidies (ODS) were established by the Merchant Marine Act of 1936 to provide parity for U.S. citizens in the operation of U.S.-built vessels with foreign competition. The construction differential subsidy (CDS), on the other hand, was designed to preserve, maintain, and advance shipbuilding technology under U.S. sovereignty. An existing body of shipyards, moreover, is one way of providing a shipyard mobilization base. As the World War II experience showed, the shipbuilding knowledge vested in their operation serves as a fund of technical and managerial knowledge which can be passed on to others in the event of mobilization. In a short war, the United States obviously would have to rely on the ships we had in existence. Given more time, we could produce ships provided that we had the shipyards in existence to build them. Finally, if the conflict lasted long enough, new ships could be obtained by expanding the shipyard mobilization base (i.e., building new shipyards).

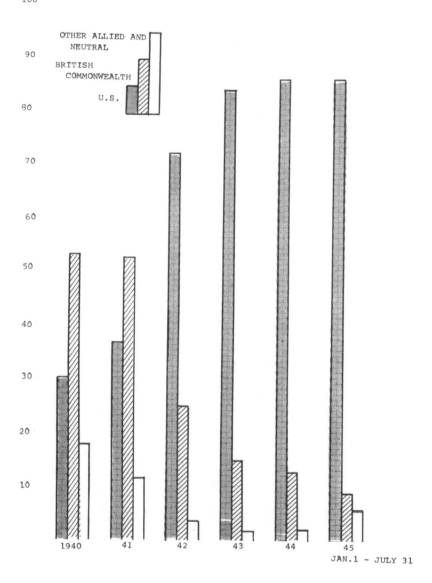

Figure 1: RELATIVE SHARES OF U.S. AND ALLIES IN MERCHANT SHIP CONSTRUCTION (GROSS TONS)

194

Figure 2: RELATIVE SHARES OF U.S. AND ALLIES IN MERCHANT SHIP INVENTORY (GROSS TONS)

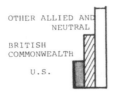

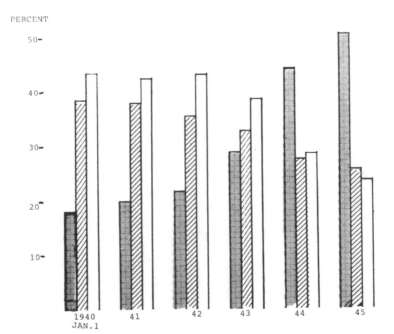

Manning the Merchant Fleet

Added to the Herculean task of building the wartime merchant fleet was the problem of how it was to be manned. Before the war started, the merchant fleet was supported by approximately sixty thousand officers and men,[47] and very early in the conflict it was apparent that maintaining an adequate pool of merchant seamen was going to be difficult. In the spring of 1942, just after the creation of the War Shipping administration (WSA), ship sailings that were delayed because of manpower shortages averaged, ominously, about forty-five a month.[48] If critical shortfalls in this area had continued, the war effort would have been hampered. The WSA and the unions worked quickly to institute recruiting and training programs. The problem was by no means an easy one to solve, and, as the war progressed, the recruiting, training, and manning of merchant ships proved a constant source of controversy.

As previously noted, before the start of the war, a series of long strikes had brought the shipping industry to a standstill, but, when negotiations ended, merchant seamen had gained many of the rights they had long been denied. From this period three very strong unions emerged: the National Maritime Union; the Sailors' Union of the Pacific; and the Seafarers' International Union.[49] When war came, it was obvious that great demands would be made on the merchant marine. Union leaders therefore vigilantly watched for any encroachment on the seamen's newly gained rights.

Unlike their naval counterparts, civilian merchant seamen were free to sign for voyages and they were free *not* to. During the first two years of Great Britain's participation in the war, her merchant sailors also maintained their civilian status. In those early years, the British also faced shortages because, since the merchant ship was not technically a weapon of war, seamen could not be compelled to go to sea. Civilian jobs were becoming more lucrative, and, as their jobs at sea became increasingly hazardous, more and more seamen were tempted to remain on land. In addition, seamen were taking longer leaves between voyages. Their home ports were already being bombed, and many opted to stay at home with their families.[50] The combination of these and various other factors created a serious shortage of merchant crews. Under the Essential Work Order of March 1941, the Minister of Labor was given the power to prevent any employee from leaving a job of national importance; nor could he be dismissed from it except in cases of grave misconduct.[51] In the same year, the Registration for Employment Order empowered the Minister of Labor to transfer men from one occupation to another. Men between eighteen and sixty years of age, who had been in the merchant service since 1936, were required to register with the Ministry of Labor. The amount of leave they could take was also set, at one month per year.[52]

Although the United States faced a similar problem, militarization of the merchant marine was avoided. This is not to say that it was not suggested. In 1942, despite the fact that the merchant marine was suffering a greater casualty rate than all the armed services,[53] reports of breaches of discipline on merchant ships and in port gained for the merchant marine some bad publicity. The demands for change included some calls for the nationalization of the merchant marine. The disadvantages of this move were fairly obvious, the least of which was that the maritime unions would never accept it. On May 2, 1942, answering a letter from Senator George L. Radcliffe, President Roosevelt wrote: "I have your letter . . . in which you refer to the current rumors that the officers and seamen of the Merchant Marine are shortly to be turned over to the Navy Department. I agree with you that at the present time such a move is not necessary, and would be unwise."[54]

Much was made in the press about the seemingly high cost of the new merchant training centers ($14 million for the station at Sheepshead Bay, N.Y.).[55] Earlier in that year, controversy over control of the training of merchant seamen created bad feeling. Reports from army and navy officers of merchant seamen's misconduct added fuel to the already hot fire. Training of merchant seamen was still, early in 1942, under the control of the U.S. Coast Guard, which had wanted to extend its control even further, to the men awaiting shipping in the pools. Admiral Land, who headed the War Shipping Administration as well as the Maritime Commission, and the union leaders both objected, and the struggle for control ended in a compromise between the WSA and the unions. The Maritime Commission and the WSA took over all recruitment, manning, and training of merchant seamen and officers from the Coast Guard. Eventually two hundred training stations were organized across the nation. Bargaining rights were guaranteed, but a temporary wage freeze was enacted. The prewar division of ships between the A.F. of L. and the C.I.O. was kept.[56]

Interagency disputes on land were echoed on board ship. Unlike their British counterparts, who were all required to take gunnery training and assume the responsibility for the defense of their ships, the corresponding responsibility in the case of U.S. merchant vessels fell on the Naval Armed Guard. Although cooperation between the Armed Guard "bluejackets" and the merchant mariners was the rule rather than the exception, when there was friction between them lack of coordination and inefficiency in operation was often the result.

This conflict stemmed from a variety of causes. The merchant seamen sometimes resented the tightly disciplined, uniformed Armed Guard. Many followed orders from the Armed Guard commander reluctantly. On the other hand, the navy bluejackets often disdained the casually dressed and casually disciplined civilian seamen. The Armed Guard gunner made $50 a month. The merchant seamen's pay was $100 per week, plus a $100 bonus for duty in the Atlantic in addition to sums of around $100 for each different war zone entered. This last bonus was eventually changed to $125 per man if an air raid occurred while the ship was in port—even if his ship was not hit.[57] Seamen who sailed the Murmansk Gauntlet could earn at least $3,200 on one voyage, which might include a several-month wait in Russia.[58] These highly publicized figures caused some hostility, but it was often forgotten that merchant seamen received no assistance for their families at home as did their naval counterparts. They also performed this dangerous and tedious task with few thanks. They were not afforded the same recognition on shore as were the men of the uniformed armed services, and they were often not welcomed in places like the U.S.O.[59] Under the auspices of Mrs. Emory S. Land, the United Seamen Service (U.S.S.) was established, giving merchant seamen around the world a place of their own.

The Armed Guard were trained at three schools in Virginia, California, and Mississippi prior to ship assignment. To the Armed Guard commander fell the duty of training a disciplined gun crew in the informal atmosphere of the merchant ship. The relationship between the commander and the master of the ship was also vital. The first duty of the master is to his men; the first duty of an Armed Guard commander, to his ship. In the face of enemy attack, it was vitally important that these two points of view somehow merged. Technically, navy personnel were to man all key positions while the merchant seamen were to perform duties such as passing ammunition, loading guns, and manning less-important stations. However, if the naval gunners were disabled or killed, the entire defense of the ship and its cargo was left to the civilian seamen. The National Maritime Union demanded the protection of naval gunners and at a later date advocated that the gun crews be drawn from merchant sailors. The navy's program to teach merchant sailors how to handle guns was a failure. Before Pearl Harbor, schools for gunnery instruction were set up in many Atlantic ports, but few seamen came. When the instruction was provided in maritime training centers, again the effort failed. In 1942, mobile gun-training units found their way to the docks and even here they were scarcely used.[60]

Protection of Merchant Ships

The Neutrality Act of 1939 not only prevented U.S. shipping from carrying goods (some of them urgently needed by Britain) into the "war zones," but also prohibited the mounting of guns for self-protection. In November 1941, the Congress voted to amend the Neutrality Act. The amendment not only permitted the arming of merchant ships but allowed them access to the war zones, in which they could now convey goods to the British Empire.[61]

There were three primary considerations in the effort to arm merchantmen. The first was the availability of equipment. The limitations of the merchant ship also had to be considered. Finally, the arms were to be primarily defensive.[62] When the program began in late 1941, guns were in short supply. Those ships not sailing in dangerous waters were not furnished with guns. Those sailing the most notorious routes, such as to Murmansk, were given top priority. Still, even in August 1942 the shortage was still critical. The vice-chief of Naval Operations issued the following directive: "Ships sailing independently should be armed. Ships sailing in regularly made-up convoys, other than ships bound to North Russia or tankers en route to the United Kingdom, may sail unarmed if the urgency of delivery of their cargo warrants it."[63] He further recommended that antiaircraft guns be removed from ships entering a port and placed on outgoing ships.[64]

There is little question that ships were not armed adequately or in time. The United States had not been in the war six months, and the merchant marine was suffering losses that were proportionately far greater than those endured by any branch of the armed services. In those six months, 350 ships were lost and with them almost three thousand men.[65]

In all, 6,236 merchant ships were armed during World War II. These included U.S. ships and certain Allied and neutral ships. Guns were the most important defense item; some fifty-three thousand of them were placed on merchant ships. In addition to the guns, an attempt was made to add twenty-five other defense items to give merchant ships their best chance of survival. No ship was given all these features, but many ships received some.[66] Among the most important were the following:

1. Degaussing
2. Deck strengthening
3. Sky lookout stations
4. Extra radio equipment
5. Lifesaving equipment
6. Darken-ship equipment
7. Extension of watertight bulkheads
8. Barrage balloons
9. Acoustic warning devices
10. Rocket flares
11. Mines
12. Gyro compasses for Alaskan vessels
13. Smoke indicators
14. Fueling-at-sea gear
15. Depth charges on tank ships

Convoying

In the early war years, the lack of adequate defense equipment on merchant vessels was not the sole reason for so many sinkings. After 1940, the British Admiralty tried to impress upon the Americans the need for a well-organized convoy system. A large convoy was usually made up of twenty-five or thirty merchant ships which sailed in columns normally about four hundred yards apart. The most efficient way to protect merchant shipping, it also provided a greater opportunity for striking back at an attacking U-boat. Despite this warning, American merchant ships continued to sail independently. They used their lights and radio equipment freely, and when German submarines entered American waters they found many easy targets.[67] Ships sank within view of people standing on shore. In the first four months of 1942, eighty-two merchant ships were torpedoed and sunk off the East Coast alone.[68]

The convoy system was not without its problems, however. Since a convoy had to sail in relatively close formation, the slower ships necessarily increased the overall sailing time of all. Additionally, unless the planning and organization was flawless —and it rarely was—congestion at both ends of the supply line was the rule rather than the exception. Convoys also meant escorts, and there was a serious lack of destroyer-escorts (DEs) during the critical phase of the German submarine campaign. However, during hostilities, there was little time to deliberate over the relative merits of the system. The Allies could not afford to lose any more ships, particularly at the rate they were being destroyed in early 1942. When the convoy system was fully adopted, the number of sinkings dropped off dramatically; of the two thousand ships convoyed in the last three months of 1942, only five were lost.[69]

Shipping the Supplies: Neutral Shipping

Before the United States ever entered the war, U.S. merchant ships were carrying goods to support the Allies in their struggle against the Germans. As early as 1939, the Allies, chiefly Britain and France, were requesting aid from the United States. That same year, at President Roosevelt's request, Congress repealed the section of the Neutrality Act that forbade the sale of U.S. munitions to foreign countries. Instead, a "cash and carry" program was adopted, and any nation that could pay for munitions could buy them.[70]

The president had begun in 1939 to push for a total repeal of the Neutrality Act, but a great majority of Americans felt that such an open show of support to the Allies would inevitably lead to our being drawn into the war. Roosevelt and his supporters continued to push for repeal of the neutrality legislation, but this would not come until a month before Pearl Harbor, two years later. While the "neutrality debate" was raging, every effort was made to circumvent the restrictions of neutrality. Because U.S.-flag ships could not enter the war zones, many were transferred to the flags of other nations, most notably Panama. Also, what constituted a "war zone" was often conveniently left unclear.

Paradoxically, the Neutrality Act may have *helped* bring the United States into the war. It was believed that the nation could help its allies without inviting the danger of enemy submarine attacks. After a time, however, Americans began to read about daily German attacks on neutral shipping. By early 1941, American hopes of staying out of the war began to dim. The Germans had already conquered much of Europe, including France, and in early 1941 Hitler declared: "Whoever believes he will be able to help England must definitely know one thing: every ship, whether with or without convoy, that comes before our torpedo tubes will be torpedoed."[71] A number of "incidents" involving U.S. ships, following this pronouncement, helped to convince Americans that Hitler's threat was sincere.

Lend-Lease

On March 11, 1941, Congress overwhelmingly passed an act authorizing a program of lend-lease with the Allies.[72] Under this act, the secretary of war, the secretary of the navy, or the head of any other agency was empowered to procure defense articles for any country whose defense was deemed important to that of the United States. Articles of defense included weapons, ammunition, vessels, aircraft, machinery, and tools.[73] That same day, the president directed the secretary of the navy to turn over to the British twenty-eight small torpedo boats and three thousand depth charges, plus a number of naval guns, gun mounts, and stores of ammunition for merchant ships.[74] The United States also transferred fifty destroyers to the British in exchange for bases in the Western Hemisphere.

U.S. merchant shipping was crucially important in the British campaigns in the Middle East, the Indian Ocean, and the Persian Gulf. In the last seven months of 1941, American merchant ships transported 48,958 vehicles, 302,698 tons of dry goods, and 814 airplanes. Many shiploads were involved; on the average, 150 vehicles could be placed on one ship.[75] Additional lend-lease shipments went directly to the British civilian population. The German submarine campaign caused a critical food shortage in England in the spring of 1941, and one of the first shipments under lend-lease sent one hundred thousand cases of evaporated milk, eleven thousand tons of cheese, and eleven thousand tons of eggs to the British people, which helped them through the worst phase of the submarine warfare.[76]

It must be remembered that the provision of the Neutrality Act prohibiting U.S. ships from sailing into war zones was not amended until November 1941. The resulting circuitous routes greatly increased the traveling time of ships and tied up much needed tonnage. In April 1941, President Roosevelt declared that the area around the Red Sea was no longer to be regarded as a war zone, and by September, American freighters were delivering cargoes of tanks and munitions to this area at the rate of one shipment a day.[77]

In 1941, the Germans turned their attacks on the Russians, who immediately became one of the major recipients of American lend-lease shipments. U.S. ships that traveled the infamous Murmansk run carried almost every imaginable article of war: explosives, guns, vehicles, machinery, oil, munitions, planes, and spare parts.[78] The voyage to Murmansk was one of the longest and most dangerous faced by merchant mariners. Once in port, many of the convoys that had managed to evade the wolf-pack tactics of German submarines faced waves of attack by the Luftwaffe based thirty-five miles away in Norway and

Finland. Nearly 21 percent[79] of the ships on this run were lost, a far higher loss rate than on any of the other routes. Still, throughout the war, merchant seamen continued to volunteer for this most hazardous of duties.

During the early part of the lend-lease program, a great deal was learned by the Americans about efficient shipping, but not before much cargo space had been wasted. Often when bulky items, such as tanks and other vehicles, were shipped, there was a great deal of space between the items. In U.S. shipments to England's Middle East campaign, shipowners filled these gaps with items that were totally useless to the British war effort. The British attempted to persuade the U.S. government to pressure U.S. shipowners to discontinue this wasteful practice, but not before some forty-one thousand tons of useless items had been dumped in the desert.[80] A similar situation developed in the Pacific when shipping space was critical. When the scarcity became obvious, ingenious methods were devised to conserve space. Dehydration cut the bulk of vegetables, eggs, and milk considerably. Fresh meat was boxed, rolled, and packed with dry ice between trucks and other heavy equipment. The same amount of meat that had taken up ten ships would now take up only four.[81]

The principal U.S. lend-lease customers were Britain and Russia, but there were others who made requests for lend-lease shipments. Although many nations were involved in carrying lend-lease cargoes, the bulk of these shipments were transported in U.S. ships. U.S. ships carried 39 percent of all civilian requirements and lend-lease cargoes in 1942, 53 percent in 1943, 62 percent in 1944, and 58 percent in the remaining months of the war.[82] In 1943 alone, U.S. merchant ships made 2,267 trips with lend-lease materials to Great Britain, 328 to Russia, and 281 to other lend-lease countries.[83]

War Shipping

After Pearl Harbor and U.S. entry into the war, it was obvious that the demands that would be placed on the merchant marine would easily tax its limits. Merchant shipping was crucial; it was needed not only to ship millions of soldiers to theaters all over the world, but to carry the weapons, equipment, food, and clothing to support them. Production of war goods required the importation of essential raw materials. Military and civilian aid to the Allies continued throughout the war, and the American civilian population also required such imported commodities. It has been estimated that two deadweight tons of shipping were continuously needed to supply a soldier in France in World War I. In World War II, weapons and equipment were bulkier and heavier. Seven or eight tons were needed to keep a soldier in Europe supplied in 1942; in Pacific theaters, that figure was doubled.[84] Between Pearl Harbor and the end of the war, the total amount of cargo lifted by the United States was 268,252,000 long tons. Of this, 203,522,000 tons were dry cargo and 64,730,000 were petroleum products. Among the thousands of items shipped were locomotives, hospital supplies, airplanes, clothing, and army tanks. Seventy-five percent of these cargoes were carried by ships controlled by the War Shipping Administration.[85] The U.S. merchant fleet also carried over seven million army personnel overseas between 1941 and 1945.

It must be remembered that, although the number of merchant ships built during World War II was impressive by World War I standards, they had to travel sea lanes that were much longer and more dangerous. Whereas our ships had to travel only three to four thousand miles to Europe in 1918-19, in World War II they sailed five thousand miles to Murmansk, nine thousand miles across the Pacific to Australia, and over fourteen thousand from New York around the Cape of Good Hope to the Persian Gulf.[86] In addition, U.S. vessels in the second war were subjected to higher attrition rates from submarine attack and the new threat from aircraft.

The importation of critical raw materials became strategically imperative after Pearl Harbor. The construction of aluminum airplanes required shipments of bauxite from South America. Imports of this crucial mineral increased from almost nothing in 1941 to two million long tons in 1942 and to three and one-half million tons in 1943.[87] Such imports were especially critical because the United States had failed to stockpile strategic materials before the war. This was most clear in the cases of rubber, tin, and scrap iron. When the Japanese attacked Pearl Harbor and cut off many of the Far Eastern sea lanes, the United States had little more than a year's supply of these goods.[88] America's importation of strategic materials and civilian goods rose sharply throughout the war. In 1943, U.S. dry-cargo ships imported 18,566,000 tons of strategic commodities, including copper, sugar, coffee, nitrates, and manganese. That same year, tankers brought in 11,200,000 tons of bulk liquids, predominantly crude petroleum.[89]

After the United States entered the war, the efficient allocation of shipping space became nearly as important as the amount of shipping that was available. The nation was now fighting a war in two major theaters, and millions of troops had to be transported and kept supplied. Aid to the Allies continued at nearly the same pace as before, and civilian populations around the globe, including Americans, were dependent on merchant shipping for food and countless other commodities. It was clear that some means had to be found to organize the distribution of shipping space among the various claimants. This was one problem that the United States was not prepared for. Interagency disputes defied attempts to coordinate efforts, and Allied criticism of U.S. utilization of shipping space continued throughout the war.

On the day following the Pearl Harbor attack, President Roosevelt created the Strategic Shipping Board, which was to be responsible for "processing or planning the procurement, production, import and export of defense articles and materials."[90] The board was established without any organizational means of making executive decisions, and it soon revealed its inability to deal with the task.

The board suggested to the president that a central shipping agency be created, and on February 7, 1942, the president signed an executive order establishing the War Shipping Administration with Admiral Land as chief administrator. The WSA was empowered to organize the operation, purchase, charter, insurance, repair, maintenance, and requisition of vessels.[91] Ships that came under the control of the WSA were to be placed in pools from which allotments were made to the army, navy, and other federal agencies and to all the Allied governments.[92]

The amount of responsibility assumed by the WSA was staggering, and the control and ingenuity exercised under its very able leadership contributed a great deal to the success of most merchant marine activities. One of the most important roles it played was in the planning of military operations. In many instances, the availability of shipping assumed decisive importance in the choice between various campaigns.[93] Throughout the war, nearly three-quarters of the ships controlled by the WSA were allotted to army and navy cargoes. Merchant ships were often turned directly over to the navy which employed them as Ordnance Replenishment Ships (AEs), Fuel Replenishment Ships (AOs), and Attack Transport Vessels (APAs).

Planning the supply of the Normandy invasion attacks proved to be one of the largest and most successfully executed programs undertaken by the merchant marine. The cargo lift began a full year before the operation, and, by the month of the invasion, May 1944, 14,050,000 tons of dry cargo and 1,071,000 men had been transported on merchant ships.[94] Well over 1,000 American merchant seamen volunteered to take part in the landings off Normandy. When operations shifted to the Pacific, WSA ships again transported thousands of tons of war material and thousands of soldiers to support the operations that led to the conclusion of the war.

No discussion of the merchant marine can be complete without mention of Anglo-American collaboration. Before U.S. entry into the war, lack of coordination between the British and American shipping authorities created much friction. They exchanged information on shipping and cargo carried, but each retained the responsibilities of operating their own facilities. There was no formal agency through which either side could make its needs clear or address its grievances. British shipping authorities often accused American shipowners of "frivolously wasting" much-needed tonnage, and American shippers contended that the British were demanding far too much.

Early in 1942, Roosevelt and Churchill laid the foundation of an agreement through which the United States and Great Britain would coordinate their utilization of merchant shipping. In what was known as the White Paper, the British and Americans agreed to pool their shipping resources.[95] In February of that year, the Combined Shipping Adjustment Board was established, which set up a board in Great Britain headed by Sir Arthur Salter and one in the United States headed by Admiral Land. The main task of the CSAB was to eliminate any duplication or overlapping in the use of merchant shipping.[96] Shortly thereafter, it was agreed that the United States would be responsible for the shipping requirements in the Western Hemisphere, and Great Britain would be responsible for the remainder. The responsibility for Russian requirements would be shared, and the United States would retain control over shipping to Iceland and American possessions in the Pacific. Two shipping pools were established, with each ally understanding that the needs of its own army and navy would be given the greatest priority.

England had entered the war with the largest merchant fleet in the world, but in the two years before the United States was drawn into the conflict, British merchant losses were tremendous. England lost three thousand merchant vessels in the first two years of the war. In a letter to the head of the War Shipping Administration in 1942, Roosevelt wrote:

> In all probability, the British are going to lose again in 1943 more ships than they can build. If we are going to keep England in the war at anything like this maximum, we must consider the supplementing of their merchant fleet as one of the military necessities of the war. Naturally, the support of our forces in the Southwest Pacific and in Africa fall into the same category.[97]

English authorities gave the Americans much useful advice on the efficient use of shipping resources, for Americans had very little experience in the science of logistics. This lack of experience was plainly visible in American operations in the Pacific. United States Pacific theater commanders were known to be using ships as "floating warehouses" which was, in British eyes, extravagant at best and, at worst, harmful to the continued operations in the Atlantic where ships were still in very short supply. Severe bottlenecks often developed on both ends of the Pacific supply line, with queues of ships waiting in various ports to unload and to load.[98] In addition, commodities were often shipped to the Pacific where they could not be used at all, or were shipped in excessive amounts and had to be sent back. President Roosevelt eventually sent a message to the military commanders in the Pacific, insisting that they put an end to these practices.[99]

In spite of the many differences in opinion that arose between the United States and Great Britain about the utilization of merchant shipping, their joint efforts in nearly every military operation throughout the war revealed a highly successful degree of planning and organization. There is no question that the merchant fleet was a critical factor in the final success of Allied war efforts. Even before the United States itself entered the war, lend-lease goods shipped on U.S. merchant vessels helped supply Allied military operations and civilian populations. Merchant ships were also urgently needed to import the raw materials that supported American war production, including the construction of what would become the largest merchant fleet in the world.

The importance of keeping the sea lanes open for merchant shipping cannot be overestimated, and this was seen very clearly by the Germans. The U-boat campaign was undertaken with the sole aim of severing the Allied supply line which supported war production. The Germans themselves, although they had a large stockpile of raw materials and military goods, had no access to a significant overseas supply. The quick-conquest strategy of the German land army would, it was believed, offset this deficiency. By late in the war, both Germany and Japan were forced to face one of the fundamental reasons of their ultimate defeat. Their war reserves were nearly depleted, and their sea lanes were cut off by the Allies. Neither could prolong a multifront war without the material needed to sustain such a tremendous task. The crucial importance of the merchant marine to a nation's military efforts had been vividly illustrated to all who would heed the lesson.

A tribute to Admiral Land and the WSA was that the lesson had been studied and the role of the U.S. merchant marine intensified in the late 1930s before its true need was realized. Through visionary strategic planning and staunch leadership, Land outlined and implemented programs for ship construction and deployment which proved decisive in victory. From the inception of the emergency shipbuilding programs to their popularization, he had one overriding objective in his policy formulation: to avoid the repetition of the "mistakes of the last war and have a lot of obsolete vessels on our hands."[100] This objective was specified in a memorandum to the president in which Land warned, "If we don't watch our step the Merchant Marine will be the 'Forgotten Man' in the national defense picture."[101] Admiral Land assured that the U.S. merchant fleet would not be relegated to such an obscure position by his active role in the emergency expansion programs which, at one point, produced approximately fifty ships per year and which helped to keep U.S. supply lines open during the war.

Appraisal of Ship Operations

Today, as in World War II, it is imperative that the sea lanes be kept open for the importation of essential raw materials and the export of military goods to our allies. Even before the United States entered the fighting in World War II, her merchant fleet was playing a strong defensive role in support of England and other Allies in the form of "cash and carry" and lend-lease shipments. Early in the war, there were many more demands on U.S.-flag ships than they could meet. Even with the tremendously successful shipbuilding program in U.S. maritime yards, our merchant fleet was not large enough to meet the total needs for a two-ocean war. Thus a major policy question becomes, How effective was the utilization of the ships we had? We can only trust that the mistakes of the past will not be repeated in the future.

Summary and Overview

This chapter has discussed the contribution of U.S. shipbuilding and merchant marine industries to the Allied cause in World War II. Before the U.S. entry into the war in 1941, the administration had embarked on an emergency program to expand shipyards and start building ships in early 1941, almost a year before those events that made U.S. entrance unavoidable. By foregoing many of the consumer goods to which Americans had been accustomed, large supplies of labor, steel, and other materials were diverted to producing ships. There was an established industry of shipbuilders who were able to pass on what they knew to a vigorous group of men who were experienced in construction, although they had never built a ship in their lives. The United States quickly adopted a basic "no frills" ship design for series production, and wisely stuck to it without major change until over twenty-seven hundred ships were built. As a result, by the time that thirty Liberty Ships had been built on the same construction way, delivery time had fallen by a factor of ten and man-hours had decreased to a third of what was required for the first ship. To ensure that these technical achievements were met, the administration had wisely used contracts that attracted the new talent by guaranteeing cost plus a minimum fee, but in which the additional fee was contingent on efficient use of resources. Finally, it was seen that plans to arm the ships had not kept pace with their construction, that merchant sailors might have been given a greater share in defending their own ships, and that, in their zeal to carry the goods, logistic planners made some mistakes in deciding the quantities and types of goods to be shipped.

In World War II, the United States was confronted with an unprecedented situation: its enemies were on different continents separated from the United States by thousands of miles of ocean. This had profound implications for the type of war that had to be fought: massive sealift was the only way to bring the military forces to the enemy. The United States had carried its army across the Atlantic in World War I; in World War II, it had to provide enough merchant ships for action on two fronts, on opposite sides of the globe. Without ships, the United States would have been unable to provide the massive support to Europe that it did, and to support its advancing forces in the western Pacific at the same time. Without this support, it would have been merely a matter of time before England fell and Europe passed under Nazi rule. It was the large and growing merchant fleet that delivered U.S. ground forces and support to Europe and prevented the Nazi conquest of Europe. *That* is the significance of what the Allied merchant marine accomplished for the free world in 1939-45.

Notes

1. Frederic C. Lane, *Ships for Victory: A History of Shipbuilding under the U.S. Maritime Commission in World War II* (Baltimore, Md.: The Johns Hopkins Press, 1951), p. 21.
2. Gross tons measure a merchant ship's internal volume: one gross ton equals 100 cubic feet. It is often used as a rough measure of the volume of cargo the ship can carry, although net tonnage (gross tonnage less space for crew, propulsion machinery, etc.) is more precise. The weight of cargo a ship can carry is indicated by its deadweight tonnage, measured in long tons (2,240 pounds). Finally, there is the weight of the ship itself, its lightship displacement (the ship must displace water equal to its weight in order to float). We will have no occasion to use the full-load displacement, which includes the weight of the cargo as well.
3. Lane, op. cit., p. 21.
4. Ibid., p. 23.
5. Ibid., p. 24.
6. Ibid., pp. 40, 42.
7. Table IV of "Aircraft and Merchant Shipping in World War II with Indicated Trends," 7 October 1949, prepared by the Aviation History Unit (Op. 501-D), U.S. Office of Naval Operations. The figures are for ships 1,000 gross tons and over.
8. Lane, op. cit., p. 43.
9. Ibid., p. 74.
10. Ibid., pp. 77, 78.
11. Ibid., p. 66.
12. Ibid., p. 37.
13. Ibid., p. 51.
14. Ibid., p. 81.
15. Ibid.
16. Ibid., p. 51.
17. Ibid., p. 47.
18. Gerald J. Fischer, *A Statistical Summary of Shipbuilding under the U.S. Maritime Commission during World War II*, Historical Reports of War Administration, United States Maritime Commission, No. 2, 1949, Tables B-3 and B-4. These figures, as do most in this chapter, refer to production organized by the Maritime Commission. The commission's program included the production of all merchant ships, whether contracted for by the commission itself or by foreign governments and some private individuals, plus some military ships built for eventual use by the army and navy. Except where noted, we will ignore the construction in private and naval shipyards of those military vessels built under direct contracts with

the army and navy.
19. Quoted in Lane, op. cit., p. 471.
20. Ibid., p. 56.
21. Ibid., p. 57.
22. Ibid., pp. 60-61.
23. Ibid., p. 64 (see figure).
24. Ibid., p. 64.
25. Ibid., p. 138.
26. Fischer, op. cit., Table B-3.
27. Lane, op. cit., p. 260.
28. Ibid., p. 272.
29. Ibid., pp. 662-63.
30. Ibid., p. 274.
31. Ibid., p. 275.
32. Ibid., pp. 284-85.
33. Ibid., pp. 279, 280, 286.
34. Ibid., pp. 306-10.
35. Ibid., p. 307.
36. Ibid., p. 245.
37. Ibid., p. 246.
38. Fischer, op. cit., Tables C-1 and E-1, p. 94.
39. Lane, op. cit., p. 182.
40. Lane estimates (pp. 347-48) that with tighter inventory control, the amount of steel in the shipbuilding pipeline could have been reduced by perhaps 300,000 tons, enough to have built 120 more Liberty Ships.
41. Fischer, op. cit., Table C-1, p. 58.
42. Lane points out (p. 457) that "from 1941 until 1945 something like nine tenths by value of all shipbuilding awards were in price-minus contracts or manhour contracts, and were about equally divided between these two types. They both provided for the reimbursement of costs, and they fixed maximum and minimum fees which were intended to give incentives to speed and efficiency."
43. Fischer, op. cit., Table D-1, p. 83.
44. The measure is based on data in Table IV of "Aircraft and Merchant Shipping in World War II with Indicated Trends."
45. We have not determined how many ships in the "other Allied and neutral" category contributed to the Allied cause, either directly or indirectly (neutrals who carried essential nonwar goods between the Allied nations released Allied ships for direct war use).
46. Because friendly ships in the "other Allied and neutral" category have been omitted, the proportional reduction in shipping associated with this hypothetical case is overstated.

47. Emory Scott Land, *Winning the War with Ships: Land, Sea and Air —Mostly Land* (New York: Robert M. McBride Co., 1958), p. 192.

48. Report of the War Shipping Administrator to the President, *The United States Merchant Marine At War* (Washington, D.C., January 15, 1946), p. 55.

49. Samuel Eliot Morison, *The Battle of the Atlantic, September 1939-May 1943* (Boston: Little, Brown and Company, 1960), p. 192.

50. C. B. A. Behrens, *Merchant Shipping and the Demands of War* (London: Longmans, Green and Co., 1955), pp. 163-64.

51. Ibid., p. 170.

52. Ibid.

53. Felix Riesenberg, Jr., *Sea War: The Story of the U.S. Merchant Marine in World War II* (New York: Rinehart & Company, 1956), p. 153.

54. Land, op. cit., p. 193.

55. Riesenberg, op. cit., p. 152.

56. Land, op. cit., p. 197.

57. Morison, op. cit., p. 299.

58. Ibid., p. 374.

59. Land, op. cit., p. 204.

60. Morison, op. cit., pp. 298-99.

61. Ibid., p. 80.

62. "Arming of Merchant Ships," U.S. Naval Administration Histories of World War II, Office of Naval History (unpublished), p. 151.

63. Morison, op. cit., p. 301.

64. Ibid.

65. Land, op. cit., p. 203.

66. "Arming of Merchant Ships," p. 151.

67. Captain S. W. Roskill, *A Merchant Fleet in War—1939-1945* (London: Alfred Hold & Co., 1962), p. 175.

68. Morison, op. cit., p. 255.

69. Robert Greenhalgh Albion and Jennie Barnes Pope, *Sea Lanes in Wartime: The American Experience, 1775-1945* (New York: W. W. Norton & Co., 1968), p. 199.

70. Ibid., p. 212.

71. Ibid., p. 263.

72. Edward R. Stettinius, Jr., *Lend-Lease: Weapon for Victory* (New York: The Macmillan Company, 1944), p. 4.

73. Committee of Records of War Administration by the War Records Section, Bureau of the Budget, *The United States at War, Development and Administration of the War Program by the Federal Government* (Washington, D.C.: Government Printing Office, 1951), p. 47.

74. Stettinius, op. cit., p. 89.

75. Behrens, op. cit., pp. 297-309.
76. Stettinius, op. cit., p. 97.
77. Albion and Pope, op. cit., p. 297.
78. Morison, op. cit., p. 161.
79. Ibid., p. 159.
80. Behrens, op. cit., p. 235.
81. Albion and Pope, op. cit., pp. 340-41.
82. *U.S. Merchant Marine at War*, p. 13.
83. Ibid., p. 14.
84. Albion and Pope, op. cit., p. 339.
85. *U.S. Merchant Marine at War*, p. 9.
86. Albion and Pope, op. cit., p. 289.
87. *U.S. Merchant Marine at War*, p. 18.
88. Albion and Pope, op. cit., pp. 296-97.
89. *U.S. Merchant Marine at War*, p. 18.
90. *United States at War*, p. 148.
91. Land, op. cit., p. 165.
92. Behrens, op. cit., p. 287.
93. Albion and Pope, op. cit., p. 369.
94. Ibid., p. 358.
95. Behrens, op. cit., pp. 287-88.
96. Ibid., p. 389.
97. Land, op. cit., p. 221.
98. Behrens, op. cit., p. 415.
99. Ibid.
100. Land, op. cit., p. 44.
101. Ibid.

7
American Maritime Power since World War II
Clark G. Reynolds

The United States emerged from World War II as the world's dominant military and economic power. Its political and economic system provided the model and standard for war-ravaged and developing nations. The nation became the hub of a great wheel of international commerce, its spokes the trade routes and hulls of international shipping. As a result of the collapse of the traditional empires of its European Allies and the defeat of the authoritarian regimes of its foes, Japan and Germany, the United States reluctantly found itself bearing the responsibility of insuring its own political, ideological, and economic stability and health by playing this dominant role. This required the restoration of the economies of Allied nations, the revitalization of former enemy countrites, and the establishment of a new order of international law based on an interchange of trade and commerce.

The international system that was established after World War II depended upon the ability of American military might to enforce its tenets. As the USSR with its closed political and economic system emerged as the major postwar counterweight to American supremacy in the late 1940s, the United States developed an increasingly effective nuclear deterrent capability and in considerable measure restored its conventional naval and amphibious forces to police the sea lanes of the world. The devastation caused by the war in Europe and Asia, the necessity for a stable international market for normal trade, and the accelerating demand for energy resources, especially oil, have combined since the 1940s to make nations everywhere economically interdependent. This interdependency was furthered by advances in technology and the growth of trade, and by the development of alliance systems as well as regional and international organizations. The nation was inspired by confidence in the new international order symbolized by the United Nations and by an accompanying belief that peace and stability were best assured by fostering the independence and well being of other nations.

The United States provided the immediate impetus for worldwide economic recovery through the Marshall Plan and other aid programs, and in merchant shipping through the Merchant Ship Sales Act of 1946. The nation's shipbuilding and shipping companies provided both the nucleus of American maritime activity and the qualitative model for maritime industries throughout the world.

With a war-developed merchant marine larger than those of all other nations combined, the United States sought, in a charitable sense which later boomeranged to plague it, to restore competition on the high seas. As one American writer said in 1945, the peace of the postwar world depended upon the creation of wealth and its distribution "through the unfettered channels of trade rather than by imperial preferences, by conquest or by international brigandry."[1] That this decision succeeded was borne out by the fact that American-flag shipping lines soon found themselves competing with nationalized foreign competitors and with lower-cost private foreign companies.

Although most American maritime shipowners again fled the American flag to foreign registries for the same prewar reasons— such as lower operating and acquisition costs, greater operating flexibility, and tax advantages—and the remainder retained American registry under the partial security of the construction and operating subsidies offered by the Merchant Marine Act of 1936 and/or trade preference policies, the financial hub of the shipping wheel has remained fixed in the United States. American citizens have owned and operated the majority of the foreign-flag registered vessels; kept their offices in the United States; shipped American goods; carried the American political, economic, and social gospel abroad; and pledged themselves to their country's defense in any national emergency. But the national objective of a shipping and shipbuilding capability under absolute U.S. sovereignty has not thereby been sustained.

Although many American shipping companies returned to prewar British or other European registries, after the war most of the others kept their convenient wartime Panamanian registrations or went to those of Honduras or Venezuela, but mostly to Liberia. The story of the International Trust Company of Liberia, formed between 1945 and 1948 by former Secretary of State Edward R. Stettinius, Jr., in an effort to keep Middle Eastern oil flowing to the United States, illustrates this development. The New York–based company, by virtue of its foreign registration, obtained exemption from paying substantial U.S. taxes and the high wages demanded by American maritime unions as well as exemption from observance of U.S. Coast Guard inspection and safety regulations. Thus, the company was able to realize large profits. Almost three decades after the company's first Liberian-registered ship, the Greek-owned tanker *World Peace*, sailed in 1949, over 80 percent of the company's stock was owned by the International Bank of Washington, D.C.[2]

In another respect, the United States has provided the qualitative standards by which other countries have operated. The American Bureau of Shipping (ABS), headquartered in New York, has continued as a major insurance classifier of world vessels.[3] American technological and managerial innovations triumphed so successfully that the other advanced nations, notably the Soviet Union, imitated them outright. Less-responsible flags of convenience, in many cases, simply gave up trying to meet the high safety, inspection, and antipollution standards set by the American-flag industry and continued to operate shipping fleets of inferior quality.

The continuing economic restoration of other nations and the expansionist drive of the Soviet Union, as it regained its internal strength, also combined to establish the pattern of erosion of U.S. dominance in the later decades of this period. Even the growing interdependence of nations placed limits on the behavior of the superpowers and complicated the solution of international problems in a world that faced increasing aspirations for national independence and economic development, as well as for a more equitable sharing of resources and benefits.

The Cold War

The two decades between the mid-1940s and the mid-1960s are generally regarded as the postwar, or Cold War, era, during which time major, strategic power realignments took place. Although both superpowers could expand and compete only by concentrating economic and political power and controls at the expense of some of their loftiest ideals, the bipolarity which resulted was a fairly predictable one. Just as World War II finally terminated the Depression and brought prosperity to the maritime as well as other industries, so too did the centralization of power in the Cold War era sustain high government spending to meet military requirements. An active defense role insured survival for the maritime industry.

During the summer months of 1945, between V-E Day and V-J Day, the U.S. government published a shipping demobilization study developed for the navy and the Maritime Commission by the Harvard Business School. It concluded, "The controlling factor in the determination of the characteristics of shipping and shipbuilding activities in the United States in peacetime as well as in wartime is the national security." Of secondary but still vital importance was national prosperity.[4] National security was then understood to mean the ability to move wartime goods essential to the nation's economy as well as the logistical sealift capability to deploy and support forces in overseas areas. This combined requirement was strengthened as American illusions of postwar tranquility were shattered. But the frustrating experiences of overseas deployment and the Korean War distracted American concern that the U.S. merchant marine was declining in its capabilities to perform such functions. Relatively unimpeded trends in the erosion of the carriage of U.S. foreign trade by U.S.-flag ships were not linked in the public mind to this security implication as the emphasis on détente and coexistence gained strength—the public seemed to take for granted the continued availability of essential U.S.

shipping and shipbuilding capabilities, regardless of the nature of future emergencies and conflicts.

National defense in the period 1945-65 revolved generally around the nuclear dimension, thus making the contribution of the maritime community, including the navy, seem miniscule. Nothing could have been farther from the truth, for the growing global commitments of the United States led to military emergencies that required conventional transportation by sea—the Korean War (1950-53); the Suez and Lebanon crises (1956-57); the Cuban blockade (1962); and the first stages of the Vietnam War (1961-65).

For all these emergencies, the government relied totally on the vessels of its Military Sea Transportation Service (MSTS) and the 1,400 mothballed World War II cargo ships and tankers of the National Defense Reserve Fleet (NDRF) in eight anchorages, backed up by whatever the privately owned merchant marine could provide, as well as chartered foreign-flag carriers operated by U.S. owners. These ships were augmented by occasional new construction such as thirty-five Mariner-class cargo ships built during the early 1950s at considerable expense to the government. In March 1951, the government established the National Shipping Authority within the Commerce Department to meet the Korean emergency and the next year vested central operational control in the commander of MSTS, a navy vice admiral. The nation met each crisis successfully but in each instance wore out more of the World War II ship inventory. Over 500 mothballed vessels were employed in Korea; about 175 in Vietnam.

As for bulk carriers, the government considered the PanLibHon (Panama, Liberia, Honduras) flag vessels to be under "effective U.S. control" in a major emergency, but the flag-of-convenience concept came under severe attack by traditional shipowners and maritime unions between 1957 and 1965. The "convenience" concept survived, although reliance upon it for defense purposes began to raise questions about the dependability of the PanLibHon companies in a crisis. The postwar (1945-65) seaborne logistical capability proved adequate, but it left no assurances—and nearly no ships—for the future.[5] Maritime America stumbled along, looking for solutions to seemingly eternal problems.

The unique problems of the industry were reflected in the industries' difficult management-labor relations.[6] Maritime management—through such organizations as the East Coast thirty-seven-company, 450-ship American Merchant Marine Institute (AMMI) and the Committee of American Steamship Lines (CASL) founded in 1953—struggled with the maritime unions. Both sides, in the postwar years, simply refused to communicate or compromise with each other. The government, bound only to insure that 75 percent of all American-flag crews be American citizens (which implied that they be paid on the American wage scale), remained unresponsive except to issue strike-halting injunctions under the Taft-Hartley Act of 1947. Its interventions as mediator were only to seek a swift solution and usually ended with management backing down, the industry suffering thereby. Finally, the unions themselves continued to fragment and wage internecine battles in the same manner as before the war.

The vigorous National Maritime Union of America (NMU), of unlicensed seamen on subsidized company ships, and the less-vocal Seafarers' International Union of North America (SIU) with its related Atlantic and Gulf District (A&G) and Sailor's Union of the Pacific (SUP), of seamen on subsidized and nonsubsidized ships, continued battling in the postwar world, though neither embraced prewar radical sympathies after 1948 when the far left-wing factions were driven out. The International Longshoremen's Union (ILU) continued to represent the dockside workers and, in the 1950s, pressed its militancy on the licensed deck officers' society, the International Organization of Masters, Mates, and Pilots (MMP), for joint action. Merchant ship engineers began to drift away from the Marine Engineers' Beneficial Association (MEBA) to the Brotherhood of Marine Engineers (BME), which was formed in 1949 as a direct challenge by the SIU but which, eight years later, merged with MEBA as the latter allied with SIU during a dispute over coal exports.

Unintentionally, the United States provided the most advanced maritime technology in the postwar world; its technological base had survived intact where others had not. Whether leading in technical progress through the research laboratories of the international ABS or the nationally directed Maritime Research Advisory Committee of the National Academy of Sciences and National Research Council (MRAC), American-based naval architects and research engineers led postwar developments in ship design and improved component parts. A dramatic advance, for example, came in 1958 when the Matson Navigation Company introduced mathematical simulation using computers to improve ship design; working through the above MRAC, Matson convinced the Maritime Administration (Marad) to undertake in 1960-61 a broad study in operation research for better merchant ships.

Change came slowly, however, because a technological plateau of merchant ship size and capability had been reached in the wartime oil-driven breakbulk carrier and tanker, with nuclear propulsion only remotely suggesting a possible alternate system. The wartime-built Victorys and C-2, C-3, and C-4 cargo ships with dry-cargo capacities of 10,000-15,000 deadweight tons comprised the postwar American-flag fleet, while the wartime 16,500-ton T-2 tankers carried the nation's oil until augmented by 25,000-35,000 deadweight-ton tankers in the late 1940s. The government funded construction of an experimental freighter, *Schuyler Otis Bland*, during the late 1940s and incorporated many of its features into the new Mariners. In 1952, the new passenger liner *United States* became a showpiece for the nation as it pushed shipbuilding technology to an upper limit of 52,000 tons and to record speeds in excess of thirty-five knots, comparable to the navy's newest aircraft carriers. Not unexpectedly, recovering foreign shipbuilders began to construct or design much larger and thus more competitive hulls, especially utilizing direct-drive diesel engines (with three times the prewar horsepower, now up to 25,000) and, later, gas turbines.

In this climate of advancement and competition, the United States, in 1956, undertook the construction and operation of the world's first nuclear-powered merchant ship, *Savannah*, to develop a possible new propulsion system. Launched in 1959 and operated during the 1960s for the Maritime Administration by States Marine Lines and then American Export Lines, she proved to be an excellent teacher in the field but—as understood from the outset—economic considerations and continuing uncertainties concerning radiation and related environmental dangers made her an evolutionary dead end for the postwar era and a questionable alternative for merchant-ship design technology— at least before the 1980s.[7]

Return to Traditional Supports

This entire period of postwar generosity on the part of the U.S. government further affected—adversely it might be claimed —the American shipping industry by the Merchant Ship Sales Act of 1946, which allowed the disposal of most of the U.S. wartime fleet by sale at small fractions of their original cost to foreign buyers (except in Germany and Japan) through 1948 and to American citizens until 1951. The final number sold was 1,113 hulls to foreigners, 843 to Americans.[8] The sales to warprostrated nations helped considerably to restore their economies, and, since the vessels had been classed according to ABS specifications, the New York-based bureau retained an almostexclusive qualitative control over worldwide shipbuilding, especially as American businesses began to contract for ships in foreign yards and under foreign registries for international and transoceanic trade.

During 1952-77, American companies, or their affiliates, have had nearly 2,000 merchant ships built in foreign shipyards. In the same period of time, American shipyards have constructed only 600 merchant vessels—less than one-third of the number built abroad. In 1977, American companies ordered 13 vessels from U.S. shipyards but almost twice that number— 25 in all—from Japanese shipyards. This unbalanced trend, extending over a quarter of a century, has hardly contributed to a strengthening of a shipbuilding industrial base which historically has been regarded am essential for national security. By 1962, the number and tonnage of vessels in class with ABS reached a record 8,221 vessels totaling over 46,500,000 gross tons. By the beginning of 1978, this figure reached 14,884 ships and passed the one hundred million mark at 102,000,000 gross tons or 183,000,000-plus deadweight tons.[9]

This veritable explosion of worldwide shipping under cheaper non-U.S. registry created a new global situation relative to maritime competition. In short, private companies were being replaced as the real competitors by national flags, a situation not unlike that of the several national joint-stock companies of Holland, England, and France during the seventeenth century. Multinational corporations and conglomerates became identified with national flags whose nations set their own rules and regulations, thereby affecting cost and tax structures. Consequently, national merchant marines—like those of the Soviet Union—or the flags of convenience—like Panama, Liberia, or Honduras—build at lower costs and sailed with lower rates. By 1960, Panama alone registered more than one thousand vessels, aggregating over 11 million deadweight tons.[10]

This development, dating from the late 1940s, left the United States, with its high standards of safety and design, unprepared to compete in the world market without returning to its prewar subsidy practices. Thus, for the twenty years after World War II, the government and maritime industry reinforced five time-honored safeguards.

1. Construction Differential Subsidies (CDS). As before, federal law required that all American-flag vessels receiving operating differential subsidies be built in the United States, which meant at roughly twice the cost of foreign shipbuilding. The American shipbuilding industry, always plagued by low peacetime demands, welcomed the Merchant Ship Sales Act of 1946 as a potential stimulus for ship construction and repair. The reduction of the wartime merchant fleet to a fraction in peacetime meant more repair than construction, and the labor-intensive skilled workmanship required in the shipyards proved too costly in the world market. So private investors, mostly commercial banks, had to be encouraged to invest in shipbuilding—to pay the unsubsidized half of the cost of the vessel. This was accordingly strengthened by new guarantees in an amendment to Title XI in 1954, while the Long Range Shipping Act of 1952 allowed construction subsidies for bulk carriers and tramps.[11] In addition, the government established a policy of "trade in and build" whereby the Department of Commerce bought up prewar vessels on the condition that the owners

would build replacements in American yards. Nevertheless, American merchant ship construction remained low throughout the period.

The Merchant Marine Act of 1970 was more visionary. It authorized construction in U.S. shipyards of three hundred merchant ships over a ten-year period for operation in U.S. foreign trade starting in 1971, extended construction assistance to bulk carriers, broadened the scope of capital construction funds (a tax-deferred mechanism to encourage U.S. ship construction), and mandated a declining level of CDS supports to 35 percent by 1976 and thereafter. Until the Middle East oil embargo of 1973 and the consequent worldwide shipping recession, these objectives were moving on schedule toward attainment. With the decreasing demand for ships in the United States and abroad, however, new orders became ever more scarce. An increasing number of shipyards began chasing a shrinking market. Bargain, below-cost prices were offered by many foreign shipbuilders in an effort to stay alive. The net result was that the declining CDS rate abruptly reversed itself and soon exceeded the statutory 50-percent ceiling. At the two-thirds mark of the planned ten-year shipbuilding program of three hundred ships, less than seventy-five vessels had been ordered from American shipbuilders.

2. Operating Differential Subsidies (ODS). As in the past, the law obliged the shipping lines to employ mostly American citizens, and, with the success of the unions in raising the standards of American seamen to the highest in the world, operating costs increased significantly. So, the ODS was perpetuated in order to equalize American carrier operating costs along the thirty or so "essential" trade routes, which meant U.S. ships operated at as much as 75-percent higher costs than foreign vessels, with 84 percent of the subsidy going into crew wages.[12] Federal regulations have helped the industry overall but also have promoted rigidity. Indeed, several shipping lines chose to remain nonsubsidized, risky as this may have been for some. Still, in all, the ODS was not as seriously contested as it might have been throughout the period, since the fleet did not carry enough of America's foreign trade to pose a serious threat to competitors.[13]

This unique status has continued uninterrupted since the end of World War II, requiring federal regulation. The War Shipping Administration came to an end in 1946 in favor of the Maritime Commission, it being replaced in 1950 by the Federal Maritime Board and the Maritime Administration; the former to regulate the industry, the later to promote it under the Department of Commerce. Included in the act of 1970 were a number of changes in the ODS program. The most important was in extending operating subsidies to bulk carriers. Other changes concerned the manner in which subsidy payments were calculated. Prior to the act, the Maritime Administration paid subsidized U.S.-flag operators the difference between the higher wages of their American officers and crew and the lower wages paid by their foreign competitors. Several deficiencies with this system emerged; most noteworthy was that it gave the operators little incentive to bargain aggressively with the maritime unions during wage negotiations. Therefore, an index system was developed for use as a standard to judge fair and reasonable wage costs. Other changes made in 1970 included an end to the subsidy for subsistence and a removal of the so-called recapture provisions for excess profits.

3. Antitrust exemption and the conference system. In a protected industry since 1916, shipping companies continued to enjoy the privilege of combining in shipping conferences to fix uniform rates and charges and to file common tariffs—with the approval of the Federal Maritime Board. The unscheduled American-flag tramp steamer had virtually disappeared during the war, leaving only the scheduled liners and private carriers (mostly oil companies), which continued to be governed by the conference system. The belief persisted, in the Congress and out, that the system not only prevented cutthroat competition and rate wars (as well as outright monopoly) but that it also preserved the very existence of the merchant marine. During this period, for example, the key North Atlantic conference system was a loose association of twenty-five flag carriers and thus not a threat to international or American traders; indeed, it seemed to be a healthy guarantor of U.S. trade. Nevertheless, by 1961, the Congress had detected at least 240 possible violations of the 1916 law governing American shippers in the con-

ferences and reacted by amending the original act to replace the inept Federal Maritime Board (FMB) with the Federal Maritime Commission (FMC). Though a strengthened body designed to thwart discriminatory rate-setting practices, the FMC was given practically no rate-making powers per se. But it did help to streamline American participation in the conferences.[14]

4. Cargo preferences. Title IX of the 1936 act continued to insure the availability of cargoes for nonsubsidized American lines and was strengthened by a cargo-preference amendment law to Title IX in 1954. Together, these laws guaranteed the shipment by American-flag carriers of a percentage of all military cargo and at least one-half of remaining government cargoes such as foreign military and economic aid, mail, and cargoes originating from Export-Import Bank loans. With the redeployment of expanded American military forces throughout the world to "fight" the cold war and with huge outlays of foreign economic aid through the Marshall Plan and other programs, the government guaranteed American-flag vessels—particularly nonsubsidized ones—ample business. By 1962, in fact, almost two-thirds of the total outbound U.S. tonnage and three-fourths of the cargoes were preferred, but at a total cost of $3 billion to $5 billion to the taxpayers between 1952 and 1972, or about twice as much money to ship preferred cargoes in American bottoms.[15] This led to such crises as the stoppage of wheat sales to the Soviet Union in 1963-64 when profit-conscious grain dealers tried to circumvent the law by shipping in foreign-flag vessels. The unions protested, and President John F. Kennedy appointed a Maritime Advisory Committee to assist him. Still, the United States could not compete with foreign shippers in the renewed wheat sales in 1965 "because of the requirement that half of such sales be shipped in U.S. bottoms when available."[16] And, as long as foreign countries depended on U.S. postwar recovery, they looked with disfavor on this monopolistic American cargo practice. But it did benefit the U.S. merchant marine during the otherwise lean Cold War years.[17]

5. Cabotage. Virtually all maritime nations of the world grant some form of direct or de facto aid or protection to their domestic shipping. Among forty-nine nations whose regulations

and promotion of domestic shipping are matters of defined public policy, twenty-six restrict their cabotage to ships of the national flag. Since its beginnings, the United States has based its policy of reserving intracoastal and intercoastal trade (cabotage) to U.S.-flag, U.S.-built ships on this overriding principle: a strong and adequate merchant marine must be promoted and maintained for economic and national security reasons and the domestic shipping fleet must always be promoted and maintained as the nucleus for expansion in times of emergency. The soundness of this principle has been repeatedly reaffirmed by the Congress. It was appropriately demonstrated at the start of World War II. Even so, there have been frequent attempts to repeal or dilute Section 27 of the Merchant Marine Act of 1920 (the Jones Act) to permit the operation of foreign ships in U.S. domestic waters, but these have been consistently rejected by the Congress. There have been few exceptions, and these have been minor in character.

Despite these incentives designed, in total, to put American-flag merchant shipping on a parity footing with foreign competitors, the industry suffered a slow, steady decline in size during the twenty years after World War II. The wartime government charters fell off from fifteen hundred in 1947 to fewer than one hundred three years later. Between 1950 and 1960, worldwide merchant tonnage grew from about 85 million to 130 million gross tons, while that of the U.S. fleet declined from 28 million (32½ percent) to 25 million (19 percent); by 1970, the figures had widened to 228 million, versus 13 million (6 percent). The amount of cargo carried declined in a similar fashion.[18] The coastal shipping trade never really recovered from the war years, nor did the passenger liner service. Both declined markedly, due to competition from railroads, trucks, and commercial airliners. But the inland waterways and the Great Lakes—particularly after the opening of the St. Lawrence Seaway in 1959—not only survived intact but burgeoned with prosperity, becoming the brightest lights in the generally dismal picture of the American-flag maritime industry.[19]

A long-term concern of the government lay in a ship-replacement policy for the 843 World War II–built vessels of the merchant marine which would reach block obsolescence in the early

1960s. Since a massive replacement program would therefore stimulate the shipbuilding industry, the government and subsidized lines in 1956 initiated the Ship Replacement Program— a plan whereby the three-hundred-plus general cargo ships of the fifteen subsidized lines would be gradually replaced by new construction over the ensuing fifteen years. Among them, three companies would each replace between forty-three and fifty-three vessels: Lykes Brothers Steamship, United States Lines, and Moore-McCormack Lines. By spreading the work over time, skilled shipbuilding labor would be steadily employed. By the early 1960s, many new ships were coming off the ways, but, regrettably, little attention was given to optimum design and opportunities for shipbuilding cost reductions through repetitive construction of nearly identical designs, such as was followed with the Mariner class ships. Basically inadequate break-bulk designs of the recent past continued to be built.[20]

In fact, for the ten years following the initiation of the Ship Replacement Program, the United States steadily lost the majority of its most valuable types of cargo to foreign competition, America's market share of liner cargoes dropping from almost 38 percent in 1956 to 22 percent in 1966. The trend was obvious to all concerned, particularly to some of the nonsubsidized lines which were obliged to seek an independent solution to their own aging World War II-vintage fleets. These lines looked to modern technology and developments abroad to find alternative solutions.[21] Sea-Land Service, Matson Navigation, and the Maritime Transportation Research Board of the National Academy of Sciences took the lead in 1959 by using computers for mathematical simulation to prove the feasibility of containerization, an experiment tried on a small basis by a few lines since 1950. The idea of preloaded, sealed cargo container boxes appealed to the subsidized Grace Lines in 1960, but its initial efforts that year were frustrated by the usual rigid government regulations, objections by job-sensitive unionized stevedores, reluctance by the steamship conferences to concur, shipper apathy, technological problems, and the sheer expense of new specialized equipment. So Grace quit its one foray into employing containerships almost immediately, and a bureaucracy-burdened federal government, already com-

American Maritime Power since World War II

mitted to subsidies for tried and true breakbulk carriers, ceased its encouragement of this innovation for the first half of the 1960s.[22]

As the fortunes of the industry continued to decline, however, independent-minded nonsubsidized lines finally, at mid-decade, took the plunge for all-out containerization. The result was a sweeping revolution throughout the maritime industry on a global scale.

The Age of Détente

The postwar/Cold War era gave way to the age of détente with greater power diffusion, intensified economic competition, accelerated advances in science and technology, and the turbulent transitional deacde of the 1960s. In 1961, the FMB was replaced by a stronger FMC, and the Maritime Administration was enlarged to direct the building and subsidy programs. The block obsolescence of merchant ships (like naval vessels), with their twenty-year life spans in the 1960s, required substantial capital outlays by the government for ship replacement construction.

The Cuban missile crisis of 1962 served to alert the superpowers about the need to reduce the risks of nuclear war, while the landing of the first human beings on the surface of the moon in 1969 symbolized a revolutionary new era of advanced science and technology. Leadership was increasingly assumed by technocrats—engineers, naval architects, inventors, financial experts, and managers. The traditional leaders—politicians, businessmen, and labor chiefs—no longer able to resolve challenges by traditional means, came closer together rather than remain divided over their archaic quarrels.

Innovative American corporate leaders realized that cargo and the handling of cargo were the key to ship design, and thus they promoted the containership which brought the worldwide maritime industry into the age of advanced technology. The nonsubsidized Sea-Land Service, founded by Malcom P. McLean, successfully engineered the containership revolution. As early as 1956, he had pioneered this revolutionary water transportation concept between the Gulf Coast and New York, expanded his operations while protected by cabotage laws, and, following Matson's and Marad's studies, took his containerships into the North Atlantic foreign trade in 1966. Simple and efficient, these vessels appeared at the right moment in the history of maritime technology and immediately swept the global industry, making the sea an extension of land transportation.[23]

The containership in one fell swoop brought about the first standardization in history of several modes of transporting goods—the intermodal carrying of cargo in the same large containers on ships, railroads, and trucks. But on international trade routes the ship remained the key, and as early as 1970 observers of the industry could declare that the goal of the American merchant marine should be "to provide the basis of an integrated international intermodal system with significant benefits in improved services and lower through costs."[24] This meant, by 1975, that containerships capable of carrying the equivalent of 2000 twenty-foot-long boxes stacked in the hold and on deck were crossing the North Atlantic at a very swift thirty-plus knots to unload and load at specially constructed port facilities with large special cranes and other loading gear at a rate of one thousand tons per berth hour over the previous 60 tons of breakbulk time. The much-enlarged capacity and speed, increased efficiency, and cargo safety of the containership (pilferage of sealed boxes being extremely difficult) made the breakbulk carrier obsolete overnight in the transportation of large bulk commodities.[25]

The containership was not an isolated technological event. Technocrats, American and foreign, designed and produced a dazzling array of revolutionary ship types from the mid-1960s on. The LASH (lighter aboard ship) and SeaBee (sea barge) vessels were developed in the United States as modified containership designs for carrying up to eighty-nine 500-ton loaded barges for coastal, shallow-water, and river traffic, enlarging the intermodal concept. In 1970, two Japanese-built, Norwegian-registered LASH ships each displaced over 43,500 tons and carried seventy-three lighters which in turn each contained 27,000 tons of cargo.[26] Lighters and barges towed up inland waterways to inland points are a challenge to more expensive trains and trucks; "LASH and SeaBee types have the

potential for a transportation revolution comparable to [the]
... 'container revolution'."[27] The Ro/Ro (roll on, roll off) ship
for trucks and trailers began with the U.S.-designed *Comet* and
soon developed into a new and efficient intermodal carrier. Toward the end of the 1970s, these four new intermodel ships were transporting some 400,000 containers. In addition, new large bulk carriers had appeared on the Great Lakes capable of loads of 40,000 to 50,000 tons.[28]

The revolution in ship architecture extended as well to fuel carriers. The super-sized oil tanker appeared, quickly doubling and tripling from the 35,000 deadweight tonnage of the 1950s to the VLCC (very large crude carrier) of 200,000-plus tons in the late 1960s and the ULCC (ultra large crude carrier) of over double that size during the 1970s. The LNG (liquified natural gas) carrier, after an experimental start in 1947, matured rapidly thirty years later; the first large American-built carrier, the 63,000-deadweight-ton (125,000 cubic meters) *LNG Aquarius*, went to sea in 1977, and the first LNG receiving terminal, in the Chesapeake Bay at Cove Point, Maryland, began operation in May 1978. Additionally, ship design experimentation, under the auspices of the navy, has grown concurrently with the development of small hydrofoil vessels and surface effect ships. Through it all, the level of automation in all ship types has been demonstrably improved.[29]

This momentous technological upheaval did not occur in a vacuum. The most pressing stimulus was the impending energy crisis of expanding Western and global industrialization. The world needed oil and natural gas. It needed foodstuffs and manufactures. And it needed them all rapidly and efficiently. Vestiges of Cold War rivalry were ever present, as when the Arab-Israeli War of 1967 closed the Suez Canal for several years and forced naval architects to design longer-range supertankers, as did an undersized Panama Canal. Scientific innovations enhanced oceanic operations and transistorized and computerized internal components; with navigation, communications, and meteorological satellites (the first of twenty-four projected NAVSTAR satellites for extremely accurate navigating went into orbit in February 1978); and with a spectrum of aerospace spinoffs applicable to ship technology.

Rampant technological-industrial expansion, however, created its own dangers, notably in terms of the fragile natural ecosystems of the planet; those in and near the sea were not among the least of those affected. Oil spillage has been a major, if not the worst, polluter, and tankers flushing tanks at sea, often illegally close to the shore, have only invited severe national and international regulation. Tanker disasters, though causing perhaps only 15 percent of the spillage, have been the most dramatic offenders. The Liberian-registered, Italian-crewed, and American-owned (by the same company) tankers *Torrey Canyon* and *Sansinena* made shocking headlines; the former breaking up on a reef in the English Channel and releasing 119,000 tons of crude oil in March 1967, the latter vessel blowing up in Los Angeles harbor in December 1976. The 40,000-ton *Argo Merchant* broke up off Cape Cod that very same month, unleashing 7.5 million gallons of oil. Foreign owned (by a subsidiary of Standard Oil of Indiana), the 233,000-ton supertanker *Amoco Cadiz* lost a third of its 68,000,000 gallons of crude oil when it ran aground off Brest in France in March 1978.[30] Toxic chemical spills, the transport of liquified natural gas, offshore seabed mining and drilling, and overfishing also pose potential dangers.

U.S. Initiative on the International Scene

As technological progress and potentially negative side effects have pointed the way to the future, the multifaceted American society has reacted at the three major levels—internationally, domestically, and intrinsically.

The international response has begun with a goal of stabilization and control of the technologically advanced, capital-intensive maritime environment. Stabilization is viewed by advocates as necessary for various reasons: the need for tightly regulated schedules to make container transfers between oceangoing ships and land vehicles during the rapid "turnaround time"; the economic dislocations caused by predatory rate-setting practices of the Soviet merchant marine; the downturn in worldwide ship construction after the peak year of 1975; and the necessity of preventing oil spills and other ship-related pollution.

These developments since the mid-1960s have produced changes in the conference systems pertaining to ocean shipping, especially in the previously loose twenty-five-member North Atlantic system. Beginning in 1968, this amalgamation became stronger, more stabilizing, and more controlling with respect to rates, practices, cargo regulations, and classifications. A common administrative machinery was formalized as the Associated North Atlantic Freight Conferences (ANAFC) in 1972, for the purpose of enforcing the rate structure of the constituent conferences with a common policing unit.[31]

This momentum contributed to the overproduction of containerships and especially of oil tankers. Unprepared for the 1973-74 rise in oil prices and the ensuing worldwide economic convulsions, the world's merchant fleet, which had more than doubled from 217,200,000 deadweight tons in 1965 to 556,600,000 deadweight tons in 1975, found itself without sufficient cargoes in the late 1970s. By mid-1978, more than 100 million tons of oil tankers were clearly excess to the requirements of the trade. The immediate response of the European and Japanese shipping leaders has been to turn to cartelization on a grand scale and extensive governmental supports for both shipping and the shipbuilding market, with a resultant controlled reduction in shipping. The lower rates of the Soviet merchant fleets, as suggested before, have also exacerbated the problem. Although the Russians held conversations with other nations and entered bilateral maritime agreements with the United States in 1972 and 1975, these agreements did nothing to stop predatory Soviet maritime practices. International shipping cartelization, the practice of replacing private companies by national flags, resulted in a trend toward bilateral trade agreements between nations. These, and the independent course of the Soviet Union, indicate the need for a motion toward more bilateral shipping arrangements as a firm foundation for an effective national maritime policy. This is not only overdue, but absolutely imperative if the United States is to exert influential leverage in world shipping and shipbuilding affairs.

In April 1961, the Intergovernmental Maritime Consultative Organization (IMCO), which had been founded in 1959 as a specialized agency of the United Nations, formed a subcommittee on Subdivision and Stability Problems. It undertook to formulate subdivision standards based upon probability studies and to examine critically the Safety of Life at Sea Convention, SOLAS 1960.

A growing realization among maritime nations of the dangers of unsymmetrical flooding had led to the convening of an international conference in 1948 from which SOLAS 1948 was developed. As the conference was dominated by the victors of World War II, the Big Five, progress was quick. SOLAS 1948 defined the heel allowable under conditions of one- and two-compartment flooding, but did not completely satisfy the U.S. delegation. A major disagreement was the difference between calculated stability and stability conditions that might arise as a result of practical operations by seamen. The concerns of the U.S. delegation proved correct.

Bad luck again influenced subsequent events when, in July 1956, rapid flooding of empty fuel-oil wing tanks, following a collision at sea, caused the *Andrea Doria* to capsize and sink. The U.S. House of Representatives Committee on Merchant Marine and Fisheries investigated the incident and called for a reappraisal of SOLAS 1948. As a result, another conference was convened in 1960. Even with clear indications that the 1948 position was deficient, agreement on major changes was elusive. However, a convention recommendation was adopted, at U.S. urging, for continued study of passenger-ship subdivision and stability.

While most of the attention in the field of stability to that point had been focused on passenger and passenger cargo ships, technological changes affecting other vessels were proceeding apace. Tankers were undergoing changes in design which increased their size rapidly and altered their damage stability characteristics. The Load Line Convention (1966), which came into effect in mid-1968, introduced international damage-condition stability standards for cargo vessels and tank ships for the first time. Then-existing tankers were found to have a high degree of safety, but the changes incorporated by virtue of the convention were needed to cope with the larger oil tankers and the bulk and bulk/ore carriers which were being built in increasing numbers.

The closing of the Suez Canal in 1967 accelerated the pace of change in tanker design. Serious concerns arose about the possibility of tankers capsizing if damaged. The *Torrey Canyon* disaster, in 1967, spurred efforts to regulate pollution and resulted in the first steps toward establishing international standards of tanker design and construction. An international conference produced an International Convention for the Prevention of Pollution from Ships, 1973. It contained requirements for segregated ballast tanks, limited tank sizes, and regulated subdivision and stability.[32]

The United States Ports and Waterways Safety Act of 1972 directed the U.S. Coast Guard to reduce cargo losses due to groundings and accidents. Any regulations to achieve this objective were authorized under the act and they would apply to all tankers operating in U.S. waters. The act has been a major influence on U.S. and international thinking since draft regulations were published in the Federal Register on June 18, 1974. It can be said that the Ports and Waterways Safety Act set the scene for the conference and that the United States took the lead by publishing regulations included in the 1973 Pollution Convention. In certain respects, U.S. thinking concerning protection of the marine environment exceeds that of its foreign counterparts.

A review of the current status of maritime conventions reveals the increasing impact of international agreements on the U.S. maritime industries and on the leadership role of the United States in support for internationally accepted standards. The United States has ratified the major international conventions related to ship safety, including stability and subdivision. Where it has not yet ratified the current revision of such conventions, it has submitted them to the Congress for ratification. In the latter cases—SOLAS 1974, Prevention of Pollution from Ships 1973, and Tonnage Measurement of Ships 1969—there are ample, adequate, and sometimes superior domestic regulations in effect.

It can be said without equivocation that the United States has led the drive among the developed nations to improve the technical basis for international maritime safety. The United States has, for the most part, acted through its own maritime laws to give effect to the spirit of such conventions when the process of national or international ratification has been slow. The IMCO Chemical Code is included in the 1973 Convention for Prevention of Pollution from Ships. However, the United States moved to adopt the code provisions and include them in U.S. laws under the authority of the Dangerous Cargo Act and the Tanker Act (46 USC 170 and 46 USC 391A) before the convention was ratified. This is another example of U.S. action in advance of other nations on matters included in international conventions.

Between May 1970, when President Nixon delivered his "oil spill" message to the Congress, and March 1977, when President Carter announced to the Congress his actions to reduce oil pollution, the United States was ahead of the balance of the world toward achievement "of the complete elimination of the willful and intentional pollution of the seas by oil and noxious substances other than oil, and the minimization of accidental spills" (IMCO Assembly Res A237, vii).[33]

Against the background of a series of oil tanker accidents, groundings, explosions, and collisions near the United States, and the need to broaden the scope of the Prevention of Pollution of the Sea by Oil convention of 1954, a subcommittee of the Seventh IMCO Assembly set out in 1971 to develop a new approach to pollution. The U.S. delegation again took the lead and achieved most of its aims when a draft International Convention for the Prevention of Pollution from Ships, 1973, was adopted. The convention aimed to eliminate marine pollution by oil and other harmful substances and to minimize accidental spills. It applies to ships, except warships and noncommercial government ships, and to fixed and floating platforms. The convention covers all aspects of pollution, from oil and harmful substances carried in bulk or in packages to sewage and garbage.

A major issue related to all types of pollution is the extent of the "waters of the United States." A new convention has been drafted and is under discussion dealing with the Law of the Sea. This convention incorporates the concepts of an exclusive economic zone (EEZ), a contiguous zone, and a continental-shelf area. Many problems arise from the fact that the area to be placed under the limits of national jurisdiction will fall within a number of these zones, some of which were previously considered to be international waters.

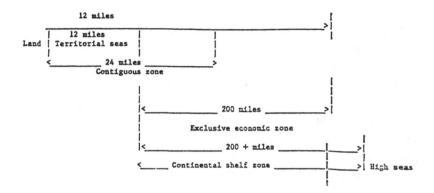

The extent of the various zones proposed in the Law of the Sea draft convention are shown in the diagram above. The "contiguous zone" overlaps the "territorial seas" zone and extends into the "exclusive economic zone" which would normally be only part of the "continental-shelf zone."

The coastal state may, by tradition, certainly exercise its rights in its territorial waters. The proposed convention also permits it to enforce security, immigration, and fiscal rights in the contiguous area. Under the Geneva Convention on the Continental Shelf (1958), a coastal state may have sovereign rights for exploration in the zone. The proposed economic zone gives to its users, the coastal states, inter alia, "preservation of the marine environment," including pollution control and abatement. Article 20(5) of Part II of the Law of the Sea draft convention provides for control of dumping and enforcement of international pollution control regulations within the EEZ. To illustrate the difficulties likely to face nations abiding by traditional international maritime law, Canada has established a shipping safety-control zone north of 60° and within one hundred miles of land. Passages within this area require Canadian approval. The justification for this action is that the Arctic environment is too fragile and important to Canada to be put at risk.

The United States published regulations on March 3, 1978, under the Federal Water Pollution Control Act, which unilaterally established a two-hundred-mile limit as one within which foreign carriers causing massive pollution would be financially responsible. Fines of up to $5 million and unlimited liability for the costs of cleanups are included in the regulations. It seems that some type of agreement must be reached among nations regarding the use of the common ocean. The Law of the Sea draft convention raises major issues which must be addressed in the age of seabed mining, offshore exploration, and Arctic gas discoveries.

In April 1974, a Code of Conduct for Liner Conferences was drafted and accepted by a large number of nations at a convention sponsored by the United Nations Conference on Trade and Development. The Code of Conduct was adopted by seventy-two to seven, with five abstentions. All of the developing countries voted in favor as did all the East European countries. The major shipping nations, Denmark, Finland, Norway, Sweden, the United Kingdom, and the United States voted against the code. Switzerland also voted against the code; West Germany, France, and Japan voted for it. Canada, Greece, Italy, the Netherlands, and New Zealand abstained. One of the major causes of disagreement among the developed nations was the inclusion in the code of the principle of cargo sharing among shipping countries in the proportion 40-40-20 percent: 40 percent originating country, 40 percent receiving country, and 20 percent third-party countries. The relevant part (Article 2) states "The group of national shipping lines of each of two countries, the foreign trade between which is carried by a conference, shall have equal rights to participate in the freight and volume of traffic generated by their mutual foreign trade and carried by the conference. Third-country shipping lines, if any, shall have the right to acquire a significant part, such as 20 percent, in the freight and volume of traffic generated by that trade." The convention will enter into force when twenty-four states with 25 percent of combined general-cargo ship and containership tonnage have deposited the instruments of accession. It is uncertain that entry into force will come in the early future.

The United States position, to this point, has been that the code is in conflict with its laws regarding antitrust and restraint of trade, and with the Shipping Act, Section 15, which provides for filing conference agreements in order to gain exemption from antitrust prosecution. The code allows for "partly closed conferences" which is a practice prohibited under U.S. law. If, through a series of bilateral negotiations, for example, the United States, which now carries a small part of its own import and export general-cargo trade, could allocate up to 40 percent of trade on a specific route to its trading partner, not a major shipping nation, at the expense of third countries, it might accomplish a lowering of total trading costs. Yet such a move could damage U.S. relations with third countries as their ships were, more and more, forced out of operations on routes affected by such bilateral agreements. It may thus be paradoxical that joining in what some see as a restraint of trade could lead to lower shipping costs.

Recently, some forecasts were made of general cargo shipping required to handle that part of U.S. trade that might be carried out under the UNCTAD Code should it come into force with U.S. approval. The forecast, made in early 1976, is now under revision; however, some idea of the scale of shipping investment needed to approach UNCTAD proportions can be presented. In 1975, the study estimates that U.S. foreign trade in general cargo ships, excluding barge carriers and part and full containerships, was carried out by about 3,995 ships. Of these 161 were U.S. flag and 86 percent of them were under fifteen thousand deadweight tons, with only 22 of larger size. By 1990, using assumptions which take into account commercial and technological changes, 4,465 general cargo ships will be required in U.S. foreign trade. The U.S.-flag component is estimated to increase to about 218 ships. While foreign operators will reduce by 21 percent the number of ships under fifteen thousand deadweight tons, U.S. operators will add 5 such ships. There will be a sharp increase, says the study, in the number of larger general-cargo ships—up to 1,206 units in total, of which increase 1,139 will be foreign and about 67 U.S. flag.

The 1975 share of U.S.-flag general cargo ships in foreign trade was about 4.7 percent of the number of total general-cargo ships. This, says the study, will rise to about 4.9 percent. To accomplish this minor change, 67 new general-cargo ships, net of scrapping, would be built. As most of the 161 U.S.-flag general cargo ships existing in 1975 were built in the pre-1970 years, scrapping could add up to 100 ships to building requirements by 1990. Thus the total general-cargo shipbuilding program facing the United States from 1975 to 1990 amounts to about 167 ships—about 10 or 11 per year.

But each 1 percent increase in the share, by numbers, of U.S.-flag general cargo ships would require forty-five new ships to be built in the period. With the introduction of considerations of cargo preference or a move toward adopting the UNCTAD Code proposals, the U.S.-flag program for building general cargo ships could increase substantially. Achievement of a 12 percent share of general cargo trade in U.S.-flag ships by 1990 would require a building program of about thirty such ships per year.

Response at the National Level

A major U.S. policy development was the Merchant Marine Act of 1970. During the 1960s, although government maritime policies continued as before, the Congress and the industry worked toward a comprehensive new policy to stimulate shipbuilding and shipping which culminated in this act. Belonging to the usual conferences, under whose rates 95 percent of all American-liner cargo has been shipped since 1965, U.S.-flag liners have accounted for about one-third of that liner carriage. However, the American merchant marine has accounted for only about 4½ percent of the total U.S. trade by tonnage,[34] contributed about $700 million to the balance of payments, and provided crucial logistical backup for the U.S. military operations in the Vietnam War.[35] But the high costs of containerization and other new ship-types (the nonsubsidized Sea-Land containership program cost $500 million for eight new SL-7s built in West Germany and Holland, for six breakbulk conversions, and for port facilities)[36] spurred the government toward measures to reduce shipbuilding costs and to preserve the shipbuilding segment of the industry. The 1970 act was the partial result.[37]

Actually a broadening of the 1936 Merchant Marine Act, the

1970 statute sought to reduce CDS subsidy levels progressively by replacing competitive bidding with shipyard-ship purchaser negotiations as to the price of the ship, the secretary of commerce deciding upon the fairness and reasonableness of the agreed-upon price. To encourage shipbuilders "to invest in equipment and procedures to reduce ship construction costs," the act was aimed at reducing the CDS ceiling from 55 percent of the total cost in the 1960s to 35 percent by 1976. An additional change was the inclusion of dry and liquid bulk carriers as well as Great Lakes ships, in addition to liners, as CDS recipients, and a capital construction fund (CCF) tax deferral was extended to all U.S. ship operators so long as their CCF was to be committed to the construction of ships in U.S. shipyards. Moreover, the 1970 act envisioned the construction of ships in series to reduce unit costs.

Anticipated as a catalyst for modernized building techniques and increased output, the legislation called for a ten-year period of ship construction during which government and industry would invest up to $6 billion to build three hundred new high-productivity ships at a rate of about thirty per year. The technological movement toward larger vessels, however, immediately lowered the goal of three hundred ships, and, in retrospect, it was probably unwise and unfortunate to include a specific number in the statute. Also, a special Commission on American Shipbuilding was established to examine shipbuilding conditions generally and to recommend to the president and the Congress actions necessary to achieve the objectives of the 1970 act.[38]

With the implicit opportunities of the 1970 act, American builders proceeded to invest heavily in capital improvements, only to be stunned by the worldwide economic crisis of the mid-1970s. Through 1977, the capital-intensive industry committed more than $1.3 billion to facility modifications and expansion, but, between 1970 and 1975, an average of only twelve CDS ships were built per fiscal year, instead of the planned thirty, for a total of fifty-eight. And then came the crash. In 1973, the Arab oil embargo and skyrocketing petroleum prices struck. Energy conservation programs led to the layup of tankers of every flag over the ensuing five years.

Although the existing American tanker fleet remained intact at some 230 hulls (active and inactive) of between 7.7 to 9.7 million deadweight tons, and the 1970 act made tanker subsidies available, the American tanker-building program dropped from sixteen new contracts in 1972 to twelve in 1973, seven in 1974 (five of these later canceled), and only three in 1975, all to be delivered by 1980.[39]

Concurrently, liner construction did not initially suffer. Even so, spiraling inflation and the devaluation of the dollar soon combined with the energy crisis to depress general world-market conditions. The continuing performance of U.S. shipbuilders in bringing the CDS level down to the mandates of the 1970 act was set back while their foreign competitors, with the assistance of governments, continued to offer to build at much lower costs. Overall, the depressed world market discouraged shipowners from building any new ships at all, even with subsidy, and during the mid-1970s contracts began to be canceled and future plans were set aside. By the middle of 1978, instead of three hundred projected ships under the 1970 act, only seventy-one had been built or contracted for, in addition to thirty-one conversions, in U.S. shipyards.[40]

The impact of the 1970 building program in conjunction with the world recession has been generally negative. For shipbuilding, U.S. and worldwide, it has been a calamitous period. While American shipyards have been vastly modernized, their loss of orders, even with the opportunity for greater governmental incentives, has not produced a long-term stability. Naval, offshore drilling rig, and repair orders, plus construction of some LNG carriers (in which the United States has to this point held a technological lead), have kept the yards busy through the 1970s, but these hold very little promise for construction beyond the early 1980s. Declining cargo needs in the depressed world market have caused American ship operators, nonsubsidized and subsidized alike, to view their foreign competitors with chagrin and envy.[41] Stimuli comparable to those that have occurred abroad, under governmental auspices, have yet to develop in the United States.

World shipping continues to be dominated by American businessmen, however, although outside U.S.-flag registry. The flag-of-convenience companies, loosely organized into the American Committee for Flags of Necessity (now called the Federation of American Controlled Shipping), built nearly 2,000 merchant ships totaling over 100 million deadweight tons in foreign shipyards between 1950 and 1974 (in contrast to 531 ships and 17,900,000 deadweight tons built in U.S. yards during the same period). By the middle of 1975, at the beginning of the shipping glut, American parent companies owned and operated 728 ships of 57,400,000 deadweight tons, most of them (513) tankers belonging to major oil companies, the others being bulk and ore carriers (129) and freighters (86).

By far, the Liberian-flag fleet continued to dominate with 370 of the 728 ships (36,400,000 deadweight tons), 85-percent financed by American shipping entrepreneurs, including major oil companies. Collectively, they owned half of the flag-of-convenience vessels in the world; most of the rest were under Greek ownership. These maintain their advantage over U.S.-flag shipping by having minimal taxation or regulation, tax breaks, lower operating costs and wages, and many incentives from their governments as well as outright financial aid in the forms of both grants and subsidies since the shipbuilding crisis began.[42] In combination, directly or indirectly, these aids outweigh anything available in the United States.

Less directly under American business control, and thus more dangerous to the stability of world shipping, are the foreign nations which are new at shipping and are extremely aggressive in their trading practices. From the oil-rich Organization of Arab Petroleum Exporting Countries (OAPEC), in 1975, came the eight-member Arab Maritime Petroleum Transport Company (AMPTC) of oil supertankers. Even more threatening has been the Soviet maritime penetration, not only in shipbuilding and advanced seaborne technology but in such practices as the refusal to join superconferences while engaging in predatory rate cutting of up to 69 percent, especially as applicable to high-priced cargoes. The Soviets even went so far as to establish, in 1976, Morflot America Shipping or MORAM, an American subsidiary of their own state shipping ministry. Based in New Jersey, its president is a native American who graduated from the U.S. Merchant Marine Academy and was a former vice president of Seatrain Lines, Inc. The Soviet Union has practiced rate cutting in cross-trading as a third-flag carrier between non-Russian ports, mainly to garner large amounts of foreign exchange because its economy "must have long-term access to Western machinery, technology management skill, and even food ... [and] the flow of exports to pay for them."[43]

The 1970 act—a plan which, by all yardsticks, has failed to revive the American Maritime industry as a commercial entity because of the changing world economic climate—was largely and rationally predicated on national-security/national-defense justifications for an American-flag merchant marine. The oil-driven U.S. Navy still needed oil tankers and dry-cargo break-bulk freighters for sealifted logistics and a stable shipbuilding base for warship construction. Indeed, by 1975, Assistant Secretary of Commerce for Maritime Affairs Robert J. Blackwell could rely upon time-tested arguments in testimony before the subcommittee on Merchant Marine of the House Committee of Merchant Marine and Fisheries; namely, that "the pivotal point of the U.S. merchant marine is national defense.... We need the fleet in time of war to support our troops. We need it for support of overseas operations [and] ... both in peace and in war to carry strategic goods for the United States."[44] The Vietnam War provided ample evidence of this essential role in that all but 2 or 3 percent of the military supplies sent into South Vietnam went by sea.[45]

Despite a record of past success, pessimism over the industry's ability to provide nearly 1,000 twenty-knot bottoms for wartime exists and has stemmed from many factors: a Military Sealift Command of only 30-some government-owned or chartered immediately available dry-cargo vessels; a skeleton remnant of 130 useful mothballed Victorys and 8 others; the potential loss of valuable commercial cargo routes if active U.S.-flag merchant ships are called up under the Sealift Readiness Program (SRP); and the doubt that the Effective U.S. Controlled (EUSC) Fleet of PanLibHon flags-of-convenience vessels and other foreign-flag ships will be available in an emergency.

Doubts about the availability, adequacy, and dependability of the effective U.S. control doctrine to carry U.S. oceanborne commerce in time of national crisis are based on many grounds.

Delays have occurred in updating contracts and agreements between the owners of the fleet and the U.S. government. Particularly, there are strong doubts concerning the fleet's actual availability and control during national emergencies. Since the doctrine is based on U.S. law, questions of international law arise concerning the extraterritoriality of possible U.S. requisition efforts. Since the overwhelming majority of the vessels are engaged in foreign cross-trading and are scattered across the globe, uncertainties exist whether these vessels could respond rapidly to U.S. commands for integration into U.S. service. Practical objections to the doctrine, in addition to the issue of availability, include the question of crew loyalty. Many nationalities man these vessels, and it is entirely possible that their loyalties may not coincide with U.S. national interests.

These issues indicate that the control and availability of the EUSC fleet is far from guaranteed. The doctrine was directly challenged in 1973 when Liberia, the major country of foreign registry, prohibited all Liberian-flag vessels from delivering war supplies to the Middle East during the Israel-Arab conflict. While the action was primarily a symbolic gesture and had little effect on U.S. military and diplomatic efforts in the Middle East, it was unprecedented and raised serious questions about U.S. maritime policy in general, and especially the EUSC doctrine, despite repeated assertions to the contrary by the Federation of American Controlled Shipping.

For wars short of a general conflict, however, the U.S. merchant marine is better equipped, especially as its newer vessels incorporate certain national defense features into their original designs. Over the first five years of construction under the 1970 act, 37 of the 58 new, contracted construction-subsidized ships enjoyed the built-in capability for directly supporting military forces—including 6 LNGs as potential oilers (the remaining 21 LNGs and VLCCs being in a more indirect defense category). In 1975, 132 of the 186 ships covered by operating subsidy— mostly breakbulk carriers and Ro/Ros—qualified, as did 45 containerships.

To overcome initial difficulties in a limited Far Eastern war, particularly the lack of container port facilities, tactical amphibious doctrines are being updated and successfully tested, as in the large-scale, joint Army LOTS (Logistics Over the Shore) and Navy/Marine Corps COTS (Container Off-loading and Transfer System) exercise in the Hampton Roads area during the summer of 1977. At that time, Lykes Brothers Steamship Lines provided a SeaBee bargeship with two SeaBee and six LASH barges; American Export Lines a containership; Hudson Waterways a C-4 heavy-lift breakbulk carrier; the army its new LACV (lighter, air cushion vehicle), a Temporary Containership Discharge Facility, and the Mobile Standard Port System data and computer-terminal van for documentation support of cargo and movements management. The navy provided an elevated 900-foot-long causeway with air-cushion turntable for trucks, and the Marine Corps provided the experimental LACH (lightweight amphibious container handler) and its advanced multipurpose surfacing system to improve automotive vehicle traction on the sand.[46]

Unfortunately, navy strategic policy planning was confronted with a crisis in the late 1970s when the cost of weapons systems became so very great that choices had to be made which would determine America's wartime posture for the remainder of the century. The three main roles of the navy, as of April 1977, remained strategic deterrence with the Polaris-Trident missile submarines, with which few people found fault; forward deployed naval forces to support worldwide units; and security of the sea lines of communications.[47] A controversy arose when aircraft-carrier-oriented navy leaders argued for retention of their offensive posture with nuclear-powered and armed strike carriers and supporting surface vessels to project strategic naval power into the Soviet Union. Opponents, led by Secretary of Defense Harold Brown, called for smaller, conventionally powered, and presumably cheaper, carriers to protect American and allied merchantmen and tankers plying the sea lines of communications and to support limited war forces. The controversy continues, delaying a long-term clarification of needs for merchant shipping.

The Innovations of Business and Labor

Concurrently with the technological revolution at the international and federal levels, business and labor groups, largely due to the efforts of the National Maritime Council (NMC), have gradually come to the conclusion that innovative responses must be made to the immense challenges ahead. Like the larger AFL/CIO, the maritime unions centralized their power during the 1960s—in 1961, the Seafarers' International Union of North America (SIU) and its contracted companies created the American Maritime Association (AMA) to represent over one hundred SIU contracted deep-sea companies before Congress and to negotiate labor costs between the SIU and these companies. That year, members of the American Merchant Marine Institute merged with the Committee of American Steamship Lines (CASL) and other management groups into the American Institute of Merchant Shipping (AIMS) to deal with management-labor questions. The impetus for this change was generated by major strikes in the industry in 1961, 1965, and 1969.

Parenthetically, it should be noted that U.S. shipyards also have not been without some labor strife. However, these strikes generally have not been too severe, but they have produced work rules less flexible than those which have been developed in other shipbuilding nations. On the management side, major U.S. shipbuilders have long looked to the Shipbuilders' Council of America (SCA) to improve the whole environment for ship construction and repair, exclusive of labor-management relations. Founded in 1921, SCA, through the years, has been increasingly effective as a national trade association in espousing the interests of its membership, but its charter does not extend to management-labor questions.

Maritime disputes between labor and management reflected the general difficulties found in the industry during this period. The federal government then took the initiative to bring the several components together to save the industry and to promote its interests in educating a public very ignorant of the industry. Taking advantage of a mutual growing awareness by management and labor of their conflicting positions, the Maritime Administration in 1971 encouraged the founding of the National Maritime Council (NMC). The NMC was founded by a voluntary coalition of labor, management, and government in an effort to promote harmony, to solve particular industry problems, and thus to contribute to the growth of the industry. So labor and management took advantage of this opportunity to promote a new spirit of cooperation to wary shippers. Unfortunately, the new NMC-centered cooperation got off to a rocky start when in 1972 the officers' unions—already embroiled for a decade over the differing wages between the higher-paid mates and the engineers—struck over the issue of whether engineers would operate engine controls on the bridge, an issue which the engineers won. Since then, however, the NMC has proved to be a practical forum for effective realization of the interdependence between shipping, shippers, shipyards, and seagoing unions.

Organized seagoing labor upgraded its training programs with new union schools in 1966 and 1967 but could not prevent the further loss of jobs. In spite of this trend, the unions strongly supported tanker automation, which they perceived to be in their long-range self-interest, due to increased productivity. Short-term reductions in ship manning, however, were inevitable. Automated tankers require 25 crew members and automated dry-cargo ships 32-40, contrasted to 40-44 and 40-49 on their respective nonautomated counterparts. For those skilled seamen in over sixty specialities who did survive, however, salaries and benefits rose, but not as rapidly as in many other industries. The industry, which requires approximately 2 men to keep 1 seagoing billet filled, dropped from 65,100 longshoremen and 65,278 billets in 1966 to 62,800 and 23,775, respectively, ten years later, plus the loss of 16,000 additional maritime-related jobs ashore.[48]

In contrast, thanks to the 1970 act, repair work, and navy programs, shipbuilding employment steadily rose to 155,500 commercial jobs by 1975. The academies and schools keep some 4,000 in training. Without the suppliers of ship component parts who employ more than another 100,000, the maritime (non-naval) work force totaled some 265,000 in 1975 just as the postboom unemployment wave began to break. Since the hiring halls in the maritime industry follow a seniority system like other industries, older seamen have gotten the jobs—in 1975 the average crewman's age was 45—thus discouraging younger men from trying to stay in the industry and increasing the danger of potential block retirement followed by a void in experienced merchant sailors. Subsequently, however, retirements have accelerated, opening up many jobs for younger officers and seamen.

Because of the new spirit exemplified by the formation of the National Maritime Council in 1971, labor and management have generally reached agreement without strikes (except for the longshoremen's strike of late 1977). But changing circumstances revealed the inadequacy of the policy context in which the NMC operated.[49]

Subsidies, it has been shown, cannot deter bankruptcy and failure. During 1978 alone, three of the nation's thirteen major subsidized lines operating in the international arena found it necessary to reorganize, or, in one case, to go out of business. Pacific Far East Lines went bankrupt outright; Prudential Lines is withering away; while a healthy American Export Line was sold by the parent company and merged into Farrell Lines; and the general health of U.S.-flag shipping leaves much to be desired.

Because of the oil depression, the independent tanker industry, supported by the shipyard industry and seagoing unions, sought to stem the trend of a lack of oil cargoes for American-flag, American-built tankers by promoting a cargo preference bill (9.5 percent) in 1977 and thus also the need for more tankers, only to have it defeated in the Congress on grounds unrelated to merit or substance. U.S.-flag subsidized ship operators and U.S. oil companies with their foreign-flag ties had prevented the prior organization, AIMS, from taking agreed-upon policy positions in support of U.S.-flag interests (AIMS survived to represent the interests of the major oil companies in shipping). Finally, in the face of rate cutting by foreign competitors, desperate American carriers have turned to the Congress for relief from the uncompetitive, predatory practices of state-controlled carriers. The subsidized lines have also separated from AIMS and organized the Council of American Ship Operators (CASO) to try to solve their problems.[50]

U.S. oceanborne foreign trade has increased dramatically in the last two decades as the U.S. merchant marine's carriage of

U.S. trade eroded. During the 1956-77 period, trade rose 184 percent in tonnage to 739.4 million tons and 710 percent in value to $166.9 billion. But the share carried by U.S.-flag vessels dropped significantly: whereas in 1956, 20.7 percent of the tonnage and 33.8 percent of the value moved in U.S. vessels, by 1977 the figures had fallen to 4.5 percent and 16.7 percent, respectively. In 1975, 1976, and 1977, U.S. liners held roughly 30 percent of this trade in both tonnage and value while U.S. nonliners and tankers carried roughly 5 percent in tonnage and 17 percent in value.

In sum, the United States has an influential but endangered maritime base.[51] By the late 1970s, adequate answers to the questions posed by the changed international environment have not been found, and there is little visible evidence or disposition on the part of government leaders to provide effective answers.

Notes

1. Robert Earle Anderson, *The Merchant Marine and World Frontiers* (Cambridge, Md.: Cornell Maritime Press, 1945), p. 180.

2. John Kifner, "Liberia: A Phantom Maritime Power Whose Fleet is Steered by Big Business," *New York Times*, February 14, 1977, p. 14.

3. "The primary functions of the American Bureau of Shipping are the establishment of rules for the design, construction and maintenance of ships and their machinery", *American Bureau of Shipping: One Hundredth Anniversary, 1862-1962*, (New York: ABS, 1978), p. 21.

4. *The Use and Disposition of Ships and Shipyards at the End of World War II*, report for the U.S. Navy and Maritime Commission by the Harvard Graduate School of Business Administration (Washington, D.C.: Government Printing Office, June 1945), pp. 5, 13-14.

5. Lane C. Kendall, "The Military Role of M.S.T.S.," *Proceedings: Naval Review, 1965* (Annapolis, Md.: U.S. Naval Institute, 1964), pp. 223, 226-28, 231-33, 236-37; Howard C. Reese, ed., *Merchant Marine Policy* (Cambridge, Md.: Cornell Maritime Press, 1963), p. 12; Wytze Gorter, *United States Shipping Policy* (New York: Harper, 1956), pp. 130, 132-33; Erling D. Naess, *The Great PanLibHon Controversy* (Epping, Eng.: Gower, 1972), passim.

6. Most of this discussion is taken from Everett P. Lunsford, Jr., "Our Merchant Mariners and Their Unions," *U.S. Naval Institute Proceedings* [hereafter *USNIP*], 101, no. 5 (May 1975), 66-85; John G. Kilgour, *The U.S. Merchant Marine: National Maritime Policy and Industrial Relations*

American Maritime Power since World War II 251

(New York: Praeger, 1975), pp. 103-50; Alfred D. Chandler, Jr., *The Visible Hand: The Managerial Revolution in American Business* (Cambridge, Mass.: Harvard University Press, 1977); statement of George Meany, president AFL/CIO, "On the Matter of Wheat Shipments to the Soviet Union," September 1965 (press release).

7. *Hearings before the Subcommittee on Merchant Marine of the Committee on Merchant Marine and Fisheries*, House of Representatives, 93rd Congress, 1st session (Washington, D.C.: Government Printing Office, 1973), pp. 39ff. See also *The Role of Nuclear Propulsion in Merchant Shipping* (New York: Atomic Industrial Forum, 1960), especially pp. 4, 8, 17-18.

8. Reese, op. cit., pp. 9-11.

9. *ABS Hundredth Anniversary*, pp. 21-22; *ABS Annual Report, 1977* (New York: ABS, 1977), p. 1.

10. James M. Morris, "Our Maritime Heritage: Maritime Developments and Their Impact on American Life," (Unpub. manuscript, 1978), p. 395; copy on file, Schuyler Otis Bland Memorial Library, U.S. Merchant Marine Academy.

11. Gorter, op. cit., pp. 1, 5, 50-53, 62-66; John W. Heilshorn, "Financing the United States Merchant Ship Replacement Program" (Unpub. paper, Rutgers University, June 1959), pp. 24-26; copy on file, Bland Library.

12. Reese, op. cit., p. 40.

13. Gorter, op. cit., pp. 102-3.

14. Ibid., pp. 159-61; *The Regulated Ocean Shipping Industry: A Report of the U.S. Department of Justice* (Washington, D.C., January 1977), pp. 4, 5, 24, 25, 34, 35, 44-47, 53-55, 59, 62, 63, 166 (hereafter Justice study).

15. Morris, op. cit., pp. 370, 385.

16. Memo, Secretary of Agriculture Orville L. Freeman to President Lyndon B. Johnson, August 6, 1965, Ex, TA 4/CO 303, LBJ Library, courtesy of Jeffrey J. Safford; also, Meany, Wheat statement, September 1965.

17. Gorter, Op. cit., pp. 106ff, 129-30; Justice study, pp. 50-51, 122-23; Heilshorn, op. cit., p. 29; Kilgour, op. cit., pp. 46-47.

18. Morris, op. cit., pp. 383-84.

19. See Oliver T. Burnham, "The Fourth Coast: Five Lakes and Five Rivers," *USNIP* 101, no. 5 (May 1975), 174-87.

20. Henry S. Morgan, *Planning Ship Replacement in the Containerization Era* (Lexington, Mass.: D. C. Heath, 1974), pp. 7-8, 11-13, 45.

21. Ibid., p. 1.

22. Ibid., pp. 27-29.

23. *Proceedings: Naval Review, 1969* (Annapolis, Md.: U.S. Naval Institute, 1969), p. 343; Kilgour, op. cit., pp. 56-59. The United Fruit Company, for example, having already switched from bunches to boxes for its banana cargoes, in 1972 received its first diesel-powered containerships from a Spanish yard, registered them with Great Britain, and based them at Galveston. Each container had its own refrigerating unit, powered by the ship's machinery at sea and by a diesel-operated unit at the dock and during transportation overland; John H. Melville, *The Great White Fleet* (New York: Vantage, 1976), pp. 215-26. United Fruit is now United Brands.

24. James R. Barker and Robert Brandwein, *The United States Merchant Marine in National Perspective* (Lexington, Mass.: D. C. Heath, 1970), pp. 18-23, 54-55.

25. Kilgour, op. cit., p. 57. A comparable technological revolution occurred in naval history with the introduction of the British battleship *Dreadnought* in 1905; Clark G. Reynolds, *Command of the Sea: The History and Strategy at Maritime Empires* (New York: William Morrow, 1974), pp. 411-12, 440-42.

26. Kilgour, op. cit., pp. 58-59.

27. Rear Admiral George H. Miller, USN (Ret.), and Max C. McLean, "The U.S. Shipping Emergency in the Seventies," *USNIP* 98, no. 5 (May 1972), 151.

28. Morris, op. cit., pp. 393, 417.

29. The commercial feasibility of such new concepts as the SES depends largely on technological factors—for the SES, optimum stability and control performance, effective lift-to-drag ratio, structure, efficient propulsion and fuel economy; *Surface Effect Ships for Ocean Commerce* (Washington, D.C.: Government Printing Office, 1966), p. 2 and passim.

30. An excellent brief overview of the tanker troubles is John Kifner's three-part series in the *New York Times* February 13-15, 1977: "Oil ... remains the single biggest pollutant and tankers the single biggest dispenser of it. ... Supertankers are the biggest moving things ever built by man, and also the most dangerous"; Noel Mostert, *Supership* (New York: Knopf, 1974), pp. 45, 130.

31. Justice study, pp. 166, 169, 174-75, 185.

32. Mostert, op. cit., pp. 196-97, 236.

33. United Fruit's M-Series diesel-driven refrigerator ships, for example, were built between 1969 and 1973 to make one entire cruise without having to ballast their fuel tanks and thus having to pump out oil-polluted ballast at sea. Also, they have their own built-in sewage processing plants, thus eliminating overboard discharge of refuse; Melville, op. cit., pp. 216-17.

34. Hearings before the Subcommittee on Merchant Marine of the Committee on Merchant Marine and Fisheries, House of Representatives, 94th Congress, 1st session (Washington, D.C.: Government Printing Office, 1976), pp. 209-12, 339, 386-87 (hereafter *1975 Hearings*).
35. Ibid., p. 211.
36. Justice study, p. 84.
37. See Kilgour, op. cit., pp. 197-203.
38. *1975 Hearings*, pp. 257, 690, 770-73, 895, 954-55; Barker and Brandwein, op. cit., pp. 13-14; Comptroller General of the United States Report to the Congress, *Government Support of the Shipbuilding Industrial Base* (Washington, D.C.: Comptroller General, February 1975), p. 8. The 1970 act also included crew size considerations and ODS extensions to bulk carriers.
39. *1975 Hearings*, pp. 331, 333, 691, 896-99. For sources on the eve of the 1970 act, see S. A. Lawrence, *United States Merchant Shipping Policies and Politics* (Washington, D.C.: The Brookings Institution, 1966), and Ran Hettena, "The U.S. Tanker Industry," *Proceedings: Naval Review* (Annapolis, Md.: U.S. Naval Institute, 1969), pp. 172-93.
40. *1975 Hearings*, pp. 690-91, 772-75, 897-98; remarks in speech by Robert J. Blackwell to the Institute of Foreign Transportation, New Orleans, April 17, 1978 (MarAd news release).
41. *New York Times*, March 6, 1978; *Journal of Commerce*, April 10, 1978; Kilgour, op. cit., pp. 207-8.
42. *1975 Hearings*, p. 899; *Foreign Flag Merchant Ships Owned by U.S. Parent Companies* (as of June 30, 1974) (Washington, D.C.: Government Printing Office, 1975), pp. 1, 2, 5-7, 9, 35, 40; *Proceedings: Naval Review* (Annapolis, Md.: U.S. Naval Institute, 1969), pp. 344-45; Blackwell 1978 New Orleans speech; Morris, op. cit., pp. 395-96.
43. Herbert E. Meyer, "The Communist Internationale Has a Capitalist Accent," *Fortune* (February 1977), 136, 137, 141, 148; *Arab Shipping: Poised for Take Off: A Seatrade Study* (n.p., 1975), pp. 3, 5; *1975 Hearings*, pp. 39-335, 870-71; *Time*, December 5, 1977, p. 59.
44. *1975 Hearings*, p. 349.
45. Lane C. Kendall, "U.S. Merchant Shipping and Vietnam," *Naval Review, 1968* (Annapolis, Md.: U.S. Naval Institute, 1968), pp. 130-31, 135-36, 140, 143-44, 146-47.
46. *1975 Hearings*, pp. 18, 369; U.S. Army Transportation Center, Fort Eustis, Va., news release, July 25, 1977, and Public Affairs brochure 878-3317 of July 1977.
47. Admiral James L. Holloway III, USN, "CNO Report" (April 1977), p. 2.
48. These and other statistics have been generously provided to the

writer by Russell F. Stryker and Richard Thomas of the Maritime Administration.

49. Lunsford, op. cit., p. 73; Justice study, p. 10; *1975 Hearings*, pp. 32-33, 264-65, 290-91, 354-55, 372-73, 896-97. On page 290 of the last, 1975 minority employment figures were 67,000 seamen, 61,000 longshoremen, and 76,000 shipyard workers.

50. *Journal of Commerce*, April 10 and 17, 1978; *New York Times*, March 6, 1978. The Jones Act continues to exempt the Virgin Islands for cabotage regulations, and foreign tankers have been moving oil to refineries there.

51. Morris, op. cit., pp. 405, 406, 492.

8
The Shipbuilding Industry: A Summary of Developments and Commentary

James M. Morris and Robert A. Kilmarx

America, from the earliest years of its colonial existence down to the present time, has been tied to the sea. These ties have been evident since the days of the small vessels ferrying men and supplies across the Atlantic Ocean and up and down the coast, in the early decades of the seventeenth century, down to the launching of one-thousand-foot behemoths for the carriage of vital commercial goods across the oceans of the world in support of world trade patterns in the 1970s. Clearly, America's links to the oceans and to the vessels which ply them have been crucial to her security and to her economic, social, and even her political strength and well-being.

Closely related to America's patterns of domestic and foreign commerce have been her shipyards, which have supplied, in whole or part, her vessels for trade and defense. Neither the vagaries of fate nor the fortunes of war and peace have changed this vital American dependence. In fact, the importance of the seas to U.S. commerce has grown because of the expansion of U.S. oceanborne trade, including growing U.S. reliance on foreign sources of oil and other essential raw materials. The United States now must import sixty-nine of the seventy-one critical commodities used in U.S. industry. Dependency is between 50 and 100 percent of our needs for over twenty of them. More than 90 percent is carried on the ships of other nations. This trend has been accompanied by a serious vulnerability deriving from the growth and modernization of the navies

The opinions expressed in this chapter are those of Robert A. Kilmarx and James M. Morris and do not necessarily reflect those held by other contributors to this volume.

of potential adversaries and the merchant fleets of friendly allies and trading partners.

The United States is an "island" nation with a heritage of maritime traditions which remains unbroken as she pursues her course into the twenty-first century, maintaining and expanding her oceanic links with other nations and peoples of the world. But, from the perspective of history, it is possible to discern certain patterns of growth and development important not only to understanding the American maritime industries as they exist today, but also to guide planning for continued effectiveness in meeting the challenges which lie ahead. These historical correlations spell out the parameters of possible change. They often clearly indicate basic problems of direction and priorities, which must be addressed, or readdressed, if the United States is to halt the drift in its maritime policies which leaves it vulnerable, perhaps helpless, in the increasingly competitive world of the late twentieth century.

This historical perspective, however, needs to be projected from the baseline of understanding present U.S. maritime industries and their near-term outlook. Merchant shipbuilding in the United States faces a period of crisis resulting from a slow rate of economic growth, a vacuum in national direction, and a loss of potential markets to government-supported foreign competition, leading to overtonnage, overcapacity, and rapidly declining work backlogs. A few years ago, the outlook for the U.S. shipbuilding industry appeared more encouraging, with contracts received for forty-seven merchant ships in 1972 and forty-one in 1973. Then came the decline: in 1975 new orders totaled eleven merchant ships and in 1976 the number was sixteen. In 1977, new orders fell to only thirteen ships. As a result of this decline, only twenty-six of these ships will remain to be delivered between 1979 and 1981. There are no present indications that an early reversal of this trend is possible. Many tens of thousands of productive jobs are therefore threatened during the next few years.

A fundamental problem is that many American companies have continued to have their ships constructed in foreign shipyards. Nearly two thousand commercial ships were constructed in foreign yards for American companies or their subsidiaries during the past twenty-five years, while only six hundred were built in the United States during the same period. Private U.S. shipbuilders continue to lose contracts to shipyards abroad which, because of governmental support, can offer reduced prices even though costs are increasing. The progressive, even accelerating, decline of the U.S. shipbuilding industry is an unmistakable result of deficient maritime policies and the absence of appropriate governmental response to the realities of foreign competition.

The Lessons of Maritime History

American history since the early seventeenth century makes it very clear that there has never been a period of time when America has not depended upon the sea lanes of the world. Numerous events, such as Jefferson's ill-fated embargo actions and the shipping crises of World War I and World War II, have graphically illustrated basic American weaknesses when the nation is denied access to sufficient shipping power. Economic statistics in the late twentieth century make it abundantly evident that dependence upon the sea is fundamental and continuing to grow, but these lessons of history seem to have become obscure, if not lost, in the minds of contemporary policymakers.

Increasing demands for ships and carrying capacity have not necessarily meant a corresponding expansion of business for U.S. shipbuilders. The presence on the high seas, and in American ports in the last thirty years, of great numbers of American-owned but foreign-registered flag-of-convenience vessels, and the ever-growing role these ships have forged in carrying American commerce, is vivid testimony to the fact that U.S. shipyards are precluded from supplying all but a fraction of the vessel capacity required by American economic imperatives. Compounding the problems faced by the U.S. maritime industries, an earlier expressed goal to rebuild the navy's fleet to about 600 ships by the mid-1980s has been abandoned. At present, the target is radically reduced to about 525 ships by the year 2000, in spite of the continuing rapid buildup of the Soviet navy.

Whatever the validity of the arguments as to the necessity of utilizing foreign registry in order to operate merchant ships at a cost advantage, the effects of the choice of non-American shipbuilding are obvious and, to many observers, a matter of serious concern. The resulting asymmetry creates a national vulnerability of significant proportions. The economic demands for American imports and exports are high and constantly multiplying, creating serious balance of trade and balance of international payments problems, yet the demand for American shipyards to supply needed vessels is low. This incongruity must be resolved within the framework of lasting national interests.

Both history and economics indicate that American shipbuilding declined in the middle decades of the nineteenth century with the transition from wood and wind to steel and steam. This loss has not been fully overcome by other subsequent factors. Despite America's technological growth in the last century and a quarter, which has been shared by the U.S. shipbuilding industry, external factors have, for the most part, inhibited the ability of that industry to compete in world ship markets. For example, no nation burdens its shipbuilding industry with as complex and costly a maze of statutory and regulatory requirements as does the United States. Undoubtedly, the condition and outlook of the industry can be explained in large measure by the lack of clear and consistent governmental policies toward the merchant marine and shipbuilding industries in this country. In contrast, British maritime industries were aided at a most crucial time in their attempt to apply technology to the sea lanes by a policy of government aid, based on the maximization of technological advances in the framework of long-range economic and maritime goals. This led, somewhat surprisingly, to the nationalization of British shipyards in mid-1977.

Moreover, the Soviet Union and other state-controlled countries have emerged as major maritime powers through government support of the industries. They have done this in a manner that makes free competition by private companies in the world's ocean trade impossible. It is not only the government-owned vessels of the USSR and Eastern Europe that have been moving inexorably to carry an ever-increasing percentage of U.S. foreign trade—their focus has been on foreign exchange earnings rather than costs or profits—but Third-World countries are also offering new ships to national companies and foreign customers at reduced costs. This is made possible by a combination of high technology, relatively inexpensive labor, favorable government-sponsored credit facilities, and government-supported ship replacement programs, thus contributing further to overtonnage and unfair competition.

But the United States has never had long-range, precisely defined, tangible maritime goals. This has kindled constant policy squabbles among various segments of the American economy, including the major political parties, the shipowners, the shipbuilders, the navy, and the agricultural and sectional interests. In this type of climate, there has been no consistency in the consideration of maritime and shipbuilding problems among involved agencies of the federal government. While potential American economic and technological advantages have foundered in a sea of government neglect of cargo carriage and rival interests, foreign maritime competitors have forged ahead, usually with government encouragement in some form, both to capture American international commerce and to build their own and flag-of-convenience vessels to carry it. It is even alleged that these foreign interests have openly, as well as subtly, lobbied the U.S. Congress to prevent the institution of an effective maritime policy which would tend to balance the scales between U.S.-flag and foreign-flag shipping in terms of U.S. exports and imports.

A major cause of the U.S. disadvantage in competing for the carriage of a significant share of its own foreign trade is the level of support given by foreign governments compared to the more limited programs of cargo stimulation provided by the U.S. government. U.S. shipping now carries only about 5 percent, by volume, of all U.S. exports and imports; in 1947 the U.S. shipping fleet carried 58 percent. The trend generally has been downward since then. In comparison, Japanese-flag ships transport more than 50 percent of that country's trade; this is also true of the Soviet Union. Comparable figures for the United Kingdom, West Germany, France, and Greece, to mention only a few, are about 30 percent.

Two major wars in the twentieth century have vividly illustrated that a high demand for ships of various types can be met by the American shipbuilding industry. The industry effectively responded to war-induced demands, central policy direction, and the coordination of facilities. Twice in this century, Herculean shipbuilding demands have been met; twice it has been demonstrated that the shipbuilding industry's limited, normal peacetime capacity has been capable of expansion and efficiency under pressure. President Truman, like his wartime predecessors, appreciated this achievement when he said at the close of World War II, "The shipbuilding accomplishments of the United States not only astonished the world but, more than that, defeated the enemy." Even with contemporary war scenarios, this experience should be a basic consideration in the formation of future policies.

Wartime efforts especially highlighted problems of lead time before the industry could be geared up to full efficiency. The lead-time requirement is constantly lengthening because of the demands of technology and size—and because of the absolute necessity for some form of centralized direction. This problem is exacerbated by a declining domestic industrial base for ships' components which arises from a declining demand for naval and merchant ships. Yet the rapid pace of advancing military technology indicates that in a future major conflict little, if any, lead time is likely to be available before the demand for ships will surge dramatically. Initial impact will very probably affect ship repairing, rather than shipbuilding, capabilities.

Problems of peacetime transition have also recurred historically. When shipyards have reverted to normal production, the persistent problems of a fluctuating order book and nonstandardized production have returned to plague the industry. It is also historically demonstrable that the federal government has intervened in U.S. shipbuilding ever since 1787 and that the role of government has expanded. Intervention has evolved from early, essentially protective, legislation against foreign competition to the present-day role of the federal government as an arbiter and contributory financier of shipbuilding.

Even so, throughout the years, the government has never followed clear and consistent policies in regard to its maritime enterprises. Goals have been ill defined and rarely specific. Intervention often has not met the needs of the industry. In recent decades, the federal government's role of providing

A *Summary of Developments and Commentary* 261

centralized direction has been marked by timidity, indecision, confusion, contradiction, and, some would say, parsimoniousness. Essentially, the government has never been able to define either the importance of the maritime industries to the nation or the most effective means of attaining the goals set.

Since 1916, the government has solemnly reiterated the essentiality of an adequate merchant marine for both commercial and national defense purposes—with the concomitant need for a strong shipbuilding base—but it has never carefully examined whether this maxim is really attainable by the means the government was willing to apply. Furthermore, the government has never been able to sway the economic factors underlining the continuing decline of the maritime industries and thus has served neither commerce nor defense adequately or appropriately. In addition, the divided authority and function of a host of governmental agencies charged with maritime affairs have probably made the effective development and implementation of maritime policy unattainable.

What is obvious to maritime interests must be made obvious to nonmaritime interests as well. Long-range commitments to maritime strength are only possible when structured on a firm foundation of general credence in maritime well-being, with constructive legislative support.

The Crucial Questions

Crucial questions must soon be confronted by federal policymakers. Washington's direction and support have become the sine qua non of the continued existence of both the merchant marine and shipbuilding and will, undoubtedly, continue to be so in the years ahead. Government, then, must confront the industry's problems squarely. If those industries are vital to American strength—and all the historical evidence demonstrates that they are—they must be preserved and advanced. If the government will not lead (but yet insists on retaining its controlling function), no one will lead, and the maritime industries will be decimated by conflicting influences.

A paramount question to all concerned is: Can American shipbuilding be made competitive with foreign shipbuilding?

And if so, under what circumstances? The conventional answers are often grounded in a profound lack of understanding of changes that have been made in the industry in recent years, and of the relative economic differences between U.S. and foreign shipbuilding. It is true that higher costs of American shipbuilders and ship operators have in some historical periods burdened U.S. competitiveness. But this relationship has been changing: the wage/fringe-benefit package for shipyard workers in several European countries, e.g., West Germany and Sweden, is now higher. Social change in other countries could soon produce similar effects. It is also true that the U.S. shipbuilding industry, because of economic verities, has at times lagged in technological advancements. This also has been changing. Large capital investments in recent years have been made in new technologies by virtually every major, privately owned U.S. shipbuilding company.

The problem of U.S. competitiveness is therefore largely a problem of benefits and incentives—also leadership and direction—provided by the governments of other nations, all competing to build ships to carry the cargoes of international waterborne commerce in order to obtain the economic benefits from that trade.

Another important question also concerns the role of government. Because of the international character of the merchant marine and shipbuilding industries, and because of other governments' active aid in those fields, should the federal government now reorient its role to assure that the U.S. shipbuilding industry has a better chance to compete? For example, would it designate certain shipyards for certain types of vessels, giving them long-run contracts, so that cost-efficient technologies could be utilized, and denying ship orders to nonefficient yards? Or should the government simply take over the shipyards and run them as nationalized industries? These points raise not only political but constitutional issues.

Would either of these steps produce the desired economies, greater efficiencies, or an adequate and competitive fleet? The high costs of nationalization have led to its repeated rejection. The experiences of other countries would seem to argue against nationalization to cure cost problems, unless a great measure of individual liberty is to be sacrificed. On the other hand, if the present limited involvement of government is not conducive to the desired effectiveness, and nationalization seems too high a price to pay, what other alternatives are possible? Why should more not be done to channel cargoes to American shipowners and so increase demand for U.S.-built merchant ships?

If it is accepted that naval shipbuilding will continue—as it surely will—then is there any justification for continuing to support both naval and private shipyards? Existing private shipyards can build naval vessels, but naval shipyards cannot build commercial vessels, and their construction costs are higher than the costs of shipbuilding in private shipyards. If both types of vessels are judged to be actually and potentially crucial to the country for commercial or defense needs, cannot the private shipyards be assigned these tasks? If shipbuilding skills and technologies must be maintained for both present demands and as baselines for shipbuilding expansion to meet national needs, cannot the private yards guarantee these skills and technologies?

Government intervention being a given fact of existence for American shipbuilding, to this point in time, other questions regarding federal policies present themselves for serious consideration and decision making. Should the government redirect its taxation policies to encourage more private investment in U.S.-flag, U.S.-built shipping trades? Should the government offer tax credits to U.S. exporters and importers using U.S.-flag, U.S.-built shipping? Should the government invest greater time and money in applied research in shipbuilding techniques? If the cost of pure and applied research in physical sciences for the "space race" was, and is, money well spent, would not an all-out effort in the essential maritime industries be an equally justifiable undertaking?

Further questions present themselves. Is American participation in shipping conferences, as now constituted, really the most effective and cost-efficient approach? Is it not possible to explore new cooperative approaches with our European allies, Japan, and the Third World to insure the protection of the interests of all? Are the vessels built to meet commercial needs as applicable as they might be to national defense and national security needs? Are they overbuilt in terms of competitive needs? Is the doctrine of effective control an outdated mechanism or a viable alternative to a merchant-fleet-in-being? Do the risks outweigh the potential benefits? Is there merit to bilateral shipping arrangements? Is a thorough, rational reorganization of the federal departments and agencies responsible for the maritime fate of the nation needed and overdue, despite the inevitable resistance of the bureaucracies and special interests involved? Or, as an alternative, is greater coordination within the present federal structure more desirable? While the evidence is not all in on these questions, there is increasing doubt that present practices should be continued without a probing reexamination.

The outlines of American merchant marine and shipbuilding history are clear. Its success and failures are clearly discernible. Its present problems are known but not sufficiently appreciated. They cry out for solutions, particularly in view of the adverse U.S. balance of payments deficit. Either all the interests involved understand the industries' past, confront the problems squarely in the present, and build for the future or the industries will continue to languish and decline in confusion and conflict.

No one segment of the industries—nor any combination of several of them—can solve these complex and interlocking problems. In whatever way all interests are brought together to solve common problems, especially the problem of assuring adequate cargoes for U.S. ships, whether at the initiative or under the direction of the government, the job of specifying goals, policies, means, and—ultimately—public support must be accomplished. Without this, America's maritime strength will not be adequate to meet future challenges.